D1561791

INVESTMENT IN PEACE

THE POLITICS OF ECONOMIC COOPERATION BETWEEN
ISRAEL, JORDAN, AND THE PALESTINIAN AUTHORITY

Investment in Peace

The Politics of Economic Cooperation between Israel, Jordan, and the Palestinian Authority

SHAUL MISHAL, RANAN D. KUPERMAN
AND DAVID BOAS

Foreword by HRH Prince El Hassan bin Talal of Jordan

sussex
ACADEMIC
PRESS

BRIGHTON • PORTLAND

The right of Shaul Mishal, Ranan D. Kuperman and David Boas to be identified as
authors of this work has been asserted in accordance with the Copyright,
Designs and Patents Act 1988.

2 4 6 8 10 9 7 5 3 1

First published 2001 in Great Britain by
SUSSEX ACADEMIC PRESS
PO Box 2950
Brighton BN2 5SP

and in the United States of America by
SUSSEX ACADEMIC PRESS
5824 N.E. Hassalo St.
Portland, Oregon 97213-3644

British Library Cataloguing in Publication Data
A CIP catalogue record for this book is available from the British Library.

Library of Congress Cataloging-in-Publication Data
Mishal, Shaul, 1945–
Investment in peace : politics of economic cooperation between Israel, Jordan, and the
Palestinian Authority / Shaul Mishal, Ranan D. Kuperman, and David Boas.
p. cm.
Includes bibliographical references and index.
ISBN 1–902210–88–3 (alk. paper)
1. Economic conversion—Israel. 2. Economic conversion—Palestine. 3. Economic
conversion—Jordan. 4. Peace—Economic aspects—Israel. 5. Peace—Economic aspects—
Palestine. 6. Peace—Economic aspects—Jordan. I. Kuperman, Ranan D.
II. Boas, David. III. Title.

HC415.25.Z9 D444 2001
337.569405695—dc21   2001020660

Printed by TJ International, Padstow, Cornwall
This book is printed on acid-free paper

Contents

———

Foreword by HRH Prince El Hassan bin Talal of Jordan   vi
Preface   viii

1   Introduction: Perceptions of War, Peace, and Economics   1
2   The Domestic Environments   20
3   The Politics of the Israeli–Jordanian–Palestinian Triangle   47
4   Trade Regimes   69
5   Transnational Economic Cooperation   95
6   Regional Infrastructure Development   119
7   Conclusion: The Future of Arab–Israeli Economic
   Relations – Risks and Opportunities   138

Bibliography   152
Index   161

Foreword by HRH Prince El Hassan bin Talal of Jordan

━━━━━━━━

This thoughtful book attempts to formulate a new relationship and a new negotiating strategy between Israel and its Arab neighbors. This strategy is defined as "perceptional pluralism," which is a way of "accommodating perceptional contradictions without succumbing to them."

The two areas of perceptional contradictions on which the authors concentrate their attention are the Israeli perception of immutable Arab hostility, and the Arab fear of Israeli economic and cultural hegemony. The innovative proposal put forward is an exchange of asymmetrical assurances: the Arabs will assure Israel that its security, and its existence, are not in danger, and Israel will assure the Arabs that it has no intention of imposing any economic or cultural hegemony. Thus it is hoped that the imbalance between Arab territorial and numerical advantage over Israel, and Israel's economic and technological advantage over the Arabs, will be compensated to the mutual advantage of both.

This is a proposal which at some later stage in the evolution of the Arab–Israeli conflict may be fruitful, but there are hurdles to be cleared before such a sophisticated approach can be practical. The fear that dominates both sides must first be attenuated, if not removed completely.

In a state of open hostility both sides are fearful for their security, and even for their very existence, and therefore define their strategies in terms of self-defense, which we know by experience to be a flexible formula. The resolution of conflict is perceived as a function of armed strength leading to either a balance of power and a state of no peace and no war, or to a military victory of one side over the other.

What I suggest is now urgently needed is to address the problem, not just of the fear of conflict, but also of the fear of peace which both sides share. For Israel, which has never known complete peace with its neighbors, peace is an "undiscovered country" where unknown dangers may lurk; a long-

———

term change, for example, in the demographic balance between its Jewish and Arab population, or a cultural dilution of the Jewish character of the state. For the Arabs complete peace, it is feared, would open the door to an Israeli "invasion" of their economic and cultural space, which it is feared by many would be the spearhead of a much wider and more powerful invasion by "western culture" of the Arab-Islamic heritage.

The fear of peace reveals a state of insecurity about their identity and their place in the world on both sides. I suggest therefore that there are four stages to be passed through before a real and sustainable peace can be achieved. In the first stage there needs to be a clear definition of how each side sees itself in terms of its history, its present condition, and its vision of the future. In the second stage there needs to be knowledge of one another, now, alas, largely lacking on both sides. In the third stage knowledge must lead to understanding, which is not the same thing. And in the fourth and hopefully final stage there needs to be an imaginative "leap" from the present state of mutual distrust and distate to a new mutual respect, a shared perception of common iterests, and a real and sincere desire to live together in peace.

There is the need therefore on both sides of the Arab–Israeli conflict for a "culture of peace." Where can this culture of peace best be nurtured and propagated other than in the mosque, the synagogue and the church; in the school and the university; and most importantly in the family, where all life and society begin, and where we are all created "free and equal"?

Preface

——————

Since the early 1990s, the Middle East has been characterized by dialogue and an ongoing peace process between Israel and its Arab neighbors. Peace and trade agreements were signed and normalization was beginning to take hold. However, at the end of the year 2000 a wave of violence between Israel and the Palestinians weakened the sense of security and stability in the region. This violence calls into question the ability of both sides to reach a final settlement that will bring an end to the conflict between Israelis and Palestinians. At the same time, both sides are weighing options regarding unilateral moves. For the Palestinians, this means a declaration of independence devoid of an agreement with Israel. For Israel, it means a disengagement from the economy in the West Bank and the Gaza Strip, and movement toward a unilateral separation of the two populations. In addition, Israel's relations with pro-Western Arab states – Egypt, Jordan, Oman, Qatar, Tunisia, and Morocco – have deteriorated and the potential for military escalation has increased on the Israeli–Lebanese and Israeli–Syrian borders.

While the peace process faces many challenges and uncertainties, a gradual but consistent change has been observed in the attitude of Arab countries *vis-à-vis* Israel and vice versa. Despite the expressions of violence, political tension and the continued procurement of arms, the attitudes of many Arabs and Palestinians toward Israel has become more pragmatic and less dogmatic. Both parties have become aware that a return to a state of violence and instability may have serious consequences. Thus, more than ever before the Israeli and Palestinian leaderships have come to understand that the conflict cannot be solved by violence, and that they have to return to the negotiating table.

The peace process has not only changed how people involved in the conflict perceive the consequences of their options, it has also transformed their priorities. This is because the various treaties that were signed between Israel and its neighbors did not merely alter the formal judiciary status of

Arab–Israeli relations. An important component of the peace process has been the day-to-day contacts and cooperative efforts between government agencies, private businesses, and individual citizens. The new bureaucratic and economic reality that has formed between Israel and its Arab neighbors has introduced a new dimension into the Arab–Israeli conflict. Whereas until the 1990s the major values motivating the antagonists were issues of territory and security, economic interests of entrepreneurs and nations have now replaced traditional military concerns. The question, however, is whether this new dimension will serve as a stabilizing factor, or whether it will produce a new source of tension that will amplify the older features of the conflict.

The optimistic view of the proliferation of economic interests envisions an economic environment based on cooperation and interdependence between Israel and the Arab parties. According to this view, the wealth produced by economic cooperation will be translated into economic development and will raise the standard of living throughout the region. The creation of business ventures that include experienced Israeli entrepreneurs with financial capability combined with the readily available supply of cheap Arab labor will also attract foreign investments. By such means, the Arab countries that suffer from high rates of unemployment can create new places of work and stimulate economic growth. These tangible benefits of economic cooperation will encourage the adversaries to seek peaceful means to overcome their differences.

A more critical view of cooperation, often referred to as the "dependency paradigm," argues that if one side is in a more advantageous position in relation to the other, the stronger partner can force the weaker party to accept an unequal share of the wealth that they produce together. According to this argument, the advantageous position of the Israelis enables them to exploit the vulnerability of the weaker Arab partners. Although Arab–Israeli economic relations will produce wealth and spur development in the region, the Arab world may become even worse off economically than it was before the peace process started. This is because the Israelis will be the major beneficiaries of the situation, while the Arabs will become economically dependent on the Israelis and be subject to Israeli domination and control.

In addition, according to the realist perspective of world politics, throughout most of the past century the fierce competition in the Middle East for territorial sovereignty induced the adversaries to build strong armies and establish rigidly hierarchical and centralist modes of government in order to control the movement of people, goods, and information across borders as well as within the jurisdiction of each state. Any action that could be interpreted as a shift in the status quo was likely to produce a crisis. Even when one of the contenders pursued seemingly peaceful policies, such as constructing an irrigation project, signing an economic transaction with a foreign country, or participating in an international organization, these material or symbolic benefits were viewed as a potential risk for the other side.

Realists frequently maintain that as long as ethnic groups aspire to achieve the ideal of statehood, the security threats posed by competing states will continue to surpass all other interests. This situation can be compared with the case of Europe following the First World War. As in the period between the two world wars, this view holds that "peace" will persist as long as one side maintains its strategic superiority. Hence, if for some reason the balance of power shifts back in favor of the Arab states, the status quo will break down, followed by possible violence. And under conditions where stability is perceived to be temporary, preference will be given to avoiding long-term commitments and confining economic exchange to trade agreements or limited forms of joint ventures.

The differences between the two competing perceptions of political–economic relations, conflict or cooperation, reflect an ongoing analytical dispute regarding the relationship between economic development and political conflict. Yet both views share a common weakness: they focus on deterministic presumptions, assume rigid cause-and-effect relations, and are preoccupied with outcomes rather than with concern for policy aspirations, social context, or political processes.

As this book will show, a departure from a deterministic and rigid mode of thinking should lead one to avoid a firm stand for or against one of the two views, and instead to ask how decision-makers perceive the political–economic relationship.

Due to the conflicting demands between national self-determination and economic well-being, one can identify a minority within the Arab business community that espouses a more liberal approach, demonstrating willingness to cooperate with Israeli partners, and at the same time protectionist elements who are still abundant within the Arab and the Israeli business community. Thus, one may argue that although the costs associated with the eruption of a large-scale war have significantly increased, the existing political reality in the Middle East is still not suitable for the establishment of large-scale regional development or long-term joint ventures. Yet, while far-reaching liberalization of Arab–Israeli relations is not acceptable to the parties, total regulation of these relations is also rejected.

The situation confronting Arabs and Jews in the Middle East to some

---

degree resembles the dilemmas that faced western Europe at the end of the Second World War. On the one hand, like the Middle East, Europe was suffering from centuries of ethnic strife and national struggle. On the other hand, driven by domestic economic interests, even the most realist leaders, such as de Gaulle, accepted, however reluctantly, the breakdown of economic barriers. Also in the case of the North American experience, there was an attempt, for many years, to maintain a well-guarded border and resist economic integration between the US and Mexico. However, during the 1960s the Mexicans encouraged the "maquiladora" factories along the border, where cheap Mexican labor produced components required for US industries. In the 1990s economic integration was further enhanced by the NAFTA agreement which reduced customs barriers between Mexico, Canada, and the US.

The European and North American experience may lead to the conclusion that it is useless to resist the forces that are binding Israel and its Arab neighbors together. However, attempting to encourage economic relations will require narrowing the gap between liberals and protectionists regarding the costs and benefits associated with economic relations. Because the Arab world is likely to interpret closer economic ties with Israel as part of an imperialist scheme to subordinate them, one may assume that adoption of an international economic regime can serve as an effective device to mitigate the tensions generated by the structural differences between Israel and its neighbors.

The chapters that follow examine the political environment and bureaucratic cultures which underlie economic relations between Israel, Jordan, and the Palestinian Authority. The analysis presented will provide a better understanding of the social mechanisms underlying foreign investments and economic cooperation among the various parties; highlight the advantages/disadvantages of encouraging patterns of economic cooperation; and present potential strategies that would lead to implementation of successful economic ventures. A central conclusion drawn from the study is that strengthening political stability and peaceful coexistence in the Middle East can only take place by encouraging innovative modes of thinking with respect to economic cooperation. Various ideas are put forward in order to begin "Investing in Peace."

His Royal Highness Prince Hassan of the Hashemite Kingdom of Jordan, an unusual man of political courage and peaceful visions, was willing to share with us his innovative ideas on how to advance economic cooperation and political coexistence in the troubled Middle East region. We deeply appreciate his contribution.

Professor Joseph Ginat of Haifa University and the Center for Peace Studies at the University of Oklahoma were instrumental in facilitating our links with HRH Prince Hassan who serves as the president of the board of advisors for the Center for Peace Studies.

This study was made possible by a research grant from the Hammer Fund for Economic Development in the Middle East at Tel Aviv University and the Chaim Herzog Center for Middle East Studies and Diplomacy at Ben-Gurion University. We wish to thank Avraham Sela and Assaf Wietman who provided their input and insight for the first version of this research. Good fortune provided us with the help of Ralph Mandel who edited our initial manuscript, and Sylvia Weinberg who bore the burden of typing the manuscript patiently and efficiently.

1

Introduction: Perceptions of War, Peace, and Economics

With the termination of the Cold War at the end of the 1980s, it was only a matter of time until the reverberations of the transforming world system reached the Middle East. The first indication of a new era was observed during the Gulf War in 1991, when a coalition of Arab states joined the United States and other international forces in a war against a "brother" Arab state (Lewis, 1992). But the more striking event that marked the advent of a new agenda in the region was the Israeli–Palestinian Declaration of Principles (DoP) of September 1993.

The decline of pan-Arabism and the thawing of Arab–Israeli relations have their origins long before the two events described above. Still, the DoP of 1993 marks a watershed in Arab–Israeli relations. Following the DoP, other leaders in the region joined the peace process and are gradually taking steps toward finding peaceful solutions to their differences with Israel and toward normalizing relations. This includes the signing of formal trade agreements and opening representation offices; allowing tourists and journalists to visit each other's countries; and managing meetings between Arab and Israeli delegates within international organizations and at international conferences. These preliminary advances have resulted in the opening of new and diverse lines of communication between Israel and its neighbors, which until the 1990s were non-existent.

The removal of the barriers that had previously existed between Israel and the Arab world has encouraged entrepreneurs on both sides to explore the new economic prospects. Despite the sporadic expressions of violence, political tension and the continued procurement of arms, as these economic contacts multiply and strengthen, the cost of breaking up the new order and trying to return to the old mode of conflictual relations will increase. This new economic reality that is forming between Israel and its Arab neighbors has introduced a new dimension into the Arab–Israeli conflict. Whereas until the 1990s the major issues were territory and security, the development of economic relations between Israel and its neighbors has added new issues, relating to the distribution of wealth and development within the region.

An optimistic view of the proliferation of economic relations envisions an economic environment based on cooperation and interdependence between Israel and the Arab parties. According to this view, instead of wasting valuable resources on a costly conflict, which has so far produced few benefits to either side, the wealth produced by economic cooperation will be translated into economic development and raise the standard of living throughout the region. These tangible benefits of economic cooperation, which can easily be forfeited and lost if the conflict is rekindled, should encourage the adversaries to seek peaceful means to overcome their differences.

Although the assumption exists that economic relations produce mutual benefits for all parties, a more critical view of economic interaction questions how the wealth generated by these relations is distributed among the partners of an economic exchange. If one side is in a more advantageous position in relation to the others, the stronger partner can force the weaker parties to accept an unequal share of the wealth that they produce together. Because Israel is in an economically favorable position in comparison to the Arab side, economic relations are unequal. The advantageous position of the Israelis enables them to exploit the vulnerability of the weaker Arab partners. Thus, according to this argument, although Arab–Israeli economic relations will produce wealth and spur development in the region, the Arab world may become even worse off economically than it was before the peace process started. This is because the Israelis will be the major beneficiaries of the situation, while the Arabs will become economically dependent on the Israelis and be subject to Israeli domination and control.

Deterministic Explanations

The difference between the two competing perceptions regarding the impact of economic relations on the future of the Arab–Israeli dispute reflects an ongoing analytical dispute regarding the relationship between economic development and political conflict. Comparative empirical research that attempts to address this issue provides contradictory results. On the one hand, studies have found a negative correlation between aggregate trade levels between states and the probability of the outbreak of an international war (Polachek, 1980; Mansfield, 1994). On the other hand, Reuveny and Kang (1996) have demonstrated that trade between states is associated with conflictive modes of behavior. While trade can lead to conflict, or conflict can lead to the development of trade relations, when a conflict breaks out, trade relations will probably be less intensive than they were before or after the crisis.

Rather than attempting to find the possible relationship between bilateral trade and inter-state conflict, some researchers have attempted to discuss whether economic dependence is associated with inter-state conflict. Barbieri (1996), measuring dependence as the proportion of a country's trade with a particular country in terms of its total international trade, concludes that the level of inter-state conflict rises as a function of dependency. O'Neal *et al.* (1996), measuring dependency as a ratio between trade with another country and the first country's GDP, observed an opposite relationship. In this case dependency reduced the probability of the outbreak of a war.

In fact, both views that emerge from the studies cited, although divergent, are feasible. In some cases, economic relations have been associated with political conflict, while in other instances conflict has been incompatible with the development of economic relations.

The possibility that economic interactions can be associated with both cooperative and conflictive political relations may raise difficulties for someone who assumes that social behavior is based on deterministic cause and effect relations. This notion of a deterministic relationship between economic and political conduct is based on two assumptions. The first is that rational choice is the prevailing method of human choice. The second assumption is that the will to survive receives priority over any ideological or moral dogma. The underlying justification of these two assumptions is the evolutionary theory of survival of the fittest. Taken to its logical conclusion, this view holds that those who do not behave in a rational manner, or who insist on acting according to moral principles, rather than materialistic values, are likely to be worse off in comparison to more "realistic" persons. Thus, according to this interpretation, groups and individuals cooperate with each other or enter into conflicts due to circumstances related to their most essential social needs.

If human conduct is strictly the consequence of environmental constraints, then the dispute between competing perceptions regarding the economic relations between Israel and its Arab neighbors can be resolved simply by calculating the costs and benefits associated with the choice between Arab–Israeli economic cooperation or preservation of the political conflict. If the benefits of economic cooperation outweigh the costs of dissociation, then those involved will find a way to maintain these fruitful relations, regardless of whatever rhetoric is invoked against economic cooperation between Arabs and Israelis. On the other hand, if the costs of economic relations between Israel and its Arab neighbors are higher than any benefits they might yield, then eventually those relations will be severed or renegotiated in a manner that will be mutually beneficial.

The cost–benefit approach described above seems to be popular among economists and analysts, since it allows them to prescribe calculated and "exact" solutions for policy questions. The problem is that calculating the different payoffs associated with social behavior is possible only if there is a consensus within each of the parties regarding basic social priorities. But different individuals may adopt opposing value systems that can sometimes lead to contrary conclusions regarding the relationship between economic and political interests. Therefore, disputes between parties cannot simply be analyzed as a competition over the distribution of valued items, they must also be addressed as the consequence of conflicting value systems. While there is no denying that the environment influences human behavior, people respond differently depending on their values and goals, and on their subjective interpretation of reality. Thus, rather than taking a stand for or against one of the two views, one should ask how decision-makers perceive the political–economic relationship. If decision-makers assume that economic interactions will lead to a political dispute they will adopt conflictive strategies. If the common belief is that economic exchange pacifies political tensions, the decision-makers will pursue cooperative policies.

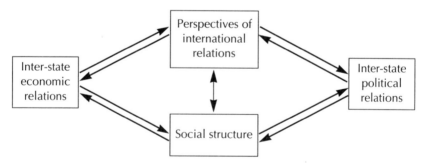

Figure 1.1 Economic and political relations

The complexity of the interaction between inter-state relations, environmental constraints, and normative perceptions can be illustrated through the work of Axelrod and Koehane (1983). They suggest that cooperative modes of international behavior are induced by the existence of systems of information regarding activities within and among states. Accordingly, the flow of information between states influences political behavior. However, systems that mediate the flow of information across national boundaries are not independent objects. The decision-makers in states have the capability to initiate and eliminate such systems.

The same can be said about economic relations. Although there are certain conditions that can encourage or inhibit the profitability of economic cooperation, social environments can be controlled and influenced by decision-makers. State leaders, if they choose, can promote policies that reduce risks and increase profits. On the other hand, if they take a negative view of economic relations, they can impose limitations and restrictions on economic activity. Thus, when attempting to analyze how inter-state political relations influence economic relations, or vice versa, one must take into account both the underlying social structure and the normative perspectives of the policy-makers. While the decision-makers' social environment and the value systems they espouse influence the nature of conflict and economic relations, they are also affected by these two variables, as well as by each other (figure 1.1).

Four Perspectives of World Order

Because policies are generated by value systems, it is crucial to identify the normative foundations that play a role in shaping the policy-makers' perceptions in different countries and the range of conflict and disagreement between them. Alternative interpretations of world order can be roughly divided into four major schools of thought.

The debate between the opposing schools of world order revolves around two sets of conflicting assumptions regarding the international system. The first two assumptions relate to the nature of the relationship between economic and political needs. The question is, do economic considerations dominate political behavior or do political interests prescribe economic behavior? The second set of assumptions relates to the distribution of resources. Is economic exchange defined as a zero-sum or nonzero-sum relationship? The zero-sum interpretation assumes that the gain of one party will necessarily be the loss of the other, while the nonzero-sum approach assumes that it is possible that both sides can gain or lose, rather than one always gaining at the expense of the other. It is these two dimensions of social reality that allow us to differentiate among four schools of thought, as shown in figure 1.2.

Priority of Interests	Distribution of resources	Zero-sum	Non zero-sum
Political interests first		Realism	Idealism
Economic interests first		Centralism	Liberalism

Figure 1.2 Four major perceptions of politics and economics

None of the four schools of thought is monolithic. Taking into account additional characteristics of political and economic behavior, each approach can be further subdivided into a number of subcategories. Although there have been vehement debates between advocates of different subcategories within each school, these differences are negligible when dealing with the basic question of the relationship between economic co-operation and political conflict. With regard to this fundamental question, the division into the four major camps is quite evident.

The realist view

The realist school envisions the world order as a system of well-defined political units, called states. Each state has clear boundaries and is ruled by a government that upholds law and order within the state, as well as being responsible for foreign policy toward other states. Unlike the domestic political system within a state, the world order is not confined by any laws, since no world government exists to maintain order. In other words, the world order is in a state of anarchy (Waltz, 1979).

Since states cannot rely on a legal and judicial system to protect themselves, each state is responsible for its own protection. This is accomplished by allocating a considerable portion of resources for the purpose of building strong armies that will deter other states from attacking. Under these circumstances, small states are in a very precarious situation. In order to preserve themselves, they tend to form alliances with larger powers. Thus, the world order is characterized by a number of blocs of states. Within each bloc, the larger powers can take advantage of the smaller states. Yet, the leverage of the stronger states is limited. If the terms of the association are unsatisfactory to the smaller state, the larger power risks the possibility that its smaller partner will try to realign with an adversarial power.

The aggregation of states into blocs with equal amount of power has been considered to have a stabilizing effect on the political order. The balance of power between rival blocs discourages the outbreak of violence since each side lacks the ability to overpower the other. However this "stability" is highly vulnerable to changes in the status quo. Shifts in the balance of power, if they are not readjusted by breaking up old alliances and creating a new and more balanced system, are liable to result in the outbreak of war (Gilpin, 1981).

A state's ability to influence and coerce other states, or to resist pressure from other states, is not a function of the absolute assets possessed by each, but of the relative distribution of capabilities. When one state gains more material benefits in comparison to another, this relative advantage can be applied in order to influence the behavior of the state with fewer resources (Carr, 1939). It is here that one should look in order to understand why the realist policy-maker tends to continually monitor, and if needed, intervene in, any economic transaction with another state. These policy-makers will be concerned about the relative benefits accruing from an economic transaction. Good prospects for economic cooperation will be likely as long as there is no fear that it will destabilize the existing balance of power between the parties. States will most probably avoid economic cooperation if their expectation is that one side will benefit more than the other, even if both economies can gain in absolute terms from such cooperation.

The idealist perspective

The idealist school differs substantially in its interpretation of relations between states. The major difference is that rather than focusing on the relative amount of power and resources available to each state, the idealists focus on the absolute amount of resources available to the citizens of the state. Since absolute assets, rather then relative power, is the central standard of analysis, it follows that the realist world is a very hazardous place. First, because states are locked in a struggle over power resources, the tendency to resort to violence is usually very high. This leads to frequent loss of life and destruction of property and the environment. Furthermore, the idealists argue that most wars do not result in a total victory. Thus, rather than conceiving the outcome of armed conflicts as a binary variable, where one side wins and the other loses, the idealists claim that this is an unduly simplistic interpretation of conflicts. If all the factors affected by armed conflicts are accounted for, it is possible to demonstrate that both sides usually lose, although one loses a bit more.

The realist answer to the idealist critic is that even though a major war can be very costly, if the enemy loses more, the war was worthwhile, since this means that the enemy will be in a less threatening position. Hence, the realist motto can be summed up as *"better to lose one eye if your opponent loses both eyes."* Such an argument is unacceptable to the idealist. The idealist response is that it is not worth sacrificing an eye, even if the enemy has more to lose. But wars are not the only issue. Even during times of peace, in a realist world large amounts of resources are squandered on military expenses instead of invested in human welfare. If instead of wasting so many resources on wars, states would adopt a legal system and surrender part of their sovereign responsibilities to a world government, differences could be resolved peacefully (Clark and Sohn, 1966). Although it is possible that in some cases international law might negate the interests of a state, the amount a state will pay for wielding power and opposing the legal solution will usually be higher than if it abides by the international law. The point is that if all states faithfully uphold the law they will save the costs of building up strong armies and suffering the rigors of war.

It is no coincidence that idealist thought developed in conjunction with democratic theory. According to Kant (1983), who was one of the precursors of idealism, the realist approach can be overcome only if states are democratic. In every state most citizens would rather not be sent to fight in a war and would prefer that most of the government's budget be earmarked for the social welfare of the community. But such preferences are usually expressed in states with governments that are accountable to their citizens. In a state ruled by an authoritarian government, the interests of the government are not necessarily compatible with the interests of the citizens. Arguably then, the realist approach serves the interests of the ruling classes, but not those of the common citizen, who bears the burden of war, and does not necessarily enjoy the benefits of victory.

Although the idealist approach has a pacifist bias, wars are justified under certain conditions. First, like most pacifists, the idealists maintain that the use of violence in self-defense is admissible (Cady, 1989). But in addition, launching a war against a state that menaces world order, or violates human rights, is also acceptable. These conditions were specifically inserted into the United Nations Charter. Of course the use of force should be a last resort, and there should be international agreement for such an action.

Like the realists, idealist policy-makers tend to view economic conduct as subordinate to political interests. However, the motives are different. While the realist is concerned about national power, the idealist focuses on the personal welfare of humanity. Thus the idealist policy-maker will urge an increase in state budgets for education, welfare, health care, environmental issues, and promote lower defense spending. The idealist will also support humanitarian aid of rich states to poor states that suffer from high rates of disease and famine. A realist, on the other hand, would never agree to assist another state for purely altruistic reasons; the state that was aided would be expected to give a quid pro quo.

The centralist school

Contrary to the realist and idealist common perception of "political interests first," the centralist approach argues that economic considerations take preference over political conduct. Apart from this difference, there are many similarities between centralist and realist thought. While the objective of the realist state is to accumulate power, the state governed by centralist policy is motivated by the desire to accumulate wealth. In order to protect those assets, a strong army will usually be required, since it is not uncommon for others to covet the state's wealth. The army can also be used to force weaker partners to accept less favorable terms in economic transactions. Those who are in a more powerful position can extract greater profits at the expense of weaker partners. Even if all partners of an economic exchange prosper, the exchange will not be considered as a co-operative association unless the profits are equally distributed among all the partners.

Following the Second World War, with the gradual independence of European colonies located mainly in the southern hemisphere, the centralist approach gained considerable influence. Underlying this development was the growing inequality of wealth between the small minority of highly developed industrial states in Europe and North America and the less developed countries. The major argument adduced by the less developed countries in the South was that the highly developed countries of the North were responsible for their dismal condition. After years of exploitation and subordination during the colonial era, when these countries gained independence, their undeveloped economies remained dependent on their former masters.

A crucial question, however, is why the less developed countries allow themselves to be exploited by the richer countries of the North. Assuming that the products of the South are essential for the economy of the North, one would expect the South to possess some degree of leverage. However, the poor and less developed countries cannot effectively exploit their resources or employ their labor without capital investment and technical knowledge from the rich states. Obtaining capital investment and knowledge means that the developing peripheral countries are forced to return most of the profits to the wealthy developed states. Any attempts by the peripheral countries to alter the existing economic order have been countered by coordinated sanctions imposed by the industrialized states of western Europe and North America (Wallerstien, 1974).

An alternative explanation, from a Marxist perspective, is that the ruling class in the less developed countries cooperates with the ruling class in the more developed countries. In return for their cooperation, the ruling classes in the North provide the ruling classes of the South with economic bonuses and with military assistance to repress the lower peripheral classes. Thus, even though the economy of a poor country may "develop," only a minority of businessmen and government officials, who collaborate with the rich investors from the North, actually enjoy the fruits of international economic cooperation. The rest of society within the world's periphery remains poor and underdeveloped. In the highly developed countries too, the peripheral lower classes suffer from this arrangement. Many laborers in the more developed countries have become unemployed, or have been subjected to declining wages, due to the transfer of labor-intensive manufacturing to the less developed countries, where it is cheaper (Frank, 1966; Gultung, 1971).

From time to time the peripheral classes of the less developed countries have attempted to overthrow the ruling regime. Such attempts have frequently led to the North's intervention in order to help the rulers in the South suppress popular resistance. In some instances, during the Cold War era, popular resistance against the ruling classes succeeded without assistance from the Soviet Union and its Eastern allies. Yet, these cases did not solve the predicament of the South, as western domination was substituted by eastern domination.

The liberal approach

An opposite version of economic order is espoused by the liberal school of thought. Although the liberals do not deny that the less developed countries are dependent on the more advanced countries, they claim that within a free market system benefits are distributed in a fair manner. The investor from the industrialized country provides the less developed country with capital and advanced technical knowledge, which are required for the establishment of an industrial base in order to utilize existing natural resources and labor that are either cheaper or not available in the North. As a result of this investment, new places of work are created, the economy takes off and all sectors of society in the periphery share in the benefits of development (Beamish, 1988). Thus, the relationship between North and South is not zero-sum. Although the North earns more than the South, in absolute terms the South also profits. And because world production depends on

cooperation between North and South, all will lose if there is no cooperation. Any attempt to resist the market forces and institute a set of
arrangements that artificially increase one group's relative material advantage at the expense of another will disrupt the productivity of the entire
system.

The liberal approach does not confine itself solely to the economic realm.
Many liberals have argued that the creation of economic cooperation,
where everybody prospers, will have a profound effect on political conflicts. This argument derives from the assumption that as economic ties
between states strengthen, the cost of terminating these relations becomes
very high. Thus, advocates of liberalism claim that the free market system
succeeds where the idealist approach failed. Even though the world lacks
an effective international government, hard-and-fast boundaries between
states are gradually fading away and international associations
between nationalities are becoming more dominant (Gilpin, 1975).

The liberal conceptualizations are accepted in part by the centralist
school. Many neo-Marxists recognize the fact that a network of cooperative links is forming between different states, but they insist that these
contacts are limited to the ruling classes. Neo-Marxists also agree that such
an international network undermines the ability of states to effectively
protect and promote political interests. Thus a decline in the incidence of
international wars is anticipated according to centralist thought. However,
unlike the liberals, neo-Marxists predicted the eruption of civil wars
between the oppressed social classes and their rulers.

The civil strife that has sometimes flared up in developing countries took
many liberals by surprise due to the liberal conviction that economic
development eventually leads to democratization. While most liberals have
not entirely abandoned the belief in the affinity between economic development and democratization, they have recognized that rapid economic
development can also produce negative social consequences. Rapid economic development tends to create new social classes that threaten the
older traditional system. The resulting tensions can foment violent social
and political conflicts. It is here one should look in order to understand
why many liberals argue that the civil strife experienced during periods of
economic development is not necessarily a reaction to economic exploitation. Rather, it reflects the social crises and instability associated with the
process of industrialization (Hirschman, 1967; Huntington, 1968).

Social Structures

Although the relationship between political and economic behavior is highly dependent on the world-view of the people participating in these interactions, this relationship is not entirely unrelated to the social structure. The problem is that social arrangements are not static; and people continually attempt to renegotiate the status quo and adjust social reality to suit their agendas as much as possible. As a result, it is possible to identify a plethora of alternative political arrangements that have emerged within different human societies.

Despite the great degree of variation of social arrangement, many political analysts tend to focus on two ideal types of social arrangements within states and social systems. All the different variants that have been created can be located somewhere in between these two extremes.

At one extreme is the state with a rigid hierarchical order. Within such a state, only those few who preside at the highest levels of command actually determine policy. This select group of leaders is the sole authority that determines whether to intervene and inhibit or to encourage international economic relations with another entity. Within such a state there is a clear chain of command and a distinct division of authority between its organizations.

An opposite view of the state, which has been termed the pluralist approach, assumes that its authoritative and functional structure is an ideal rather than a reality. Officials whose task is to execute the policies handed down by their superiors have their own agenda, which they are interested in implementing. Furthermore, policies are often only vaguely formulated, providing the lower-level bureaucrats considerable discretion. Also the division of labor between organizations is not always well defined. Consequently, internal conflicts often arise between different bureaucracies, as well as between the government and private groups (Allison, 1971).

The two social arrangements described above are the product of many factors and interests. Thus, for example, Hobbes argued in favor of the hierarchical arrangement, claiming that this was a more stable social system, which could preserve law and security. The founding fathers of the United States, on the other hand, advocated a more pluralist approach, contending that the hierarchical structure infringed on people's freedom.

When considering the utility of the two systems in the context of world politics, the realists and centralists will usually favor a hierarchical state, while idealists and liberals will prefer the pluralist model. Pluralism is preferred by idealists and liberals because such a system allows groups within the state to freely associate with external groups and thus form cooperative links across borders (Alger, 1977). However, such a system will be incompatible for leaders who attempt to promote realist or even centralist policies, which entail intervention in international economic relations.

It is possible that there might be a contradiction between alternative perceptions of social order. Still, while people may be motivated by opposing purposes, this does not mean that such incompatibilities cannot be resolved and new social realities cannot be forged. Thus, decision-makers can advocate seemingly contradicting policies while attempting to reorganize the existing social system. The upshot is that realist perceptions have succeeded in flourishing even within democratic states. In such instances, while the government assumed pluralist characteristics, the security forces continued to preserve their hierarchical and centralized attributes.

Social orders therefore include both hierarchical and pluralistic elements. Furthermore, they have the capacity to change over time and oscillate between various degrees of centralization and decentralization. Such developments can even be detected in the case of the Middle East. During most of the twentieth century the Middle East was, overall, extremely hierarchical. However, over the past two decades one can discern hesitant beginnings of pluralist thought. At present, while the hierarchical state order is still quite evident, transition in the direction of pluralism is struggling for a better place on the state agenda.

Inter-State Political Relations

Political relations between states are frequently identified on the basis of behavioral patterns that are assumed to be associated with conflictive, competitive or cooperative policies. Conflictive actions spring from subjective feelings of threat and intimidation, in the perception of at least one party. Because increasing one's advantage is perceived as a threat to another party, attempts to change the status quo will encounter stiff opposition and readiness to initiate a crisis, which could culminate in an outbreak of violence.

When relations between parties are competitive, rather than conflictive, any disagreements that may arise are not considered vital by any party. Because an advantage gained by one party at the expense of another is not viewed as a threat, there is no need to maintain military deterrence and there will be a tendency to avoid escalatory behavior and crises. Thus, despite disagreements, the likelihood of a violent eruption is low. These types of relations can be perceived within all four perceptions of world political order.

The third pattern of relations is cooperative. Cooperative relationships reflect the liberal and ideal types of international association, although they are also expected between allies within a realist or centralist system. In this case, rather than disagreement over certain matters, both parties share common or symbiotic interests. Cooperation between two parties is expected if it will promote the interests of both. The fact that one side might obtain certain gains in relation to the other will not be viewed as an advantage that comes at the other's expense.

Although disagreements can emerge even within the context of cooperative relations, the method for resolving these differences is significantly different from that in competitive or conflictive relations. When relations become cooperative, disagreements are treated as a problem that must, and can, be resolved. Each side discloses its needs and attempts to give the other party the greatest possible leeway to pursue its interests. A famous example invoked by problem-solvers is the case of two people finding an orange and squabbling over its possession. If they are problem-solvers, each will reveal his or her interest in possessing the orange, thus perhaps discovering that one of them wants to drink its juice and the other to use its peel. Thus the conflict over the orange is easily resolved and both parties share it.

When relations are dominated by conflict and competition it is more difficult to resolve differences. This is because almost everything is open to bargaining, including items that are valued slightly. In competitive and conflictive relations, a dispute can arise even if the interests being pursued by one party do not infringe on the interests of others, as the fear is that if any party is allowed to freely achieve its interests, it will improve its position in comparison to others. As a result, opponents will attempt to interfere whenever they recognize that one party is successfully achieving its interests.

In the case of two bargainers the story of finding the orange will develop quite differently. In contrast to cooperative problem-solvers, who disclose interests, the opposite occurs: each side attempts to conceal its priorities. In this manner, even interests that are of low priority can be bargained over at a high price. Even though each party really wants only a part of the orange, it will demand tribute for conceding the parts it does not want.

Like the social organization of the state, political relations between states are also dynamic and value priorities can change over time. On the one hand, this can generate new disagreements that did not previously exist; on the other hand, ideological change can lead to the dissipation of the initial feelings of threat. In the case of the Middle East, certain social values seem to be losing their prominence in comparison to others. For example, in the past the Jewish claim regarding the right of return to the historical home-land, or the Palestinian claim of self-determination, were portrayed as highly threatening to the other side. In fact these two issues were tradition-ally held up as the crux of the Arab–Israeli conflict. However, over the years these issues lost their dramatic significance. Each side agreed to accept, or at least acknowledge, the existence of these two rights in the historical and political consciousness of each of the two peoples, as a fact of life.

Inter-State Economic Relations

International economic interactions can roughly be divided into three distinct types: trade, joint ventures, and regional infrastructure develop-ment. The major criterion used for distinguishing between risks and opportunities associated with each of these three types of economic relationships is based on the "costs of dissociation."

In order to calculate the "cost of dissociation," it is necessary to evaluate the relative ease with which each side can obtain a similar input from alternative sources (Ben Shahar *et al.*, 1989: 11–13). In this respect, it should be noted that because economic relations are not necessarily balanced, the costs of dissociation might be different for each party involved.

Trade relations

Most economic exchanges between states can usually be defined as trade transactions. The volume of bilateral trade between countries, however, is influenced by the formal political arrangements between them. These arrangements, which affect the profitability of trade, depend on the ideo-logical orientation of the states involved. Liberal economic leadership advocates freedom of trade, while centralist or realist concerns might justify imposing limitations that will reduce the profitability of trade in order to protect the state's economy or national security.

Buying and selling commodities is normally defined as zero-sum, and has a natural tendency toward bargaining, as each partner attempts to demand the highest possible return for the exchange. However, such a relationship can become cooperative if a trade relationship is long lasting and all the partners participating in the transaction are satisfied with the terms of the exchange. In order to maintain the relationship and preserve a steady flow of exports or imports, it will be worthwhile to behave cooperatively and to compromise instead of bargaining, so as not to break off the relationship. However, if one or even all of the partners believe they have been coerced to settle for a deal at unreasonable terms, then the relationship can be viewed as competitive or even in extreme cases as threatening.

Liberals assume that the creation of a free market is the most suitable arrangement to encourage cooperative trade relationships and avoid situations where one partner becomes dependent on and exploited by others. In this manner, due to competition among sellers of similar types of merchandise, the market forces determine the optimal values of trade transactions (depending on the number of buyers and sellers). On the other hand, centralists are very suspicious about the benefits of a so-called free market. They argue that even within such a system, weaker trading partners are exploited and coerced. Thus, the scarcity of a particular product (including an artificial shortage caused by monopolization) can force consumers to buy commodities at prices much higher than their actual costs of production. On the other hand, the abundance of a certain product, or a small pool of buyers, can compel a producer to sell at prices below the actual production costs.

Joint ventures

Although aggregate trade volumes are one of the most popular methods used to measure economic cooperation between states, there is a major qualitative difference between regular trade transactions and the transfer of capital within the framework of a joint venture. Trade entails the lowest level of economic cooperation and involves lower risks, as it requires only minimal formal cooperation between the parties. Unlike trade, where two or more parties cut a deal, the parties form a new institutional structure, to which they both belong, for the purpose of producing a product that is intended for their mutual benefit. As in trade, there is a certain degree of bargaining between the partners. Each has an interest in investing as little as possible and in reaping the greatest possible profits. On the other hand, the creation of a joint venture requires far greater coordination and a higher degree of trust between the partners, since the costs of dissociation are much higher. If one partner fails to produce his or her share of production, the joint venture will fail and both stand to lose. Thus, the risks associated with joint ventures are much higher than they are with trade. As a result, while trade can proliferate between states that do not have formal diplomatic relations, this is more difficult in the case of joint ventures.

Indeed, even formal relations between states are not enough to reduce the risks associated with the creation of joint ventures. Again, as with trade, there are many alternative ways to establish joint economic institutions. When relations are cooperative, these arrangements are perceived by all partners as providing a fair distribution of costs and benefits, but when relations are tainted by a competitive atmosphere, it is possible that some members may feel exploited and disadvantaged.

Regional infrastructure development

The highest costs of dissociation are expected when parties attempt to develop shared infrastructures. As in the case of joint economic enterprise, the relationship can be viewed as either mutually beneficial or one-sided. However, unlike joint ventures, which can be conducted by private firms, a shared infrastructure requires some degree of government involvement, and some form of cooperation at the government level must be established. Thus, various political considerations will probably be incorporated into such a partnership and each party might have to compromise a portion of its national sovereignty.

Sharing infrastructures does not correspond very well with realist political thought. Although soft infrastructure developments, such as international governmental organizations or communications networks, can successfully be established between allies within a realist international system, a project that requires intervention in the environment, such as building a tunnel or a canal, will probably be avoided even by allies. The point is that according to the realist view, alliances are temporary political situations.

As indicated above, economic relations interweave cooperative, competitive, and conflictive characteristics. Of the three types of economic exchange, trade is the poorest indicator of cooperation. Quite frequently trade relations will involve a great deal of bargaining, especially if they are ephemeral. The formation of shared infrastructures is probably the best indicator of cooperation. Although this type of interaction can be characterized by bargaining and competition, if partners are unwilling to invest a considerable degree of problem-solving, the attempt to construct shared infrastructure is likely to fail.

The Israeli, Jordanian, and Palestinian Triangle: The Interactive Perspective

The analysis presented in the following chapters focuses on the interaction between economic and political relations in the case of Israel, Jordan, and the Palestinian Authority. On the basis of the experience that has accumulated since the signing of the Israeli–Palestinian DoP in 1993 and the Israeli–Jordanian peace treaty in 1994, it is possible to gain some insight into the question of whether or not Arab–Israeli economic relations are dominated by problem-solving or bargaining tactics.

Our major thesis is that normative perceptions have been the key variable affecting the attitudes of Arabs and Israelis toward the assumed benefits to be gained from these new economic ties. However, to a great extent the regional political conflict, different social structures, and different economic features nurture these perceptions. These issues will be discussed in chapters 2 and 3.

Following a brief summary of the structural and historical constraints affecting Israeli–Jordanian, and Palestinian relations, the remaining chapters will analyze the establishment of economic relations between the three parties, since 1994. As economic relations should be divided between three different levels of association – trade, joint ventures and regional infrastructure development – each of these three forms of economic exchange will be analyzed separately. Chapter 4 is dedicated to the simplest and most rudimentary form of economic relations – trade; chapter 5 concentrates on the establishment of transnational economic ventures; and chapter 6 addresses the complications involved in the creation of shared regional infrastructure development.

As will be shown in chapters 4–6, Arab–Israeli relations are mainly characterized by bargaining types of negotiations. Although trade was flourishing between Israel and the Palestinian Authority, most Palestinians felt that they were in a disadvantageous position. So far, sharing infrastructures has not been very successful, and joint ventures are still limited to exceptional cases where the partners have succeeded in shifting the relationship from bargaining to problem-solving.

To a certain extent, one might have expected that after a prolonged conflict Israeli–Jordanian and Israeli–Palestinian economic relations would necessarily be conceived within an atmosphere of bargaining. Still, the major question is under what circumstances can these relations shift toward more benign and problem-solving modes of interaction. This crucial question will be addressed in chapter 7. It will be suggested that Arab and Israeli negotiators could benefit from taking a different course of action. Instead of each side attempting to force the other to comprehend and accept each other's perspectives, both sides should make an effort to create an international regime of *perceptional pluralism*.

While each side continues to adhere to their subjective perceptions, each side is granted relative advantages in comparison to the other, regarding those highly crucial issues according to their subjective point of view.

It should be emphasized that a regime of perceptional pluralism is not always a feasible solution for all international conflicts. However, in the specific constellation of the Arab–Israeli conflict, once the territorial issues are resolved, the remaining sources of disagreement can be settled on the basis of perceptional pluralism.

2

The Domestic Environments

———————

Political and economic attitudes and perceptions are in constant interaction with the social environment. This chapter provides a general background regarding some of the basic aspects of the Israeli, Jordanian, and Palestinian social and economic environments. Readers who are well informed about one or more of these three societies and their political–economic structure may choose to skip the relevant sections; those who are unfamiliar with any of these three social and economic entities may wish to consult the bibliography for better understanding.

The Israeli Polity

The political system

Israel is considered the most democratic country in the Middle East (Moustafa, 1996). The foundations of Israeli democracy can be traced back to the beginnings of the Zionist movement. From the end of the nineteenth century Zionists organized in political parties and elected candidates to the World Zionist Congress, which convened every two years. During the period of the British Mandate in Palestine, the Jewish community also voted a number of times for representatives to the Knesset Yisrael, which was responsible for administering civil matters in Palestine, including welfare, health, and education (Arian, 1973). The political norms and structures that were established prior to Israel's independence served as the basis for the Israeli regime. Thus, Israeli citizens vote in national elections to the Israeli Parliament (the Knesset), they are granted the right to demonstrate and to organize political parties, as well as the freedom to express their opinions (Arian, 1985).

Like many other democracies, Israel is tainted by violations of human rights as well as attempts to limit freedom of speech, information, and mobility. For example, Israeli law allows censorship of any information that the authorities consider threatening to the country's security. Until 1966, Palestinians living in Israel were subject to military law, even though they were granted full citizenship, including the right to organize and to vote for their own political representatives. Still, despite a sometimes unflattering record, the historical trend seems to uphold liberal–democratic values. In recent years, the Israeli Knesset has ratified a number of more liberal laws, such as the Basic Law of Human Dignity and Liberty (1992) and the Basic Law of Freedom of Occupation (1994). There are also indications that government and security officials are under a higher degree of public and judicial scrutiny than in the past. During the 1990s the police force has shown determination to investigate the behavior of government officials, including high-ranking members of the police and security forces. In addition the Israeli government and High Court of Justice have also been taking steps to impose limits on the methods used to interrogate suspects (High Court of Justice, 1999).

Jewish immigrants

In 1949, Israel's population stood at only 670,000. During its first fifty years of existence, Israel absorbed a total of 2.4 million immigrants, and at the end of 1999 the country's population was estimated to be slightly more than six million. Overall, the new immigrants boosted Israel's economy, enlarging the workforce and increasing domestic consumption. But in the short term, new immigrants put a strain on the economy. The state, together with the Jewish Agency, provided housing and considerable financial support to help new immigrants integrate into the Israeli society.

For many years the state's official policy was to settle the new immigrants on the periphery in "frontier settlements" or "development towns." The economies of the frontier settlements were usually based on agricultural production, while the development towns were oriented toward industry. Until the Arab–Israeli war of 1967, the establishment of these settlements was motivated mainly by security concerns. The idea was to populate empty areas or regions where few Jews resided (for example, see Ben-Gurion, September 30, 1949). Besides the fact that these towns and settlements frequently suffered from attacks by terrorists who infiltrated into Israel or who shelled them from across the border, the settlements failed to keep stride with the economic development of the urban centers. Many of the frontier settlements went bankrupt, while most of the development towns suffer from high unemployment.

The majority of the immigrants entering Israel's middle and upper classes originated from European countries, while a large portion of the immigrants from the Arab countries joined the lower socioeconomic classes. Although many members of the second generation of Middle East immigrants acquired professions and a better education, their very success induced them to leave their home towns on the periphery and move to urban centers, relegating the periphery to a permanent status of underdevelopment.

Religious Jews

In addition to the social division between "Orientals" (from Middle Eastern countries) and Europeans, Israel's Jewish population is divided between religious and secular groups. While the Nationalist Religious Orthodox community attempts to coexist with secular society, the Ultra-Orthodox deliberately separate themselves from the mainstream of Israeli society. Preferring study to work, this sector is supported by the state or by philanthropic organizations. In recent years, public subsidies for the Ultra-Orthodox have increased in line with the dramatic rise in their political power. For example, it is estimated that nearly 0.5 percent of the 1999 budget was earmarked to support yeshivas that belong to this sector (*Globes*, February 3, 1999).

The Arabs in Israel

The Arabs in Israel, who in 1996 accounted for almost 20 percent of Israel's total population, also suffer from a lower economic status. In 1982, over 50 percent of the Israeli Arab labor force were employed in either agriculture or construction, the less desired sectors of employment in Israel. Over the years, the plight of Israel's Arab citizens has improved, although their socioeconomic status remains well below the Jewish average. A 1992 survey estimated that nearly 30 percent of the non-Jewish labor force in Israel was employed in unskilled work or agriculture and about 20 percent were professionals. Among the Jewish population, about 50 percent were categorized as professionals and fewer than 20 percent were unskilled workers or employed in agriculture (Heiberg and Ovensen, 1994).

Discrimination against the Arab population, in contrast to the Jewish peripheral sectors, is state sponsored. Many positions are not open to Arabs because they require a "security clearance" or prior service in the Israel Defense Forces (IDF). However, Muslims and Christians are exempt from military service. Similarly, for many years Arabs were not eligible for many social benefits, which by law were available only to IDF veterans. In addition, Arab education, social welfare services, religious services, municipalities, and local councils consistently receive fewer funds than their Jewish counterparts (Haider, 1995).

An extremely sensitive and complicated issue is the fear that the Arabs are expanding geographically at the expense of Jewish localities. Israeli governments have therefore stepped up the expansion of Jewish settlements and agricultural land, while limiting the expansion of Arab settlements and confiscating Arab land. This issue has occasionally sparked violent riots by Arabs.

Foreign laborers

The expansion of the Israeli economy during the 1990s brought about an influx of foreign workers from poor countries. The demand for foreign labor was enhanced by the outbreak of the Palestinian uprising (the "*Intifada*") in December 1987, which was characterized by the frequent closure of cities and work strikes in the West Bank and Gaza Strip (WBGS). Increasingly, foreign workers replaced the residents of the Occupied Territories in the low paying jobs.

The number of foreign workers in Israel in 1998 was estimated at about 250,000 (Pines, 1998), far exceeding the workforce of Palestinians from the WBGS and from South Lebanon who work in Israel.

The Israeli Economy

Despite the fact that Israel is a small country (about 20,000 square kilometers) with virtually no natural resources, it succeeded in transforming itself from an agrarian-based economy into the most advanced industrial state in the Middle East. However, compared to western Europe or North America, Israel's economy is less developed; even in comparison to eastern Europe or Latin America, Israel's industrialization levels are significantly lower. Still, with a GDP (gross domestic product) of $68.7 billion in 1998 and a per capita GDP of $15,485, Israel is ranked as a "high-income economy" (World Bank, 1995).

In contrast to Jordan or the WBGS, which are considered "middle-income economies" according to World Bank criteria, the Israeli economy is gargantuan. Jordan's GDP in 1995 was only $6.6 billion, less than 10 percent of the Israeli GDP, and its per capita GDP stood at $1,574, one-tenth of Israel's. The GDP of the small Palestinian Authority in 1995 was half the size of Jordan's, although its per capita GDP, estimated at \$1,336;[1] was only slightly lower than that of Jordan.

Table 2.1 Composition of domestic product in percentages

Sector	Israel[1] (1994)	Jordan[2] (1997)	WBGS[3] (1994)
Industry	27	17	8
Agriculture	4	9	33
Construction	9	10	17
Other	60	64	42

Source: [1] David Boas Ltd. (1996); [2] IPR (1998); [3] Palnet (1998).

Table 2.1 illustrates that the larger Israeli GDP is coupled with characteristics of a more advanced economy, i.e., a larger portion of industrial production compared to agricultural production. In 1993 the GDP of Israel's industry was estimated to have reached a level of \$17 billion. In comparison, Jordan's industrial GDP was only \$800 million (less than 5 percent of Israel's). The industrial GDP of the Palestinian Authority was even smaller, estimated at only \$200 million.

Industry and trade

The composition of Israel's industries clearly reflects characteristics of an advanced economy. In 1994, the manufacture of electrical and electronic equipment accounted for 22.5 percent of the industrial GDP. Industries that specialize in metals contributed 17.1 percent of the industrial portion of the GDP, and the chemical and plastic industries a further 16.8 percent. These types of advanced industries are far less developed in Jordan and the WBGS, accounting for less than 8 percent of the industrial GDP in both of those regions in 1994.

In order to support an advanced industrial base in such a small country, Israel relies heavily on the export of its manufactured products (Richards and Waterbury, 1990: 30). In 1998 Israel exported about \$35 billion worth of goods, more than 70 percent to the United States and Europe. One consequence of the export-oriented approach is Israel's eagerness to form trade agreements with other countries that serve as potential markets for its products. Israel is currently a signatory to more than ten different international trade agreements that allow customs free transfers of commodities.

Because Israel has very few natural resources, local industry must import most of its raw materials. A case in point is the diamond industry, which in 1996 exported goods worth $5.2 billion, or 25 percent of Israeli exports. However, the diamond industry imported raw materials worth an estimated $5 billion during the same year (CBS, 1997). Altogether, about 60 percent of all Israeli imports are earmarked for industrial production. In addition, Israel imports large quantities of weapons and other military products. As a result, Israel suffers from a negative trade balance. Total Israeli imports in 1998 (estimated at $43.2 billion) were 23 percent higher than exports for that year (JCSS, 1998).

Economic growth

Israeli economic development can be divided into three distinct periods. The first is the period of 1948–1973, which was characterized by rapid economic growth. Between 1950 and 1973, Israel experienced an average growth rate of nearly 10 percent per year. The second period, which lasted until 1985, saw a slowdown in economic growth. From 1973 to 1981, GNP (gross national product) increased by an average of only 3.4 percent per year (Metzer, 1989). During the 1980s, as a result of the new oil crisis in 1979, Israel's economic performance actually worsened. Unemployment rates rose, inflation soared to an annual rate of nearly 400 percent, the GNP stopped growing, per capita GNP declined, and Israel's external debt approached a critical point.

The economic slowdown, which began in the aftermath of the 1973 October war, can be attributed to three factors. First, like many other countries Israel had to cope with the steep hike in oil prices. This, however, was compounded by the fact that the Israeli economy was highly dependent on international trade; the negative effect of the oil crisis on the economies of Israel's trading partners brought about a reduction in Israeli exports while increasing the prices of imports (Ben Porath, 1989). In addition, the traumatic effect of the war drove Israel into a spiraling arms race. The portion of military expenses and imports accelerated from about 20 percent of the GNP in 1972 to nearly 35 percent in 1974 (Bergles, 1989). As a consequence the Israeli budget started to swell to unprecedented proportions. According to Gabbay (1979), the fiscal 1978 budget (from April 1, 1978, to March 31, 1979) was estimated to have equaled 87 percent of the total GNP. The expansion of the budget generated a dramatic rise in the balance of payments deficit. Before the war, Israel's net external debt was less than $2 billion; within eleven years, by 1984, it was nearly $20 billion.

In 1985 the economic crisis induced the government to launch a strict recovery program. This included a price freeze on essential products, a sharp devaluation of the Israeli currency, cuts in subsidies, and greater taxation of higher income sectors. In addition, the defense budget was drastically cut and the government moved to liberalize the Israeli market system and curtail government intervention. Among other measures the government relaxed many of the restrictions that had been imposed on financial transactions, creating new investment alternatives and facilitating the opportunities of businesses to obtain loans and funding. Another form of liberalization was the privatization of government-owned corporations (Razin and Sadka, 1993), a still ongoing process.

The recovery program was initially quite successful. Inflation fell, unemployment decreased and GNP growth rates picked up, reaching an annual rate of 5.7 percent during the first half of 1987. Israel's negative balance of payments also reversed its previous trend. Between 1985 and 1992, government expenditure declined from 34.5 percent of the GDP to 26.4 percent. The net external debt was reduced from $19.4 billion in 1985 to $15.0 billion in 1991. In real terms (taking into account the devaluation of the dollar) the debt was cut by more than a third. However, the 1987 energy crisis combined with the outbreak of the *Intifada* undercut the optimistic projections. The Israeli economy once again entered a slowdown. Unemployment swelled to 9.3 percent of the labor force in 1989 (Razin and Sadka, 1993), the highest rate of unemployment Israel had experienced since the recession of 1966.

The economic slump of the late 1980s ended with the influx of immigrants from the former Soviet Union. Even though the sudden surge in the population intensified unemployment (which climbed to 11.6 percent of the workforce in the first quarter of 1992), most of the new immigrants, especially the professionals among them, successfully integrated into the Israeli economy.

The 1993 Oslo agreement raised expectations that at last a new era of economic prosperity would descend upon the Middle East. The assumption was that significant political stabilization within the region would attract foreign investors. The prospects of a peace settlement also signaled a reduction in the military budget and investment in more productive areas. In addition, the decision of the Arab states to terminate the boycott against companies trading with Israel allowed Israel to expand its foreign markets and attract investments that were denied in the past.

Despite the optimistic climate, the refusal of Syria and other Arab states to join the peace process, followed by the stalemate in the peace negotiations, discouraged potential investors and deterred tourists. This eventually led to a new economic slowdown in 1997 and unemployment rates rose to a level of 8.6 percent of the workforce by the end of 1998. In addition the gradual trend of reducing Israel's foreign debt which began in 1985 was reversed. Between 1992 and 1997 the foreign debt grew to $17.9 billion (JCSS, 1998).

Poverty and unemployment

In the face of the acute social divisions within Israeli society, successive governments have tried to maintain poverty at a minimal level: food and housing are subsidized, as is land leasing for agricultural production; most Israelis have some form of health insurance; all working residents are insured by social security; strong labor unions ensure the existence of a minimum wage for each sector; primary and secondary education is free and until 1980, tuition in Israel's universities (which are all public) was not expensive.

Because of government intervention in the economy, unemployment in Israel was usually low in comparison to many other countries. With the exception of the economic recession in 1966/7, until 1980, unemployment never rose above 3 percent of the labor force. However, attempts by the government to maintain a progressive welfare state have taken their toll on Israel's budget, which is anyway overburdened by excessive defense demands (Richards and Waterbury, 1990: 213). For example, in 1973 the public sector (employment + consumption) contributed nearly 40 percent of the GDP; in comparison, in most European countries the public sector accounted for less than 20 percent of GDP (Spechler, 1979).

Since Israel embarked on the liberalization policy in the 1980s, the shrinkage of the national debt has been accompanied by the gradual elimination of many of the special government subsidies and welfare programs. In addition, the privatization of government companies has aggravated unemployment. Thus, even though the growth rate of the economy started to pick up, as in other industrialized nations this has exacted a social price at the margins of society, which is characterized by rising levels of poverty, homelessness, and crime.

The Jordanian Polity

The government

Jordan was granted independence in 1946. However, unlike Israel or the Palestinian Authority, which are political entities that emerged out of a struggle for national self-determination, Jordan was created as a British protectorate. Following the First World War, the British nominated their Arab ally 'Abdallah as the Emir of Transjordan, which later became the Hashemite Kingdom of Jordan. 'Abdallah was one of the leaders of the Arab revolt against the Turks during the First World War. He belonged to a distinguished Arab family, known as the Hashemites, who were considered to be the descendants of Fatima, the daughter of the Prophet Mohammed. For more than a millennium this family served as the guardians of the Muslim holy shrines in Mecca and Medina.

After the First World War, 'Abdallah's brother Faisal was crowned as King of Iraq and his father Hussein King of Hijaz. 'Abdallah, on the other hand, was initially appointed by the British as governor of Transjordan for only six months (Dann, 1984). However, 'Abdallah established a monarchical dynasty which, in contrast to the rest of his family, has survived numerous attempts to topple it. Eighty years after 'Abdallah arrived in Jordan, the Hashemite family still remains the highest authority in the Kingdom.

Like most non-European twentieth-century monarchies, the Hashemites did not encourage democratic principles of government. Still, for a short period during the 1950s, and again since 1989, it is possible to identify a certain degree of liberalization: a parliament was established and multiple-party elections to the lower House of Deputies were introduced. In fact, several scholars maintain that since 1989 Jordan has become the most democratic Arab country (Moustafa, 1996; Malik, 1999). Still, unlike what one would expect in a democratic state, the Jordanian parliament and the judicial system have no real power over the executive branch. The King appoints and dismisses the government and can reject bills presented by the legislative branch, unless a two-thirds majority in both houses of parliament ratifies the law. Taking into account that members of the upper House of Senators are appointed exclusively by the King himself, such an exceptional situation is unlikely to arise (Jordan Bureau of Information, 2000). In addition to the rather limited authority of the parliament, the Jordanian security service can arrest suspects indefinitely without warrant, as well as censor information deemed to threaten Jordan's security (Anderson, 1997).

Social divisions

Over 60 percent of Jordan's citizens are thought to be of Palestinian origin (Kanovsky, 1997; Sobelman, 1998). The large number of Palestinians obtained Jordanian citizenship as a consequence of the Arab–Israeli War of 1948. After the war, the 460,000 Palestinian residents from the West Bank and the 450,000 Palestinian refugees who had fled from Israel into the West Bank were granted full Jordanian citizenship. At the time, the population residing in the East Bank was about 400,000.

The April 1950 decision of King 'Abdallah to annex the West Bank was very beneficial for the Jordanian economy. The annexation increased the population of the kingdom, thus boosting the workforce. Second, it improved the general educational level, as the new Palestinian residents were better educated than the original population in Transjordan. However, as in Israel, the Jordanian authorities had misgivings about the Palestinians' loyalty to the state. As such, they were excluded from many positions within the government, with the result that the private sector in Jordan is dominated by Palestinians, who own more than 80 percent of the country's business sector (Hamarneh, 1997).

Jordan's poorly developed economy drove many professionals and skilled workers to seek employment abroad in the rich Arab states. And because of the poor conditions of employment within the private sector, those who remain in the country prefer to pursue a career in the government bureaucracy (Barham, 1997). This dual thrust – to work in the public sector or to seek employment abroad – created the need for foreign labor. In 1997, it was estimated that 500,000 foreigners were residing in Jordan, which has a population of about 4 million.

While non-Palestinians dominate the bureaucratic class, Bedouin have dominated the Arab Legion, the primary military force in Jordan, since the 1930s. The alliance between the Bedouin and the Hashemites has been a major pillar in the stability of the Jordanian monarchy. Whenever disturbances have erupted, the Arab Legion has demonstrated a high degree of loyalty toward the King.

As in Israel, since the late 1980s, a privatization process has been set in motion. However, the Jordanian government was extremely reluctant to liberalize the economy significantly. As demonstrated in the riots that erupted in April 1989 and in August 1996, subsidy cuts can easily trigger popular violence (Jaber, 1997).

The death of Hussein in 1999 and the succession of his son, King 'Abdallah II, has had a pronounced effect on the liberalization process. Unlike his father, King 'Abdallah is a strong believer in liberal economics. As a consequence, despite the opposition of the parliament, one can discern for the first time a serious move toward privatization and an improvement in services, even though 'Abdallah is risking the possibility that Jordanian unemployment might rise even further (Huri, 1999).

Besides privatization, King 'Abdallah has also adopted another western standard: employment on the basis of personal merit, rather than ethnic affiliation. Thus, there is a willingness to employ Palestinians in government positions, which were traditionally fiefdoms of trusted families. Again, as in the case of privatization, while the new policy will probably improve the government's performance, the risk is that 'Abdallah will forfeit the loyalty of his traditional allies.

The Jordanian Economy

Although Jordan is larger than Israel and the WBGS, it is still a relatively small country, with an area of about 89,200 square kilometers, of which three-quarters is desert. Jordan, again like Israel and the WBGS, has a small population, estimated at between 4.2 million (JCSS, 1998) to 4.4 million in 1996 (*Jordan Economic Monitor*, January 1998), and hardly any natural resources. However, in contrast to Israel, Jordan has not succeeded in developing an advanced industrial base.

Industry and trade

The majority of Jordanian private enterprises are relatively undeveloped and oriented toward local needs. According to a 1994 survey, 71.6 percent of all Jordanian businesses employed fewer than four workers. The major heavy industries, chemicals and the extraction of potash and phosphate are export oriented, and are primarily owned by the government. In any event, their contribution to the GDP is small. Thus, like Israel, Jordan suffers from a negative trade balance. But the situation in Jordan is much worse. In 1997, Jordan's exports amounted to only about half of its imports; its exports that year were around $2.1 billion (IPR, 1998) – less than 10 percent the size of the Israeli total. While most of Israel's exports derive from industrial manufacturing, this sector contributed only 19 percent of Jordan's exports in 1994. And while over 50 percent of Israel's exports are directed at the United States and Europe, only a small fraction of Jordan's exports go to western Europe, and until 1997 Jordanian exports to the United States were non-existent.

Economic growth

Even though the Jordanian economy did not develop as rapidly as Israel's, the yearly rise in GNP following the war of 1948 was impressive. Between 1949 and 1966, GNP increased at a rate of 7 percent to 8 percent per year.

By 1966, Jordan had the highest per capita GNP of any Arab state (Ben Zvi, 1993).

After the 1967 war, GNP continued to grow, but the per capita GNP remained stable. This was due to the immigration of 260,000 residents from the West Bank who fled from the Israeli occupiers, compounded by large military expenditures associated with hostile activity in the Jordan Rift Valley in the war's aftermath.

Following the Arab–Israeli war of 1973, economic growth in many countries decreased due largely to the sharp rise in world oil prices. In Jordan, though, as in many other Arab Middle Eastern states, the surge in oil revenues stimulated economic growth. Between 1972 and 1982 Jordan's GDP increased at an average rate of 7.9 percent a year; the per capita GDP grew at an average yearly rate of 2.7 percent. Although Jordan is not an oil producer, it benefited from the vast oil resources in the form of generous aid from the oil-rich states. In addition, many Jordanians moved to these countries in order to support their families, who remained in Jordan. Between 1974 and 1982, the economic aid and the money sent by Jordanians living abroad constituted 58 percent of Jordan's GDP.

As could be expected in a developing country, the portion of the work-force devoted to agricultural production steadily declined, from 17 percent in 1972 to around 5–7 percent in 1990. Concomitantly, the number of people employed in industry, construction, and transportation doubled between 1972 and 1990. But it was the public sector that dominated Jordan's workforce. Already in 1972, one-third of the total workforce was employed by the state, and by 1990 the public sector had tripled in size and accounted for more than half of Jordan's workforce.

The expansion of the public sector at the expense of the industrial sector may seem surprising. Usually the expansion of the government bureau-cracy requires increasing the tax base; the higher the income of the population, the more taxes the state can collect in order to pay the public sector. Yet, many Arab countries have lacked such incentives. This is because their economy is not based on production, but on rent – leasing land for exploitation of natural resources. Because the revenues from oil, the major natural resource in the area, were so high, there was no need to develop the economy and create a large tax base (Luciani, 1990).

Jordan too, even though it lacks oil reserves, developed an economy that resembles the rentier model. In this case, the Jordanians leased their armed forces to protect foreign interests. Until the 1960s, the major allies were Britain and the United States. Arab radical regimes perceived Jordan as a potential force in the forefront of the war against Israel (Augé, 1997).

Much of the foreign economic aid received by the Jordanian government was diverted toward enhancing the services available to the country's citizens. Thus, despite the relatively low per capita GNP, the standard of living improved and unemployment levels dropped to nearly zero (Ben Zvi, 1993). Even though the standard of living in Jordan remained lower than in Israel, living conditions in Jordan surpassed those in the WBGS. For example, annual electricity consumption in Jordan was 1130 kilowatt-hours per capita in 1991. In the WBGS it was only 680 kilowatt-hours per capita in 1991. The number of telephone subscribers in Jordan was 67 per 1,000 persons; in the WBGS it was only 22 per 1,000 persons. The urban water consumption in Jordan was 137 liters per capita per year, while in the WBGS it stood at only 60 liters per capita. Health services were also more abundant than in the WBGS, although health conditions in the WBGS are better, mainly because the Palestinians have access to Israeli health services.

Table 2.2   Indicators of standard of living in the WBGS and Jordan, as of 1991

	WBGS	JORDAN
Telephone subscribers per 1000	22	67
Electricity consumption (kwh per capita/year)	680	1130
Households with electricity (%)	85	98
Urban water consumption (liters per capita/year)	60	137
Households with safe water (%)	90	96
Persons per physician	847	767
Persons per hospital bed	658	519

Source: World Bank (1993a), p. 8.

Between 1983 and 1987, Jordan's GNP increased on average by only 2.1 percent per year, while the per capita GNP declined by an average rate of –1.7 percent per year. Jordanian industry, which accounted for 8.3 percent of the GDP in 1972, constituted 14.2 percent of the GDP in 1980. But between 1980 and 1990 the portion of industry in the total GDP barely rose, reaching only 15 percent.

The major reason for the stagnation of the economy was the depreciation in the price of oil. The foreign aid that Jordan had been receiving from the oil-rich Arab states fell from $1.1 billion in 1981 to less then $600 million in 1989. The decline in oil prices also hurt Jordanian exports to these countries. Another factor was the Iran–Iraq war. Iraq, a major trading partner with Jordan, imported fewer Jordanian goods, due to the economic burden of its prolonged war with Iran.

The lower productivity combined with high population growth led to increased unemployment and brought about a decline in the per capita GNP. However, the government continued to maintain the special subsidies and public services it had provided during the years when economic aid was abundant. This generated a deficit in the balance of payments, which by 1984 stood at $3.5 billion and three years later reached $7.4 billion. Jordan's foreign reserves also dwindled rapidly, falling from $1 billion to $400 million, between 1981 and 1985.

By 1988 Jordan was on the verge of an economic crisis. The GDP declined that year by 1.6 percent and the government was defaulting on loan repayments. To stem the erosion of the economy, the government raised taxes and imposed strict limitations on imports. Yet, the following year GDP plunged by another 13.4 percent, and the Jordanian government requested the IMF to restructure its loan payments. The IMF agreed, on condition that Jordan initiate a five-year recovery plan. However, following the 1990 Gulf crisis, Jordan in accordance with Security Council Resolution 661, had to cease all trade with Iraq, which was a major trading partner. In addition Jordan had to cope with the masses of foreigners who fled from Iraq and streamed into the country. In the first six months following the Iraqi invasion of Kuwait, an estimated 750,000 refugees entered Jordan. Many of them lacked financial means and were unable to return to their home countries. Finally, due to King Hussein's siding with Iraq, foreign aid from the Gulf states was terminated and Jordanian citizens living in those countries were expelled. Thus another important source of income was lost. Most of the expelled Jordanian citizens, numbering between 250,000 and 300,000, returned to Jordan, increasing its population by 10 percent, and as a consequence, sending the unemployment rate to a record high of 25 percent (Feiler, 1993). After the war, the IMF again agreed to assist Jordan and with the introduction of a new economic recovery plan, which included drastic cuts in public sector spending and a tax hike (Ben Zvi, 1993), GDP ceased to decline and even slightly increased (JCSS, 1998).

Indicators since 1992 showed that the Jordanian economy had at last begun to recover, or at least to stabilize. The GDP grew by 38 percent between 1991 and 1995 and the per capita GDP by 13 percent, while the external debt decreased in real terms. This positive trend can be attributed to a number of factors. First, the Jordanian government, abiding by the guidelines of the recovery plan, reduced the budget and liberalized the economy. In addition, the large number of Jordanian citizens expelled from the Gulf states brought with them considerable capital, which was invested in construction and business ventures. In the meantime Jordan's trade deficit eased slightly as a by-product of the oil-for-food deal between the United Nations and Iraq. Furthermore, the Gulf states renewed their financial assistance and again allowed Jordanian citizens to work in them (EIU, 1998).

Since 1995, access to the Israeli market has also offered new economic opportunities for Jordan. Israel serves as a good source of trade, tourism, investment, and connections with European markets. Close proximity to Jordan renders cheap transportation of products to and from Israel. In addition, in 1995 the Jordanian government took a number of steps to encourage investment, especially from abroad. Taxes were reduced and bureaucratic procedures were simplified. Since the peace agreement, Jordan has been undergoing a renewed process of industrialization. According to IPR (1998) data, the industrial portion of GDP increased from 15 percent to 17 percent between 1995 and 1997. In 1996 Jordanian exports to the fifteen states of the European Union expanded to around $200 million, nearly five times the total amount of exports to these countries in 1994. In 1997, 8 percent of Jordan's exports were directed to the European Community and another one percent to the United States.

Still, a large portion of the budget is dedicated to covering the external debt, which remains high (at the end of 1997 it stood at $6.8 billion), has required reducing the size of the public sector. Thus, the positive trends described above had a limited effect on the unemployment rates, which in 1998 were estimated to be approaching 30 percent of the labor force; per capita GDP continued to decrease (Jaber, 1997; Sobelman, 1998).

The Palestinian Polity

The government

The Palestinian Authority (PA), although considered an autonomous non-state territory, bears many of the attributes of a state. Within a very short time the Palestinians established legislative and executive bodies, a judicial system, and a complex array of bureaucratic institutions. However, unlike a normal state, the PA does not have its own currency, lacks an army, and does not have full control over all the territories designated as the WBGS.

Like most Arab states (including Jordan), the PA is a semi-authoritarian regime. Although the government holds periodic elections where voters are required to choose among a number of different party platforms, the parliament and judicial system have no real control over the executive branch. In comparison to Israel, freedom of information, speech, and association is quite limited, and basic human rights are frequently violated (Amnesty International, 1996; 1999). An illustration of the PA's sweeping control is the order it issued requiring all Palestinians to stay at home on the first day of the third millennium. This demand was respected almost unconditionally and without protest (Channel 2 News [Israel], January 1, 2000).

Social divisions

The creation of the PA was accompanied by the establishment of a bureaucratic class. Most of the members of this class are Palestinian refugees, formerly employed by the Palestine Liberation Organization (PLO) abroad, who moved to the WBGS following an agreement between the PLO and Israel in 1994. The purpose of this large bureaucracy is to control areas of the PA; this comprehensive control has affected every aspect of political, social, and economic life.

As in the Arab states, an entrepreneur in the PA who does not develop an "appropriate" relationship with the proper government official stands no chance. This means that the businessman must either have "family connections" or pay off PA officials who will "protect" the business. This centralized form of control actually reduces the incentive to establish competing industries and break the local monopolies.

Regional divisions

As in Israel and Jordan, economic development in the WBGS is uneven. The situation of the Palestinian residents of the West Bank is far better than that of the population in the Gaza Strip. This situation derives from the high population density in the Gaza Strip. Although the Gaza Strip is very small (370,000 square kilometers), only 6 percent of the area of the West Bank, more than a million Palestinians live there, while less than two million Palestinians reside in the West Bank. Per capita GDP in the West Bank (excluding East Jerusalem) was estimated to be $1,410 in 1994, while in the Gaza Strip it was even lower at $1,079 (PCBS, 1998). For many years the health system in the Gaza Strip was also inferior, although the disparity between the Gaza Strip and the West Bank in this sphere has narrowed. According to the CIA *World Fact Book* (1997), by 1996 the infant mortality rate and average life expectancy in the West Bank and the Gaza Strip were about equal.

The economic gap between the Gaza Strip and the West Bank was mainly the result of the 1948 Arab–Israeli War. Unlike in the West Bank, the number of Palestinian refugees in the Gaza Strip exceeded the indigenous population. Egypt did not annex the Gaza Strip or integrate its economy into Egypt's, and it maintained the region under a military government. Although the standard of living and the economic welfare of the residents in the Gaza Strip improved after the Israeli occupation, the disparity with the West Bank was never eliminated.

The Palestinian Economy in the West Bank and Gaza Strip

The WBGS is even smaller than Israel, with no natural resources and a population of 2.9 million (including 210,000 Palestinian residents of East Jerusalem). In 1967 Israel conquered the West Bank from Jordan and the Gaza Strip from Egypt. In contrast to the pre-1967 period, the first fifteen years of the Israeli occupation can be considered a period of economic prosperity for the Palestinian residents of these territories. Between 1967 and 1972, per capita GNP of the WBGS doubled from $670 to $1,350 (estimates measured according to the value of the US dollar in 1990), or an average annual growth rate of 17 percent. The following decade saw a moderation in the GNP growth rate. In 1982, the per capita GNP stood at $2,200 (Sagea *et al.* 1992), or an average increase of about 5 percent per year. Although less impressive than the previous period, this is still a relatively high growth rate.

Standard of living

The economic growth in the WBGS brought about an improvement in the standard of living. Thus, as table 2.3 shows, the proportion of households connected to the electricity grid more than doubled between 1970 and 1980; and by 1991, 85 percent of the households in the WBGS enjoyed electric power. Concomitantly, the number of households with electric refrigeration increased almost eightfold within two decades. While in 1970 only 11 percent of households were equipped with refrigerators, by 1980 some 57 percent of the households had refrigerators and in 1991, 85 percent of the households possessed a refrigerator (World Bank, 1993a).

Another result of the Israeli occupation was a spurt in the natural growth of the population. This was due to improved healthcare introduced by Israel, which reduced infant mortality (IMR). Between 1970 and 1996, the IMR declined in the West Bank from 38.1 per 1,000 live births to 28.6; in the Gaza Strip the effect was truly dramatic, IMR plunging from 86.0 to

27.5 per 1,000 live births in the same period (CIA, 1997; Feiler, 1993). In comparison, between 1970 and 1996 the IMR dropped in Jordan from 82 to 31.5 per 1,000 live births (CIA, 1997; Eurostat, 1996).

Table 2.3 Standard of Living Indicators in the WBGS (percentages)

	1970	1980	1991
Households with electricity	30	66	85
Households with safe water	15	47	90
Households with refrigerators	11	57	85
Households with washing machines	–	23	61
Households with automobiles	2	–	16

Source: The World Bank (1993a).

The life-span of the population also increased. In 1995 average life expectancy in the WBGS was 71.1 years, higher even than Jordan (69.7 years). By comparison, in 1970 average life expectancy in the WBGS and in Jordan was only 56 years.[2] Still, in comparison to Israel, both the standard of living and health conditions are inferior. For example, in 1995 average life expectancy in Israel stood at 77.4 years (JCSS, 1998). Similarly, the IMR among Israeli Jews stood at 5.0 per 1,000 live births in 1996, and among Israeli Arabs at 10.1 per 1,000 live births (CBS, 1997).

Industrial production

The growth of the Palestinian economy and rising living standard during the 1970s was not accompanied by the expected indicators of economic development. Fearing competition from WBGS industries, the Israeli authorities were reluctant to provide Palestinian entrepreneurs with license permits to establish new ventures. Would-be Palestinian manufacturers were usually required to subcontract from an Israeli firm (Institute for Social and Economic Policy in the Middle East, 1994). The upshot was that between 1967 and 1982 industrial production in the WBGS showed only marginal growth. Although industrial production in the Gaza Strip increased significantly, this was offset by stagnation of the industrial sector in the West Bank. Thus, by 1994 the WBGS industrial production had reached only 8.2 percent of the total GDP, a poorer performance than most Third World countries.

The leading industry in the WBGS is the manufacture of non-metallic products, which in 1994 accounted for 30.8 percent ($246.5 million) of the gross manufacturing output. The gross output of the food and beverage industries stood at $137.4 million, and the clothing apparel industries at $100.5 million, contributing 17 percent and 12.3 percent, respectively, to the total manufacturing output of the WBGS. Advanced industries, such as electronics and electrical production, major industrial branches in Israel, were confined to the manufacture of electrical machinery, with a gross output of only $2.9 million in 1994. There are also small metallic, chemical, and plastic and rubber industries.

Tourism, which once accounted for a major portion of the GDP in the WBGS (especially the West Bank) has receded since the Israeli occupation. In 1967 the tourist industry was even more developed than in Israel or the Jordanian East Bank. The market included 47 tour agents and 206 tour guides, and hotel capacity was 2,000 rooms. In comparison, Israel had only 35 tour agents and virtually no tour guides, though hotel capacity was considerably larger, at about 5,000 rooms. Tourism in the Jordanian East Bank was very limited, with only 96 hotels and 17 registered travel agencies in 1966. By 1992 the situation was reversed; Israel had 206 tour agents and 4,300 tour guides, whereas in the WBGS, there were only 36 tour agents and 70 tour guides, fewer than in 1967. The number of hotel rooms in the WBGS in 1992 was about the same as in 1967, whereas in Israel the number of hotel rooms had multiplied more than sixfold to 31,000. The major reasons for the stagnation of the Palestinian tourism industry were the poor facilities available in those areas and the stringent criteria imposed by Israel for obtaining permits and licenses (World Bank, 1993b: 13).

The workforce

As in other places with an undeveloped industrial base, agricultural production has remained a dominant sector in the WBGS. In 1994, one-third of the labor force there was employed in agriculture, contributing 33 percent of the total GDP (JCSS, 1998). In comparison, agricultural production in Jordan accounted for 9 percent of the total GDP in 1997 (IPR, 1998) and only 4 percent of Israel's GDP in 1994 (JCSS, 1998). Concomitantly, only 5.8 percent of the Jordanian workforce was employed in agriculture in 1990 (Findlay, 1994: 153), while the comparable figure for Israel in 1996 was only 2.5 percent (CBS, 1997).

Industrial manufacturing in the WBGS is very similar to the Jordanian model, consisting of cottage industries and enterprises of individuals supplying limited local market needs. In 1991 it was estimated that 60 percent of the enterprises in the WBGS employed fewer than four persons and that only 7.5 percent had more than ten persons (World Bank, 1993b). Many of these businesses target local communities and maintain a monopolistic control over their domain of distribution.

As in Jordan, the Palestinian workers in the WBGS are short on social benefits. In the Gaza Strip, which until 1999 was still following the 1967 Egyptian law, employers are not required to provide benefits such as a pension, health insurance, or compensation for work-related injuries. The labor force in the West Bank is in a slightly better position. According to the prevailing Jordanian labor laws, employers are required to pay for annual leave and are liable for severance pay and compensation for work-related injuries. However, as in the Gaza Strip, employers are under no obligation to provide many other common benefits such as a pension or health insurance.

Employment in Israel

The increased GDP in the WBGS, despite the underdeveloped economy, was a result of the Palestinians' work in Israel. Israeli employers welcomed this source of cheap labor, who were willing to work in the most menial, lowest-paying jobs. Agriculture and construction, the two sectors that in the past had attracted many Israeli Arabs, were now drawing the Palestinians from the Occupied Territories. By 1987, it was estimated that residents of the WBGS comprised 42 percent of the construction workers in Israel.

While the wages paid to the Palestinians of the WBGS were considered low according to Israeli standards, they were relatively high in comparison to the average income of the population in the WBGS. Thus, working in Israel was very attractive, causing the number of Palestinian residents of the WBGS working in Israel to steadily increase, while the total number of Palestinians working within the WBGS barely changed, as shown in figure 2.1 (overleaf).

By 1974, over one-third of the total workforce in both the West Bank and the Gaza Strip was employed in Israel, contributing 25 percent of the total GNP of these territories. The proportion of West Bank residents employed in Israel persisted until 1988, even though the total workforce increased during this period by more than 30 percent. But in the Gaza Strip the portion of the workforce employed in Israel continued to expand, and by 1986, 50 percent of all working persons in the Gaza Strip were employed in Israel.

Although they earn more than those employed in Palestinian businesses or agriculture, Palestinians working in Israel do not fare any better than their colleagues employed in the WBGS. Most of the Palestinians employed in Israel work on a daily or weekly basis, and have neither a permanent place of work nor any guarantee of employment. They have no union backing or social insurance protection, even though they pay social security taxes like the Israelis. The payments made to the Israeli social security benefit the residents of the WBGS indirectly; the money is transferred to the Civil Administration of the Occupied Territories and hence to the Palestinian Authority.

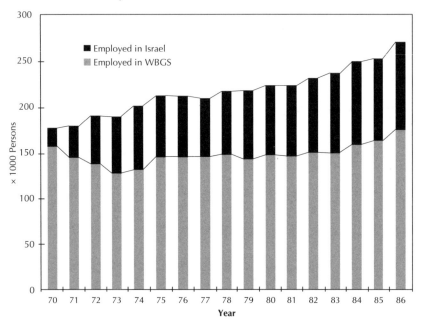

Figure 2.1 Number of Palestinians working in Israel out of the total labor force.

Source: Tuma (1991).

Most of the Palestinians from the WBGS who work in Israel are legally employed. Usually they are recruited through Israeli government employment offices, although many are also hired directly by private firms and public organizations. At the same time, an illegal employment market also developed, in which illegal workers congregate at "labor markets" where they hope to be hired and get a reasonable daily wage. A smaller proportion of illegal workers are recruited directly from their villages or neighborhoods by contractors; it is mainly Palestinian women who prefer this form of employment. Working for a contractor is the easiest and most convenient method for both the employer and the employee. The employers deal only with one person and the laborers do not have to worry about transportation. However, because the laborers earn much less than they would if they were hired directly, without the mediation of the contractor, most illegal workers shun this method (Portugali, 1996).

The reliability of the periodic estimates made by the Israeli Central Bureau of Statistics (CBS) regarding the size of the illegal labor force is questionable (Benvenisti, 1986: 5). Thus, the labor employment statistics cited above are only approximate. During the 1980s it was assumed that at least a quarter of the labor force employed in Israel was illegal (Gharaibeh, 1985: 50). Since 1994, after Israel imposed closures on the WBGS in response to a wave of terrorist attacks, illegal employment has become a key source of income. It is estimated that by 1999, over 60,000 illegal laborers from the WBGS had been working in Israel; this is more than the legal workforce (UNSCO, 1999).

Illegal employment in Israel has two advantages for the workers and their employers. First, illegal workers pay no taxes. Second, workers do not apply for a permit to enter and work in Israel, which is a time-consuming process and not always successful. But illegal labor also has its drawbacks. Since the would-be worker has no guarantee that he or she will find a job, the time and money spent on reaching the labor market might be wasted. In addition, there is the risk of being caught by Israeli security forces, leading to possible arrest and imprisonment. Another drawback, which applies to legal employees as well, is that workers from the WBGS can easily be fired because employers do not have to worry about paying compensation or dealing with organized protest strikes that might break out. To make matters worse, unlike an Israeli citizen who loses his or her job, the resident of the WBGS cannot obtain unemployment compensation from social security.

Since most of the jobs available for residents of the WBGS (inside the territories or in Israel) are oriented toward unskilled labor, professionals and skilled laborers usually have to emigrate to other Arab countries (as in Jordan). This has been an additional important source of income, which has helped raise the standard of living in the WBGS despite its lack of development.

Trade

Coinciding with Palestinian employment trends, the merchants and manufacturers of the WBGS also set their eyes on the Israeli markets. The true scope of trade between the WBGS and Israel is not known, since as with the labor market, not all transactions are reported. Still, even on the basis of the inaccurate data, it is clear that despite the "open bridges" policy with Jordan following the 1967 war, which allowed the residents of the West Bank to travel to and trade with Jordan, the Israeli market got the lion's share.

In 1993, 22 percent of the exports from the Gaza Strip reached Jordan, while Israel received 78 percent of the exports. Jordan also lost its status as a major exporter to the West Bank. In 1968, 45 percent of the goods imported by the West Bank came from Jordan. By 1991, Jordanian products accounted for only 15 percent of the imports in the West Bank. The Gaza Strip did not import any goods from Jordan (in 1993), while 88 percent of its imports came from Israel (David Boas *et al.*, 1996). The preference for trade with Israel is due mainly to the fact that it is cheaper to import Israeli products (Awartani, 1991). However, another factor is that the WBGS cannot export or import directly with other countries. Thus, in many cases Israeli or Jordanian merchants serve as middlemen between the WBGS and the rest of the world.

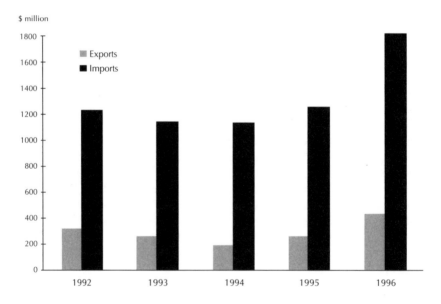

Figure 2.2 Unofficial estimates of imports and exports between the WBGS and other countries (including Israel)

Source: Jaffee Center for Strategic Studies

From the beginning of the occupation, the Israeli authorities hindered export from the WBGS to Israel or abroad. Agricultural products, which accounted for 33 percent of the total exports from the WBGS, required special permits. Agricultural produce that was supplied in sufficient quantities by Israeli farmers was not permitted to enter Israel or to be exported abroad. Only in 1988, as a consequence of international pressure that built up in response to the *Intifada*, were citrus fruits from the Gaza Strip allowed to be exported directly (Razin and Sadka, 1993: 95). However, the tariffs that the Israelis demanded for transferring these products were very high (Awartani, 1991). A still on-going problem of trading via Israel is the Israeli demand to inspect the Palestinian products before they are shipped abroad (*The Jerusalem Post,* December 21, 1998). Frequently the Palestinian exporter is denied a permit to enter Israel in order to oversee the Israeli border inspectors.

Nonetheless, according to the Palestinian Trade Center (1999), importing and exporting via Israeli intermediaries is more efficient than trading via Jordan or Egypt. First, Jordan and Egypt impose quotas on Palestinian products. Second, Palestinian products moving through Jordanian and Egyptian ports are subject to delays, something rarely encountered in Israeli ports.

The growing dependence of the economies of the WBGS on Israel, which brought about the boom years during the 1970s, showed its negative side in the following decade. The slowdown in Israel's economic growth during the 1980s, and rising unemployment, directly affected the employment of the Palestinians in Israel, which reached a saturation point, stabilizing at about 110,000 workers. The sluggish growth of the Israeli economy also impacted negatively on exports to Israel. To make matters worse, during these years, because of the depreciation in oil prices, many Palestinians from the WBGS who had sought employment in the Gulf states lost their jobs. In 1983, as a consequence of its economic recession, Jordan imposed strict restrictions on immigration from the WBGS, allowing only 1,000 persons per year to enter. As a result, the per capita GDP in the WBGS, which had reached a level of $1,310 in 1980, increased by only 5 percent over the next six years.

The Intifada

In December 1987 a civil uprising, known as the *Intifada*, erupted in the WBGS. Among other measures, the Palestinians attempted to boycott Israeli products (Mishal and Aharoni, 1994). Initially, the boycott seemed to create a positive economic momentum. Industrial production surged from 8 percent of the total GDP to 13 percent. However, this is misleading. Because of the closures of towns and villages imposed by the IDF, as well as strikes initiated by the Palestinians, the total amount of working hours by Palestinians in Israel and within the Occupied Territories declined. The CBS has estimated that during the first three months of 1988, the number of hours worked by residents of the Occupied Territories in Israel fell by 42.8 percent. Although the total number of work hours has gradually increased since then, it has never again reached the levels of the pre-*Intifada* period.

In addition, exports to Israel fell drastically from $395 million in 1987 to $248 million in 1991 (a decline of 37.2 percent). Thus, by 1991 the per capita GDP had fallen to a level of $1,275, which was lower than its real value (in 1991 prices) in 1980.

In the aftermath of the Gulf War in 1991, the already depleted economy of the WBGS deteriorated even further. Because the Palestine Liberation Organization (PLO) sided with Iraq, many Palestinians working in the Gulf states lost their jobs. Moreover, during the war Israel barred the entry of Palestinians from the Occupied Territories, resulting in the loss of an additional source of income.

The establishment of the PA and economic development

The Oslo agreement offered the Palestinians the hope that their political and economic situation would finally improve. Following the 1993 Declaration of Principles between the PLO and Israel, the Israelis agreed to cancel the tariffs on exports from the WBGS into Israel. Israel also agreed to remove the former quotas on all but five agricultural products, and to cancel these within four years (Fischer and Hausman, 1994).

Although the implementation of the economic agreement between the two parties was hindered by the Israeli closures that followed Palestinian terrorist attacks, by early 1998 all trade barriers between the WBGS and Israel had been removed (Israeli Foreign Ministry, 1998). The shifting trends in Palestinian exports in the wake of Oslo are clearly shown in figure 2.2. Even though the figures from 1993 on are unofficial estimates, the total volume of exports apparently increased between 1994 to 1996 by well over 100 percent, from $164.5 million to about $400 million, thus approaching the pre-*Intifada* levels. However, as figure 2.2 shows, imports also increased, driving up the trade deficit. This is due mainly to the purchase of production inputs from Israel (EIU, 1997).

Another economic field that suffered under the limitations of the Israeli occupation was construction. Housing costs were relatively high, due to the limited land available for building, the bureaucracy involved in the authorization of building permits, and the high prices of building materials imported from Israel. A new home was therefore incredibly expensive (World Bank, 1993b). Since the establishment of the Palestinian Authority in 1994 there has been a surge in the rate of construction. The previous building restrictions were canceled and there has been a profusion of foreign aid and private investment in housing. One result was a dramatic increase in the labor force working in construction, from 10.4 percent of the employed labor force in 1991 to 46.6 percent in 1993 (Pianet, 1998).

Another area that for many years remained undeveloped is finance. In 1993 there were only two Arab banks in the WBGS, but four years later there were twenty, with the number of branches increasing from 13 to nearly 90. Deposits in these banks grew by about 300 percent between 1993 and 1997, reaching about $1.9 billion. Total bank lending grew by about 400 percent during this period, despite the fact that the loan-to-deposit ratio remained under 30 per cent, as compared to 64 percent and 82 percent in Jordan and Israel, respectively. In addition, in 1996 a stock exchange was opened in Nablus (UNSCO, 1998).

According to PCBS statistics, the Palestinian economy has produced significant economic growth. Between 1994 and 1996, GDP leaped from $3.0 billion to $4.0 billion (a 25 percent spurt), though the per capita GDP increased by only 15 percent from $1,329 to $1,537. However, as in Jordan, unemployment has remained very high. Taking into account the high unemployment rates, the EIU (1997) estimated that the economy of the PA actually collapsed immediately after the Oslo agreement. The GDP fell from $2.14 billion in 1994 to $1.63 billion in 1995, while per capita GDP was estimated to be only $682 in 1995 – a 50 percent drop within one year.

Indeed, to a great extent, the difficulties encountered by the Palestinian economy can be traced to the Oslo agreement in September 1993 and the creation of the Palestinian Authority in mid-1994. Like developing countries, the Palestinian Authority established a large bureaucratic class to run its affairs, including an enormous security force that employs over 35,000 policemen (Shikaki, 1998). Many of these officials have exhibited corrupt practices and have squandered the PA's budget. In addition, the PA has created its own companies to monopolize the local market (*Israel Business Arena*, August 6, 1997). This behavior has deterred many potential foreign investors (Roy, 1996). In January 1998, the EU explicitly insisted that the PA honor its commitment to maintain transparency of its finances as a condition for continuing aid (*Israel Business Arena*, January 19, 1998).

To a certain extent, Israel has cooperated with the inappropriate public policies of the PA. For example, under the Israeli–Palestinian economic agreement of 1994, Israel agreed to transfer to the PA taxes collected from Palestinians. At a Cabinet meeting in July 1998, Minister of Industry and Trade Natan Sharansky inquired about the fact that the Israeli Finance Ministry had transferred 30 percent of these taxes directly into PA Chairman Yasser Arafat's personal bank account. While Sharansky and Foreign Minister Ariel Sharon demanded a halt to this procedure, Prime Minister Netanyahu's response was that he "would look into the matter" (*Globes*, July 12, 1998).

Notes

1   This data is based on the estimates of the Economist Intelligence Unit (EIU). However, according to the official estimates, the 1995 GDP published by the Palestinian Monetary Authority was lower, standing at $2.16 billion (EIU, 1997).

2   These figures are based on the data of the Israeli Central Bureau of Statistics (CBS). However, there are claims that these are underestimates, as not all births or child deaths were recorded, and the base census figures from 1967 were incorrect (no new census was carried out until 1997). Alternative reports (e.g., World Bank, 1993a; Heiberg and Ovensen, 1994) found that the IMR was as high as the CBS data indicated. Similarly, average life expectancy was said to be three years lower than the CBS reported, while the population in the WBGS was 10–15 percent higher than officially reported by Israel.

The CBS dismisses these charges. Because the 1967 census was conducted under a curfew, the CBS believes its reliability. As far as the claim that births were not recorded, this would be economically irrational, since residents were liable to lose social benefits granted on the basis of family size, although this could also serve as an incentive not to report child mortality (World Bank, 1993a: 3; Roy, 1996).

Regardless of the exact figures, all researchers agree that the general health of the Palestinian population in the WBGS has improved since the Israeli occupation; the debate is over the level of that improvement.

3

The Politics of the
Israeli–Jordanian–Palestinian
Triangle

The origins of the Arab–Israeli conflict lie in the attempt of both the Jewish and the Palestinian-Arab national movements to establish an independent sovereign state within the confines of the same territorial boundaries. The ethnic conflict between the Jews and the Palestinian-Arabs along with the supporting Arab states, started at the beginning of the twentieth century, as a direct consequence of Zionist settlement in Palestine. While the Jews and the Palestinian-Arabs viewed this conflict as an existential threat, the rest of the Arab world perceived it in terms of a more limited political dispute. Thus, despite the Arab denial of Israel's legitimacy, these relations bear a much higher resemblance to competitive relations, rather than conflictive relations. Unlike the Palestinians who continually attempt to intensify and aggravate tensions, the Arab states have preferred to maintain a more low-key profile, declaring their animosity toward Israel and refusing to recognize it, though being reluctant to engage in an all-out confrontation.

The conflict between Israel and the Palestinians has not been the only point of friction in the Middle East. An additional inter-ethnic conflict, of a more surreptitious nature, developed parallel to the Israeli–Palestinian rivalry, between Palestinians and Jordanians (Mishal, 1978: 1–17). Its roots lie in the large Palestinian population living in Jordan. As in the case of Israel and the Palestinian Arabs, the Palestinians and Jordanians also perceive each other as a potential threat.

The result has been the emergence of a triangular system of conflicts, consisting of two inter-ethnic conflicts: an overt conflict between Israel and the Palestinians, and a tacit, covert, and controlled conflict between Jordan and the Palestinians. A third conflict, between Israel and Jordan, can be viewed as part of the general Arab–Israeli inter-state system.

The triangular system of conflict has produced seemingly aberrant behavior, with two rival parties temporarily cooperating in order to confront the third common enemy. Thus, for example, due to Israel's powerful status in relation to both Jordan and the Palestinians, these two parties have been inclined to overcome their differences and cooperate with each other. However, in some instances Jordanians and Palestinians have sought Israeli aid as part of their struggle against each other.

The Arab–Israeli Conflict: The Dominance of the Realist Perspective

The Arab–Israeli conflict began as an inter-ethnic conflict between an indigenous population and a group of European Jews. However, as the process of de-colonization started, especially after the Second World War and the independence of Israel in 1948, the conflict in Palestine was transformed into an inter-state rivalry between Israel and its Arab neighbors.

Following the Second World War, the United Nations, along with the major powers, attempted to implement the idealist approach. In November 1947 the UN General Assembly voted to split Palestine into two states. During the war that erupted afterward, the United Nations made efforts to persuade the parties to reach a settlement and imposed an arms embargo on the Middle East. Although this initiative failed, the cease-fire agreements included an international mechanism for resolving differences between Israel and its neighbors (the mixed armistice commission) and a UN force (UNTSO – UN Truce Supervision Observers) to oversee the cease-fire. The United Nations also established a special organization (UNRWA – UN Relief Works Agency) to look after the welfare of the Palestinian refugees until a settlement was reached (*United Nations Yearbook*, 1949).

The idealist approach was not very successful. Since the United Nations, unlike a sovereign government, could not impose its resolutions, both sides routinely ignored the resolutions of the UN Security Council and the rulings of the Arab–Israeli mixed armistice commission. The Arab states refused to establish diplomatic relations with Israel and imposed an economic boycott on Israel and on all foreign companies that traded with Israel. This proved to be a very costly policy. First, all trade and transportation links that had previously existed through Palestine were severed. The Arab states thereby lost access to the port in Haifa on the

Mediterranean and to land routes linking Egypt and North Africa with Syria and Lebanon. All trade links between the Palestinian Arabs living in Israel and the Palestinians on the other side of the cease-fire lines were also totally cut off, as was the trade route between the Gaza Strip and the West Bank. The Palestinian refugees who fled or were expelled from their homes during the 1948 war paid an especially heavy price. They could not return to their homes or even reclaim the property they abandoned during the war.

In the long run, the Arab boycott became highly counter-productive. Many goods that could have been bought cheaply from Israel had to be imported from other countries at higher prices. In some areas, such as agricultural products for arid climates, Israel had become the world's major supplier of know-how and technology. In this case, the Arabs, who were obviously interested in these types of products, could only purchase them indirectly through third parties, thus needlessly multiplying the cost. The secondary boycott against foreign companies cooperating with Israel also backfired in the long run. As the Israeli economy developed, Israel became a more attractive market for high quality expensive products. Thus the boycott was effective mainly against Israeli trade with less developed countries, rather than with the highly developed countries, which preferred the Israeli market.

Besides the boycott, the political instability and the military conflict in the Middle East had additional costs. Since most investors sought stable regions, foreign investment was low and regional development suffered. A large portion of whatever wealth was accumulated was wasted on procuring arms and military build-up instead of being invested in social welfare. Although in the 1970s, with the increase of oil prices, foreign capital poured into many Arab countries, the direct beneficiaries were not necessarily Israel's immediate Arab neighbors; they had to bear the burden of the conflict and rely on the contributions of the oil-rich states. Furthermore, the rise in oil prices increased the cost of production in the industrialized countries, thus raising prices of imports. While the oil-rich countries could afford these higher prices, the countries lacking large oil reserves suffered from negative trade balances.

Despite the dominance of the realist approach, the idealist attempts to intervene in the conflict did exert a certain influence. Although the borders between Israel and its neighbors were never quiet, the conflict was guided by certain rules of conduct. Usually, when possible escalation loomed, the opponents would negotiate with the mediation of the United Nations, or the United States and the USSR, and reach an agreement to reduce tension. However, the intervention of the world powers had the effect of perpetuating regional tensions because of Israel's association with the United

States and the Arab affiliation with the Soviet Union. Thus stability was maintained mainly by the mechanism of the balance of power. This was at best a limited method of conflict management and could not prevent the occasional eruption of wars.

The Arab–Israeli war of 1973 can be viewed as a turning point; it marked the beginning of the decline of the realist school in Middle East politics. The war came as a surprise to the Israelis. The element of surprise lay not only in the ability of the Egyptian and Syrian armies to make secret plans without Israeli intelligence discovering them. Even without knowledge of the plans, there were indications that the Egyptians and Syrians were preparing an offensive. But this made no sense from a realist point of view, for even in a surprise attack the Arab armies were in no position to defeat Israel.

What the Israelis failed to comprehend was that the success of the Arab offensive was not the issue. The key outcome of the war was that it motivated the superpowers and the United Nations to intervene and impose a new settlement on Israel and its neighbors. Thus, even though Israel defeated the Arab armies, they could not resist the foreign pressure and eventually agreed to withdraw from all territories conquered during the war of 1973, as well as some territories occupied in 1967, and allow the entry of a UN peacekeeping force.

Despite the unpredictable Arab military strategy, the Israelis were unwilling to abandon the realist paradigm. The perceived lesson of the war of 1973 for Israel was to increase its military power *vis-à-vis* its Arab neighbors. Thus the Israeli government expanded the size of the army and stepped up arms procurement. This required expanding the government's budget. Eventually, the defense burden became so great that the national debt and inflation began to spin out of control.

It took Israel another war to finally entertain seriously the limits of realism. The 1982 invasion of Lebanon reflected Israel's most extreme attempt to implement the realist vision. Its purpose was to eliminate the PLO's military and political presence and impose a peace settlement on Lebanon (Schiff and Ya'ari, 1984; Naor, 1986; Evron, 1987). Since the Israeli army was far more powerful than the PLO, this made complete sense from a realist perspective. Yet, even though the Israeli army occupied the southern half of Lebanon and defeated the Syrian army units stationed in Lebanon, the military and political outcomes were unsatisfactory.

The Israeli leaders repeated the same mistake that the United States made in Vietnam and the Soviet Union in Afghanistan. Although, as a powerful state, Israel had the capability to conquer and control a weaker state, the price of exerting power was intolerable to domestic and world public opinion alike. The general public was unwilling to tolerate the moral and political price of a military occupation, especially the terrible toll on human life. Hence, just as the Americans and the Soviets eventually retreated, Israeli forces began gradually withdrawing from south Lebanon. The Palestinian uprising against Israel, the *Intifada*, which began at the end of 1987, further heightened the doubts regarding the utility of Israeli occupation by force. Yet a shift in the global balance of power was required in order to draw the Middle East out of the clutches of realism. Hence, only after the Cold War came to an end and Russia stopped supporting its previous allies, were the radical parties in the Middle East critically weakened, enabling more moderate elements who sought a peaceful resolution to prevail.

The most obvious demonstration of the new political order was the reaction to the 1990 Iraqi invasion of Kuwait. The Iraqis, who were also under the influence of the realist doctrine, calculated that given their relative power in comparison to Kuwait, there was no reason why they should not conquer that small country. Probably the Iraqis expected the denunciation of their aggressive conduct by other governments and by the UN Security Council. However, they failed to foresee that their military initiative would bring about the formation of an international coalition, including countries in the region that would be willing to confront the Iraqis in a military conflict in order to implement a UN resolution demanding an Iraqi withdrawal.

The 1991 Gulf War can be viewed as the initial catalyst of the Israeli–Palestinian peace process. The ability of the United States to overcome the opposition of the USSR and garner the support of most of the world, as well as persuade Israel to exercise restraint in the face of Iraqi provocations, created an appropriate atmosphere for conceiving the 1991 Madrid Conference after the war. Thus, for the first time since the Geneva Conference, which followed the 1973 Arab–Israeli war, Israel and its Arab neighbors entered a multilateral negotiation.

Like its predecessor in Geneva, the Madrid Conference at first also seemed to be a failure. The idealist prescription was not working. The leaders on both sides were intransigent. But the anti-realist mode of thinking had already taken hold, and in 1992 the hawkish Israeli government was ousted, paving the way for the 1993 Oslo initiative to be accepted by both the Israeli government and the PLO.

The Jordanian–Palestinian Conflict

New incongruities

The new political order that emerged in the territory of Mandatory Palestine after the 1948 war afforded the Jewish community in Palestine sovereign status and the Emirate of Transjordan political authority for its independence. The war, the movement of the Palestinian population to the West Bank, the control of the region by the Jordanian Army (the Arab Legion), and its annexation to Jordan in April 1950, transformed Jordanian–Palestinian into intra-state relations. Jordan became a dualistic society with two main political communities: Palestinian and Transjordanian. Annexation of the West Bank tripled the population under Jordan's rule. In 1948 Transjordan's population was almost 400,000; the annexation added about 900,000 Palestinians, half of whom were inhabitants of the West Bank, while the rest were refugees (United Nations, 1951: 4; Abidi, 1965: 63).

The existence of three societies – Jewish, Palestinian Arab, and Transjordanian – in two states – Israel and Jordan – heightened the incongruence between the political boundaries fixed by the armistice agreement and the boundaries demarcated in the Palestinians' collective identity. The disparity intensified the desire of Palestinians inside and outside the West Bank, to regain Palestine within the Mandatory boundaries. Palestinian aspirations, which contradicted Jordanian interests in the West Bank, generated a focus for potential conflict between the Palestinians and the Jordanian regime.

There had always been some Palestinian leaders, during the 1948 war and in the first years after the annexation, who challenged Jordan's activities on the West Bank and who sought to express Palestinian allegiance through Palestinian, pan-Arab, or pan-Islamic options. In September 1949, for instance, Palestinian leaders established, under the auspices of the Arab League, the ill-fated All-Palestine Government in the Gaza Strip to regain Palestine within the Mandatory boundaries (Aref al-'Aref, undated: 89, 703–705; Abidi, 1965: 49–52). Beginning in 1954, political groupings in the West Bank like al-Ba'th and the National Socialists tended to manifest their Palestinian allegiance through the pan-Arab option that was associated with the Nasser regime, although some saw it embodied in the Damascus Ba'thist regime. Others, like the Muslim Brethren and the Liberation Party, sought to realize their political desires in Palestine through activity in pan-Islamic movements (Cohen, 1982: 24–6).

Some Palestinian leaders in the West Bank, especially those who belonged to the Nashashibi faction, supported King 'Abdallah's political goal of incorporating Palestinian territories into his kingdom. However, many of them tended to make their support conditional on his willingness to annex all of Palestine and on the termination of the political independence of the Jewish community there. This attitude was most strikingly articulated by the Jerusalem and Ramallah delegates to the Palestinian Congress, also known as the Jericho Conference, held on December 1, 1948. The meeting was arranged by King 'Abdallah and his Palestinian supporters to legitimize his annexation of Palestinian territories to Jordan. Only a few of the delegates, Shaykh Muhammad 'Ali al-Ja'bari of Hebron and Wadi' Da'mas of Beth Jalla, were willing to give 'Abdallah a free hand in solving the Palestine problem (Shihadah, 1970: 166). The attitude of the Jerusalem and Ramallah representatives were reflected in some of the resolutions adopted by this conference. It was resolved, for example, that "the Conference sees Palestine as a single indivisible unit. Any solution incompatible with this situation will not be considered final. The Conference recognizes His Majesty King 'Abdallah as King of all Palestine and greets him and his gallant army as well as the Arab armies that fought and are still fighting in defense of Palestine" (Aref al-'Aref, undated: 877–8).

One can conclude that despite internecine conflict over a broad range of issues, Palestinian leaders inside as well as outside the West Bank strongly agreed about the need to preserve the Arab character of Palestine. Consequently, they were unanimous in their desire for the establishment of an Arab political authority that would include the whole territory of British Mandatory Palestine, though the exact form and operation of this authority were a subject of controversy among the various political streams.

In this respect, for the king's Palestinian opponents as well as many of his supporters, the struggle between the Arab and Jewish communities over Palestine was a fundamental issue that involved a total opposition of interests. But 'Abdallah, who sought cooperation with the Jewish community in Palestine and later with Israel, preferred to see the conflict as a problem to be handled by processes of political bargaining with due regard for the balance of power in the region (al-Tall, 1964; Kimche, 1973: 263).

These opposing interpretations were mostly a result of the divergent political goals of 'Abdallah and the Palestinians during the Mandate period – a contradiction that stemmed from 'Abdallah's desire to prevent the creation of an independent Palestinian political entity in Palestine, which he perceived as a potential rival (Nevo, 1975, chs. 3, 4). Contrasting evaluations of the outcome of the 1948 war reflected this contradiction. From the standpoint of the Palestinian Arabs, the war had ended in utter defeat; for King 'Abdallah, however, it had enhanced the political authority of Jordan and increased his military power.

These differing evaluations of the war's outcome critically affected the way each side defined its objectives in the conflict with Israel. King 'Abdallah tended to treat the Arab–Israeli issue as a residual border conflict. The Palestinians, on the other hand, considered it a clash of destinies, which required a radical solution (Safran, 1969: 22). In this respect, Amman defined its political objectives in terms of the actual needs of the existing Jordanian state, while the West Bank population defined its political objectives in terms of the realization of the national ambitions of the Arab people of Palestine. Amman tended to stabilize the status quo with Israel by embarking on a process of political arrangements; the Palestinian leaders in the West Bank strove to change the status quo by military means.

Under these circumstances one might have expected that the tension between Palestinian desires and Jordanian interests would increase separatist currents within the Palestinian community, engender a Palestinian appeal for an autonomous existence, and culminate in an inevitable clash between the two political communities. After all, Palestinians had become the majority in Jordan. They were better off socioeconomically and exhibited a higher level of political awareness. But in reality, no strong separatist current emerged on the West Bank for most of the years of Jordanian rule. Instead, Palestinian leaders in the West Bank showed themselves willing to work economically and politically with the regime in Amman, even though such cooperation had a negative effect on the West Bank political leadership by restricting it to local bases and to dealing with day-to-day political issues.

Cooperation as a mutual need

The Palestinians' tendencies toward moderating conflicts and strengthening participation and cooperation with the Jordanian center derived from mutual needs of the population on the West and East Banks. The disparity in the level of development of the two populations heightened the feeling of mutual dependence after the annexation and encouraged an exchange relationship between the two groups.

Different levels of modernization and of social and political development had characterized the two political communities before and during the Mandate period. Palestinians ranked higher than Transjordanians on a range of socio-demographic measures: urbanization, educational level,

54

health standards, exposure to communications media, and growth of per capita income (Lerner, 1958). Despite this, the West Bankers' situation after 1948 – the crushing defeat in the war, the proximity to a hostile and threatening Israel, the annexation by a suspicious Transjordan, and the lack of a border with any third party – heightened their sense of political dependence on the East Bank. Their inferior political status was aggravated by the Hashemites' monopoly of both military and economic power, which sealed the dependence of the West Bank on Amman.

The West Bankers' superior socioeconomic development, coupled with their sense of political inferiority, provided the basis for exchanges with the administrative center in Amman. Palestinians supplied skilled manpower to fill vital economic, administrative, and public service functions. In return, Amman allowed them some scope for action and freedom of maneuver in both the political and economic spheres. This interdependence increased during the years of Jordanian rule of the West Bank.

The balance struck between conflictual pressures and cooperative interests was also expressed ideologically, as both parties tended to define their political identity flexibly rather than adhere strictly to such concepts as nation-state or national collective. After the annexation, the West Bank Palestinians had at least three sources to draw on in order to shape and define their political identity: pan-Arab, Jordanian, and Palestinian. Their attachment to pan-Arab and Palestinian political symbols and beliefs was based on voluntary acceptance, while their affiliation with the political entity of Jordan materialized mostly in participation in its political life and in concrete dependence on resources allocated by the Jordanian government in Amman.

Even the East Bank population, however, was ambiguous about the content of Jordanian identity. Some political circles in Amman did not accept the finality of Jordan's national boundaries. 'Abdallah still saw the realization of the Hashemites' political dream in a "Greater Syria" that would encompass Syria, Lebanon, Palestine, and Transjordan (King 'Abdallah, 1951: 307–8; al-Hayat, February 18, 1958). By sharing with the Palestinians an ambivalence about the delineation of collective boundaries, the Jordanians opened the way for various possibilities of practical cooperation, even with their rivals among the Palestinians. Thus, without unequivocally committing itself to accepting the central symbols of the Jordanian government, the West Bank leadership could cooperate with Amman in terms of "temporary arrangements," which could in fact persist for a relatively long time.

The perception of temporary arrangements had two aspects. On the one hand, it reflected the feeling of the political elite in the West Bank that they were involved in an unresolved conflict. It thus entailed non-acceptance of the status quo, at least in terms of ultimate goals. On the other hand, defining the existing situation as transitory meant that West Bank political circles could reconcile themselves to it in the short run until they acquired the means to realize their goals. The perception of transitory arrangements, then, allowed not only for the existence of a *potential* for change, but also for the possibility of maintaining the status quo.

Cooperation without integration

Ideologically, the roots of the tacit acceptance by West Bank leaders of the status quo in Jordan as a temporary arrangement lay in their flexible definition of the political boundaries of the Palestinian collective. Their definition emphasized the transitory aspects of the Palestinians' present existence. These leaders were cognizant of Amman's monopoly of both military power and foreign economic aid, which underscored the subordinate position of the West Bank. By regarding the situation of the Palestinians as a kind of interim condition, the West Bank elite could put off confronting Amman over issues that had a high potential for immediate conflict, such as the question of political identity and the nature of long-term relations between the two population groups.

Amman contributed to the perception of the arrangements as temporary for the most part by developing a strategy for pacifying the West Bank political elite and seeking compromises with it rather than direct confrontation. Despite the emphasis on accommodation by the two sides, however, their mutually suspicious attitudes limited the possibilities for transforming the relationship of coexistence into full-fledged integration. The coexistence patterns between Amman and the West Bank remained viable as long as many of the political groups in the West Bank were inclined to consider the solution of the Palestine problem as a long-term, pan-Arab matter.

The emergence of radical Palestinian factions outside the West Bank, particularly the Palestine Liberation Organization (PLO) and Fatah Organization in the mid-1960s, constituted a serious challenge to the locally based landowning West Bank leadership that was willing to settle for coexistence through acquiescence in temporary arrangements. In order to regain for the Palestinians a central role in the political and military struggle for Palestine, the radicals sought to bypass concern with temporary arrangements and focus attention on the long-range question of a solution to the problem of Palestine.

However, lacking a basis for political activity in the form of grassroots political parties, the national-oriented leadership found it difficult to effectively give voice to its positions within the framework of the existing regime. The opposition forces were therefore left with two options: either to terminate opposition activities in an effort to blend into the Jordanian establishment and enjoy the material benefits that this entailed, or to continue opposition activities within Jordan and outside it within the Palestinian or other radical Arab frameworks. The existence of the first option and the legitimacy enjoyed by those who acted outside Jordan weakened the pressure to change the Palestinian leadership in areas under Jordanian control, and this leadership continued to follow the pattern of pragmatic and localized action.

Another reason for the absence of any real pressure to replace the Palestinian leadership in Jordan was that the leadership was able to vest its pragmatic activities in a nationalist garb. This was due to its success in presenting the political union of the two banks of the Jordan as a strictly temporary one that would continue to exist only until such conditions arose as would enable the favorable conclusion of the Arab–Israeli conflict. The Palestinian leadership in Jordan was able to acquiesce to this description of the current state of affairs as a temporary situation. By simultaneously professing their unwillingness in principle to view the present situation as permanent, while accepting it at the practical level, the leadership could interpret Palestinian national goals in ways that were convenient for it while at the same time acting to serve its own interests. Close cooperation with the Jordanian regime was, therefore, viewed as legitimate, as a necessary evil, compared to other options that were held to be unrealistic.

Jordan and the PLO in the post-1967 era

The patterns of coexistence and cooperation between Jordan and the Palestinians continued to exist after the Israeli conquest of the West Bank in 1967, becoming entrenched as an arrangement preferable to a direct and open conflict between the two parties. The gradual consolidation of the Israeli military occupation in the West Bank and Gaza, the fact that Israel defined its presence in those territories as temporary (until a permanent settlement could be worked out), and the struggle between Jordan and the PLO over political influence and domination over the Palestinian population, all encouraged Israel, Jordan, and the PLO, as well as the local Palestinian elite, to search for a working formula of negotiated coexistence and controlled cooperation between them.

The heightened prestige of the PLO in the 1970s, in both the inter-Arab and the international arenas, generated a surge of national feeling among the Palestinians. These sentiments were channeled by the PLO into political activity in the West Bank and Gaza. In the mid-1970s, the PLO's efforts began to bear fruit. PLO influence was palpable in municipalities and in local bodies such as universities, student organizations, trade unions, charitable societies, and the press. In addition, new bodies, such as youth organizations, were established which operated under PLO auspices.

Nevertheless, Jordan retained considerable political influence in the West Bank; the Hashemite Kingdom remained a political force to be reckoned with by the PLO. Relations between the PLO and Jordan were hardly fraternal. A deep conflict of interest divided them regarding the nature of the eventual political settlement in the West Bank and Gaza. At the same time, the PLO was conscious of the possible adverse effects were it to exploit its success among the Palestinian population in order to spark an all-out confrontation with Jordan. Cooperation and coexistence with Amman was the order of the day.

Compelled to take into account the categorical Israeli rejection of the idea of a Palestinian state in the West Bank and Gaza, the PLO espoused instead a political settlement with Jordanian participation. As long as this Israeli stand prevailed, the PLO could not rule out the possibility that its unwillingness to compromise was liable to vitiate its status among the Palestinians – who were anxious to see an end to the Israeli occupation – and push them into the arms of Jordan. It is here that one should look to understand the statement of Arafat's political adviser, Hani al-Hasan, that "no Palestinian strategist can afford to remove his eyes from Jordan for even a minute. The only Arab state able to replace us [as a party to a political settlement] is Jordan." Furthermore, "no Palestinian strategist can ignore the geographical fact that the Palestinian state-to-be will have two entrances: one from the East Bank and the second from Gaza. There can be no chance to ensure free access to the West Bank other than by having cooperative ties with Jordan" (*Filastin al-Thawra,* April 21, 1984).

The day-to-day reality of the local Palestinian population added to the PLO's considerations in favor of cooperation and of maintaining open channels of communication with Jordan. Indeed, ties with Jordan were a *sine qua non* for obtaining essential goods and services. These included the export of agricultural produce and other goods via the Jordan River bridges; Amman's continued payment of salaries to civil servants who had served under Jordanian rule prior to the war of 1967; approval of development projects; exit permits and passports; matriculation certificates required for admittance to universities abroad; import and export licenses; and so forth. In none of these spheres could the PLO replace Jordan. The prolonged Israeli occupation and growing Israeli–Jordanian interaction on routine matters, made the PLO increasingly inclined to accept the ties linking the residents of the territories to Jordan as a fact to be taken into account in its quest for political status there. Moreover, as the PLO moved toward a political process and sought ways to participate in negotiations that would assure it a territorial *quid pro quo* in the West Bank and Gaza, it was disposed to redefine its priorities in terms of the "here and now" reality rather than adhere to a dogmatic all or nothing approach. Dialogue and cooperation with Jordan became a key component in PLO policy toward the occupied territories.

A similar conclusion – that cooperation and dialogue were preferable to confrontation – had been reached in Amman. Jordan was intensely conscious of its profound differences with the PLO regarding the desired solution in the West Bank. PLO domination in the West Bank and the establishment of a PLO-led independent entity could threaten the very existence of the Hashemite Kingdom, in which Palestinians constituted approximately half of the population. One might argue that the logical course of action following from this premise entailed a head-on clash with the PLO similar to the civil war of 1970. But other considerations were also at work: the political status acquired by the PLO in the Arab world and among the Palestinians since the mid-1970s; demographic trends in Jordan which favored the Palestinian side; the exposure of the Palestinian population on both banks of the Jordan to outside radical influences; and the constantly shifting alignments in the Arab world, which were not always to Jordan's advantage. Amman was disinclined to view the option of a frontal clash with the PLO as a preferable alternative to the existing political order. Such a confrontation could prove disastrously destabilizing for the regime, possibly even causing its collapse.

Recognizing the limitations of its power to neutralize the PLO in one swift blow as a political rival for West Bank hegemony, Jordan turned to more flexible political methods. Amman's policy was guided by the principle that the less it infringed on Palestinian national symbols, the less friction would be generated with the PLO. A moderate level of friction would facilitate the continuation of Jordanian activity in the West Bank without the accompanying perception that such activity was detrimental to Palestinian national aspirations. Thus, in its public statements Jordan endeavored to play down the importance of its disagreements with the Palestinians on the political future of the territories. Jordan continually declared that its political goals were identical with those of the Palestinians. It was careful not to challenge publicly resolutions of the highest inter-Arab forum, the Arab summit, which recognized the Palestinians as a separate entity with the right to establish their own sovereign state. As presented by Amman, any differences between the two sides were artificial and temporary, deriving less from a dispute over the Palestinians' right to self-determination than from a choice of tactics.

The Jordanian and PLO interest of preferring cooperation over confrontation spawned a pattern of relations most aptly described as coexistence within a prolonged conflict. Both sides were well aware of the gulf dividing them and the difficulty of reaching an agreement that would enable them to live side by side in political harmony. Yet, each side recognized its limitations to press for a solution of "one in place of the other." While both sides were clearly unwilling to accept each other fully, they were equally loath to adopt a position of total rejection. In the dusty reality of the Middle East arena the price each side would pay in attempting to remove the other from the political stage was intolerable. Both therefore preferred to pursue a strategy which would mitigate the disadvantages of coexistence rather than strive for a new political order that would exclude the other side. According to this perception, it was more promising for each side to concentrate on improving its positions and to beef up its bargaining ability *vis-à-vis* the other side, instead of pursuing an "all or nothing" policy to advance ultimate political goals. Coexistence within a prolonged conflict was perceived by both sides as the lesser evil and as a situation preferable to any of the alternatives.

The rise of the Palestinian local leadership

The pattern of coexistence worked out by Jordan and the PLO was profoundly influential in shaping the attitude of the Palestinian local leadership toward each of the two parties. As will be seen, the character of the relationship that developed between the West Bank and Jordan on the one hand, and between the West Bank and the PLO on the other hand, exercised a moderating influence on the stand of the Palestinian leadership in the territories toward Israel.

The state of coexistence between Jordan and the PLO spared the local Palestinian leadership the need to choose between the two and enabled them to maintain ties with both sides alike. This was the case with both the traditional pro-Jordanian leaders, who dominated West Bank politics until the municipal elections of 1976, and the pro-PLO leaders who were victorious in those elections. Despite their pro-Jordanian leanings, the traditional leaders maintained contacts with the PLO, particularly after the latter began to evince an interest in a political settlement following the 1973 war. The same was true of the pro-PLO leaders centered in the National Guidance Committee, established in 1978. True, these leaders, especially the four mayors – Bassam al-Shak'a in Nablus, Karim Khalaf in Ramallah,

Fahd Qawasima in Hebron, and Muhammad Milhim in Halhul – identified strongly with the PLO and viewed the organization as an equal party in any future negotiations on the territories. Yet they did not balk at dealing and cooperating with Amman on everyday affairs.

The conditions prevailing in the West Bank left the local leadership no real choice but to seek support from both Jordan and the PLO. The absence of a tradition of political independence in the West Bank, combined with the lack of a distinctive ideology and a self-sustaining economy, and the fact that the only common border with the Arab world was with Jordan, precluded the creation of an autonomous power base which might have impelled the West Bank leadership to pursue political initiatives beyond the parameters of Jordanian–PLO coexistence. An Israeli approach to the local leadership as a political partner for negotiations on a permanent settlement, if accompanied by far-reaching territorial concessions, might have created a convenient political climate to build such a power base. Without that willingness, it was unrealistic to expect the emergence of an independent power base in the West Bank (Gazit, 1985: 151–61, 335).

The coexistence between the PLO and Jordan, as well as the West Bank's economic dependence on Jordan, ideological allegiance with the PLO, and political reliance on both alike, created a situation in which any attempt by the local leadership to court one of the two parties at the expense of the other could jeopardize its very existence. Total submission to the PLO would trigger Jordan's wrath, undermining the local leadership's economic mainstay; while unequivocal affiliation with Jordan would have dragged the local leadership into a confrontation with the PLO, eroding its public standing.

As the local leadership became more aware that its bread was buttered by both Jordan and the PLO, it was increasingly disinclined to embark on a new path which could be perceived as a threat to either side's vital interests. The leadership scrupulously refrained from initiating or taking part in political activity beyond the day-to-day level – be it negotiations on a political settlement detached from the PLO, from Jordan or from both; or full-scale civil disobedience against the Israeli authorities. Both types of activity conflicted with PLO and Jordanian interests. Civil disobedience, entailing a severance of contact with the Israelis, would lead to a forceful Israeli reaction. This, in turn, could harm the local institutions that assisted both Jordan and the PLO to tighten their grip on the Palestinian population. By the same token, talks by the local leadership with Israel on a political settlement would undercut the demand of both Jordan and the PLO to play a dominant role in decisions concerning the future of the territories.

As the PLO's civilian activities among the local population increased, and as the base of coexistence between the PLO and Jordan solidified, the local leadership became increasingly unwilling to accept the Israeli occupation, while avoiding direct confrontation and continuing to maintain dialogue and cooperation with Israel on day-to-day issues. This pattern of activity was manifested by pro-PLO and pro-Jordanian local leaders alike. The pro-Jordanians' moderate approach toward Israel was attended by declarations of support for the PLO as the embodiment of the Palestinians' national aspirations; while the radical stand of pro-PLO circles was tempered by pragmatism where contacts with Israel were concerned. Both camps denounced Israeli actions in the territories such as land expropriations, settlements, taxation, arrests, and house demolitions. Radical leaders organized strikes and mass demonstrations and voiced publicly their unequivocal support for the PLO as their sole representative in any political settlement. Nevertheless, the radicals, and certainly the more moderates, were careful not to strain their relations with Israel irrevocably. They maintained constant contact with the Military Government in order to ensure the continued operation of the local governments and of essential services in the realms of health, welfare, education, and commerce. As long as Jordanian–PLO coexistence prevailed, and as long as Israel continued to pin its hopes on political settlements with Arab partners outside the territories, simultaneous reliance on the PLO and Jordan, followed by cooperative relations with Israel, remained the West Bank's preferred mode of action.

Israeli intervention: conflict and coexistence

In Israel, political stands regarding the West Bank and the Gaza Strip (WBGS) derived primarily from two political perceptions: the Greater Israel vision associated with the rightist Likud, and the territorial compromise approach espoused by the Labor Alignment.

The Alignment, which was in power until 1977, viewed the West Bank and Gaza in terms of security considerations, whereas the Likud, which succeeded Labor, spoke in terms of historic rights as well. The Alignment, fearful of what demography portended, sought a political settlement that would enable Israel to rid itself of densely populated Arab areas, while the Likud, with an eye on geography – the whole Land of Israel – urged a permanent Israeli presence throughout the West Bank and Gaza. The Alignment advocated selective settlement, chiefly in the Jordan Rift Valley and the Etzion Bloc south of Jerusalem, whereas for the Likud the entire West Bank was a legitimate, indeed vital, target for Jewish settlement.

Under the Likud government the pace of settlement in the West Bank intensified, the settler population increased, and budgetary allocations for the physical infrastructure in the West Bank were multiplied. Yet, Israeli policy toward the local leadership and the Palestinian population as a whole remained unchanged. Under three defense ministers – Moshe Dayan and Shimon Peres from the Alignment, and Ezer Weizman from the Likud – Israel gave priority to securing calm in the territories through cooperation with the local leadership on day-to-day matters. At the same time, Israel refused to consider these leaders as potential partners for talks on a permanent settlement. Two repercussions followed from the Israeli policy. First, the disinclination to conduct political negotiations with the local leadership encouraged that leadership's continued cultivation of political and economic ties with Jordan, and later on with the PLO; and second, Israel's desire to maintain calm relations with the Palestinian population through cooperation with the local leadership meant Israel's acquiescence in the continued influence of Jordan and the PLO in the West Bank.

Manifestations of Israel's acceptance of a continuing Jordanian influence in the West Bank were clearly visible as early as 1970. Beginning in that year, Israel permitted Jordan to pump money into the territories to pay the salaries of those who had been employed in the Jordanian civil service until 1967. These included municipal clerks, teachers, doctors, lawyers, and clerics. Israel also allowed Jordan to provide financial aid to local governments and to educational, religious, cultural, and social institutions (Ma'oz, 1984: 77, 171–2). The interaction between Jordan and the West Bank was given an additional boost by the Israeli policy of maintaining open bridges across the Jordan River for two-way traffic of persons and goods, and in growing cooperation with Jordan in agriculture, education, health, and various economic spheres. A similar, albeit less obvious, tendency characterized Israeli policy toward the PLO's role in the West Bank. From the mid-1970s, the Military Government tacitly agreed to the injection of funds originating with the PLO for local governments and other civilian bodies. The money reached the West Bank via international or inter-Arab organizations.

Israel continued to acquiesce in the local leadership's affiliation with both the PLO and Jordan even after the 1976 West Bank municipal elections. The victory of pro-PLO candidates such as Bassam al-Shak'a in Nablus, Fahd Qawasima in Hebron, Karim Khalaf in Ramallah, Ibrahim Tawil in al-Bira, Muhammad Milhim in Halhul, Hilmi Hanun in Tulkarm, Amin al-Nassir in Qalqilya, Wahid Hamdallah in 'Anabta, and Bishara Dawud in Beit Jala did not prevent the Military Government from appointing them as mayors. Furthermore, Israel allowed the mayors to visit Amman and other Arab capitals for meetings with Jordanian person-alities and senior PLO officials. Israel took no steps to block the continued transfer of funds by Jordan and the PLO to local governments and other institutions. In May 1977, for example, Jordan earmarked half a million dinars for town governments. Earlier that year, Nablus had received a grant of three million dinars made up of contributions collected from Palestinians in Saudi Arabia. In 1980, Hebron received a grant of ten million dinars from al-Madina in Saudi Arabia as part of a "twin cities" pact sponsored by the PLO.

From Israel's point of view, the continued reliance of the Palestinians in the territories on both the PLO and Jordan, even at the price of the mode of controlled radicalism, seemed the lesser evil. While Israel was hardly pleased by these developments, the probable consequences of a policy entailing the removal of the local pro-PLO leadership seemed worse by far.

It was this cautious approach that guided Alignment policy toward the local leadership up to 1977, and the Likud during the first government of Menachem Begin, when Moshe Dayan served as foreign minister and Ezer Weizman as defense minister. Both had recognized the limitations of Israel's power to neutralize the PLO as a politically potent element in the West Bank. Absolute truths and millennial visions were alien to their politi-cal thought.

The 1981 appointment of Ariel Sharon as defense minister signaled a turning point in Israeli policy toward Palestinian local leaders. Sharon believed that the political reality that had developed in the occupied terri-tories was detrimental to Israel's national interest of maintaining a permanent presence there. He therefore adopted a policy aimed at severing ties between the PLO and the Palestinians in the West Bank, while creating conditions that would reconcile the Palestinians to the idea that Israel was in the territories to stay. To this end, Sharon availed himself of the services of the Civil Administration in the territories, established as an adjunct to the Military Government at the time he took over at the Defense Ministry, to effect the removal of the pro-PLO urban leadership. In March 1982, the mayors of Nablus, Ramallah, and al-Bira were dismissed and Israeli officers appointed in their place. In the same month the National Guidance Committee was outlawed on the ground that it was an arm of the PLO. Bir Zeit University was shut down. Strict censorship was imposed on news-papers published in East Jerusalem and their distribution in the West Bank was prohibited.

The 1982 Lebanon war and the outbreak of the *Intifada* in 1987 under-scored Israel's inability to dictate terms that were unacceptable to the PLO or Jordan. King Hussein's declaration of August 1998 on administrative and legal separation between Jordan and the West Bank paved the way for a clear differentiation between the boundaries of sovereignty and responsibility of the Hashemite Kingdom as distinct from the West Bank. This move contributed significantly to dissipating the tensions between the PLO and Jordan over representation of the West Bank in a future political settlement, and to the creation of a broader base for economic and political cooperation between the two parties. On the other hand, this declaration, along with the PLO's decision to recognize Israel, required the Israelis to come to terms with the legitimacy of the PLO as the legitimate organization representing the WBGS. However, such a radical admission by Israel was not possible, and the PLO was officially denied from participating in the 1991 Madrid Conference, although it was obvious to all that the local leadership of the WBGS that attended the conference was well coordinated with the PLO. It was then only a matter of time for Israel to recognize the PLO as the major actor representing the WBGS, and to directly negotiate the 1993 DoP, while keeping the Jordanians out of the picture.

The Post-Oslo Period – New Dilemmas

Despite the Israeli–Palestinian 1993 DoP and the 1994 peace treaty between Israel and Jordan, the tension between realist and idealist interpretations of Middle Eastern politics has remained a major factor, and a political settlement acceptable to the majority of the contending parties in the Middle East has not yet been achieved. Still, progress in the direction of peace negotiations has had a profound effect on the Middle East, with open lines of communication between Israel and its Arab neighbors continually expanding. However, due to the sharp contrast between the Arab and Israeli social and economic systems, different expectations regarding the nature of economic relations are gradually becoming a current issue in Arab–Israeli relations.

The proponents – both Arabs and Jews – of full normalization of relations between Israel and its neighbors have tended to interpret the peace process in terms of the liberal perspective. As such, economic cooperation is viewed as beneficial to all parties and to regional interdependence. According to the liberal approach, business ventures that include experienced Israeli entrepreneurs with financial capability, on top of the readily available supply of cheap Arab labor, will attract foreign investments. By such means, the Arab countries that suffer from high rates of unemployment can create new places of work and stimulate economic growth. The high cost of breaking down these cooperative economic bonds will minimize the chance of violent conflict.

The Israeli opposition to the peace process, basing its arguments on realist theory, is against economic integration between Israel and its Arab neighbors. Evacuation of territories occupied since the 1967 war is perceived as giving up indispensable resources required to maintain Israeli power, thereby making Israel vulnerable to aggression, which realist theory perceives as inevitable. Moreover, since, according to realism, political interests prevail over economic interests, economic interdependence cannot be viewed as a reliable guarantee for preserving peace. At the same time, because the Arab economies do not threaten Israel, most Israeli realists would not oppose economic cooperation with Arab countries, as long as the proper security arrangements are maintained.

Still, Israeli realists, while willing to accept Arab–Israeli economic relations that are based on trade, oppose relying on the Palestinian or Jordanian workforce as a source of cheap labor. The risks associated with allowing free mobility across the borders are considered too high. Cross-border labor mobility will be exploited by Arab terrorists, who consistently target Israeli citizens and property. In any case, Israeli demand for Palestinian and Jordanian labor is not considered that critical. Because foreign workers from eastern Europe and the Far East are not currently viewed as a serious social problem, no advantage is seen in the fact that the Jordanian and Palestinian laborers do not have to reside in Israel. Indeed, foreign labor is usually cheaper than Palestinian labor.

Similarly, there is relatively low interest in Jordan and the WBGS in long-term Israeli economic policy. This is because most of the comparatively expensive and high-quality Israeli products are oriented toward industrial countries. The market for Israeli products in Jordan and the WBGS is assumed to be limited. The result is that economic relations between Israel, Jordan and the WBGS remain at a low level.

While the Israeli opposition to the peace process can be described in realist terms, both realist and centralist principles motivate the Arab opponents of the process. The fact that Israel has a more developed economy is considered a potential threat that must be offset. Thus, Arab realists advocate maintaining strong military capability and forging an Arab alliance in order to deter Israeli expansionism. Economic relations with Israel must also be avoided, as Israel could utilize them for coercion. This conceptualization of Arab–Israeli relations has led many Arab realists to prefer a settlement of a provisional character with Israel rather than one that will spur normalization.

The Arab centralist school has reached similar conclusions to the realists, although their arguments differ. Arab centralists view Israel in similar terms to the European industrial states, fearing that if Israeli investors obtain access to Arab markets they will immediately exploit them and reap most of the profits. Thus, they advocate placing limitations on economic relations with Israel, though they do not necessarily oppose reaching a limited type of agreement to end the state of war, so that more Arab resources can be invested in economic development.

Although Jordan and the PA would seem to face a very similar problem – how to avoid Israeli exploitation and dominance – there is a big difference. It stems from the fact that the Palestinians and the Jordanians have emerged from the Arab–Israeli conflict in entirely different positions. The Jordanians are interested in taking advantage of the new economic opportunities that Israel might be able to provide. However, when they look at the situation of the Palestinians, they are aware that they risk becoming dependent on Israel. The Palestinians are in exactly the opposite situation. The peace process has given them the opportunity to free themselves from the clutches of Israeli dominance. But when they contemplate the economic situation in Jordan, it becomes clear that breaking their ties with Israel might entail high economic costs. Thus, while there is a genuine desire to cast off Israeli dominance, it is tempered by caution and hesitance.

From the perspective of the conflicting Arab attitudes toward Israel, the Jordanians and Palestinians are confronted with a paradox. On the one hand, Israel is a potential source of income. Since 1967, the Palestinians have capitalized on this potential mainly in the form of finding employment and as subcontractors for Israeli industries. On the other hand, from the Palestinians' point of view, dependence on the Israeli economy is fraught with risk. First, reliance on Israel reduces the incentive for autonomous economic development. Second, when the Israeli economy lags or Israel decides to close its borders, the consequences can be harsh.

Since Israel granted the WBGS a degree of economic autonomy, the Palestinians have had the potential to reduce their dependence on Israel by investing in development programs and promoting trade with other countries besides Israel. In practice, however, this is largely a utopian aspiration. The Palestinians' economic plight is immediate and acute, while the costs of development and creating new economic markets are very high: it is much easier and far cheaper to import and export through Israeli channels.

As for the Jordanians, their temptation to forge economic ties with Israel may lead to competition and even conflict with the PA. The Jordanians in fact have two advantages over the Palestinians. First, because the cost of living in Jordan is cheaper than in the WBGS, Jordanian laborers are willing to accept lower wages than Palestinians. Second, since cooperation between the Israeli and Jordanian security services has a long and positive record, it is easier for Jordanians to get a security clearance in order to enter Israel.

Any analysis of how the Israelis, Jordanians, and Palestinians have actually coped with their mutually contradictory interests must take into account that none of these entities is fully hierarchical. That is, although the government of each party might have a clear agenda, individuals as well as bureaucrats have found ways to push their own policies.

When we observe the underlying political nature of the economic relations between the three parties since the 1993 Oslo agreement, we should take into account that at different levels of interaction, behavior based on the various conceptual underpinnings has been manifested at one time or other. When the conduct of the participating parties reflected realist or centralist perceptions they engaged in bargaining tactics, while behavior inspired by liberal and idealist visions were inclined toward a problem-solving approach. Thus, merely to identify conflictive or cooperative modes of behavior is not sufficient. The crux of the matter lies in the general trend and in the prospects that economic relations will produce a co-operative social reality rather than conflictive or competitive interaction.

4

Trade Regimes

The Debate over Free Trade

Trade is the oldest type of international economic relationship and requires the least amount of cooperation. Even during the period of the state of war, when diplomatic and economic relations with Israel were forbidden by Arab governments, Israeli and Arab merchants engaged in trade with the aid of third parties. However, such trade was limited due to its high ancillary costs (Klienman, 1998).

Due to the close geographical proximity between Israel and the Arab world, trade was expected to proliferate rapidly with the lifting of the Arab boycott, as it occurred between Israel and the WBGS following the war of 1967. Indeed, despite the stagnation in the peace process following the election of the Netanyahu government in 1996 and the Arab League's subsequent recommendation to resume the boycott, the volume of Arab–Israeli trade continued (*Globes*, June 17, 1998).

Like most countries, Israel and the Arab states have not been indifferent to the development of mutual trade relations. The general expectation was that the onset of the peace process and the concomitant exposure of the Arab and Israeli markets to each other's goods would influence their respective economies. That influence could be either positive or negative for particular sectors as well as for the national economy overall. It is here one should look in order to understand the interaction between each side's preferred trade regime and choice of suitable trade arrangements, and the political and social consequences of each side's policies (Arad and Hirsch, 1981). However, there is considerable disagreement on how to measure the potential costs and benefits of each of the alternative trade regimes. Ultimately, it boils down to one's view of the relationship between economics and politics.

The liberal school advocates the establishment of a *common market*, which allows free movement of goods and factors of production. This increases the size of the market by providing producers with new consumers. According to Ricardo's theorem, free trade increases the amount of wealth a state accumulates in comparison to a situation where international trade is denied. The reason is that in a free trade regime, each nation will manufacture the most profitable products for it to produce, while importing goods that are less profitable for it to produce. If trade were prevented, states would produce fewer quantities of their most profitable goods (because the market would be smaller), while at the same time production of less profitable items (which could otherwise have been imported) would have to be done locally (O'Brien, 1975: 172–82).

There is of course a certain cost associated with unrestricted international trade, at least in the short term. Local sectors that are less efficient might be unable to compete against foreign imports that are cheaper or of better quality and will go out of business or at least sustain reduced profits. In addition, if there are no limitations on labor mobility, countries with a strong economy will attract immigrants from impoverished countries.

Advocates of the liberal economic doctrine argue that the benefits of a common market outweigh the costs. Immigration of qualified laborers and professionals will boost economic growth, and the elimination of low efficiency sectors due to foreign competition and immigration will provide consumers with higher quality products at lower prices. Thus the less efficient producers or laborers will face the choice of either improving themselves or changing their profession and starting to produce commodities that carry a competitive edge. Similar problems also arise within the confines of the domestic economy.

Taking issue with the liberal interpretation, many economists, influenced by centralist perspectives, have argued against the "simplistic" classical assumptions. The movement of professionals and laborers across borders produces negative social effects in both the highly developed and the less developed countries, they maintain. In this view, emigration inhibits the development of less developed countries, as the most qualified people leave, attracted by higher paying jobs in wealthier countries. The result is that the periphery is left with less qualified workers who are paid less but also contribute less to economic development (Weisskopf, 1972). At the same time, the centralists say, the influx of highly qualified foreigners also creates problems in the developed countries. The new arrivals often encounter intense hostility in the more developed countries, where they are perceived as a potential threat to the livelihood and to the fundamental cultural values of the local inhabitants. Such reactions have been manifested even in countries that traditionally absorbed new immigrants such as the United States (Walker, 1896).

A slightly less liberal approach, which coincides with the national and sectoral interests associated with labor mobility, involves the creation of a *customs union*. Like a common market, a customs union seeks to break down all tariffs between members of the union, while limiting labor mobility. However, allowing free trade while restricting immigration creates economic inequality between different regions within the customs union. Normally, in a common market, one would expect people to emigrate from densely populated areas with few resources to regions that are blessed with abundant resources and opportunities. This is what characterized the emigration from Europe to the "New World." But once the freedom to immigrate is denied, nations with many resources and a small population will be in a better position to maintain their economic advantage in relation to nations with a large population and fewer resources (Myrdal, 1956).

Not only the quantity but also the type of resources available can generate inequality. Inflexible products, such as oil and coal, place the suppliers at an advantage, while producers of flexible goods, such as agricultural foodstuffs, are in a less advantageous position (Polachek, 1980). According to Boulding (1975), countries depending on a small range of alternative trading opportunities are more vulnerable than those with a large variety of alternatives; hence they are more likely to become involved in conflicts than countries with more trade opportunities.

Liberal economists, however, contend that the unequal distribution of the world's resources does not necessarily place nations with fewer resources at a disadvantage. Their argument is based on the Heckscher–Ohlin theorem, which proposes that countries with fewer resources can specialize in labor-intensive industries, while those countries with greater resources can specialize in capital-intensive industries. On the basis of this form of the division of labor, Lawrence (1995) suggested that in the case of Israel, Jordan, and the WBGS, a customs union would provide mutual benefits to all parties. The Jordanians and Palestinians would invest in labor-intensive industries, while the Israelis would invest in hi-tech, capital-intensive industries.

The Heckscher–Ohlin theorem also has its critics. According to the Stolper–Samuelson theorem, specialization in either labor-intensive industries or capital-intensive industries has a profound sectoral effect on the local economy. Higher rates of unemployment and low wages can be expected in the capital abundant states, since their labor-intensive industries will be unable to compete with foreign producers in states with abundant labor resources. At the same time, the price of capital in the capital abundant states will rise in response to the increase in demand from abroad for capital-intensive products. The opposite process will occur in labor abundant states. As labor-intensive production increases, more laborers will be required, leading to a demand for higher wages, while capital-intensive industries will suffer due to foreign competition from states that specialize in capital-intensive industries.

The Stolper–Samuelson theorem is based on the assumption that prices differ between countries. However, if two countries share the same production technology and are joined together in a perfectly competitive common market, then according to the factor-price equalization theorem the costs of the different factors (capital and labor) will eventually be equalized between them. This is because within a perfectly competitive market, factor costs are based on the value of their marginal productivity, which in turn depends upon the output prices of the goods produced. The implication is that the effects predicted by the Stolper–Samuelson theorem are expected only during the initial stage of free trade; but over time the wages of workers and the rentals earned on capital throughout a customs union will equalize.

Empirical observations based on US labor statistics partially support the predictions of the Stolper–Samuelson theorem. Contrary to expectations, the ratio between skilled and unskilled modes of production has not changed. However, the wages of unskilled laborers in comparison to skilled laborers have been declining since the 1970s (Freenstra and Hanson, 1996). Opinion is divided over whether this was a consequence of cheaper labor abroad or of domestic economic developments in the United States, unrelated to foreign competition (Lawrence, 1994). Testing the relevance of the Stolper–Samuelson theorem in labor-intensive countries is even more difficult because in the short term unemployment is projected to increase as laborers transfer from unprofitable capital-intensive industries to labor-intensive industries (Lee, 1996). The surging unemployment rates during the transition period can have a destabilizing impact within the labor abundant countries, culminating in political turmoil and internal violence. This can completely disrupt the transformation process, debilitating the local economy and ultimately preserving the high levels of unemployment that were created during the opening of the market to free trade.

Even if a labor abundant country succeeds in establishing an economy based on labor-intensive industries, in the long run, Myrdal (1956) argues, nations that possess high technology and capital will have an advantage over nations that rely on labor-intensive industries or produce only primary products. The reason is that the products of the highly developed nations are sold at a higher profit than primary products or products based on unskilled labor. Furthermore, the uneven flow of capital will be maintained because the development of higher-level industry within a less developed economy will be inhibited. Attempts to produce such products locally will fail due to lack of technical knowledge and sources of investment.

The problems described above led many countries to adopt centralist policies, oppose free trade and protect their economy from a leakage of capital by imposing high tariffs on imports or subsidizing local industries to encourage local production. However, attempts to prevent a negative trade balance have not necessarily improved the local economy. Because of lack of competition and poor technical capability, local products are of low standard and likely to be unattractive. An opposite argument, in favor of foreign competition, proposes that while in the short run foreign hi-tech production is in a better position, in the long run these technologies can be learned and copied. But even if a state has the technological capacity to produce a certain product, without a sufficiently large local market import substitution will not be feasible (Richards and Waterbury, 1990).

In many cases, free trade, rather than eliminating a particular industry due to foreign competition, has caused a fragmentation of the production processes. Once the costs of moving merchandise across the border are removed, production is divided among a number of sites in different countries, with each state involved specializing in a particular aspect of production (Lawrence, 1995).

The Debate over the Appropriate Trade Regime between Israel and its Neighbors

Although it has been acknowledged that fragmentation of production will encourage economic development for Jordan and the PA, many Arab economists have expressed little enthusiasm about the prospects of a customs union with Israel. According to their understanding, because the Israeli economy is much larger than the Jordanian and the Palestinian economies, the impact will not be symmetrical. The result will be to encourage the development of industries that are dependent on Israel. Thus, economic shifts in Israel will have a serious effect on the small economies of Jordan and the WBGS, since their relative shares of trade with Israel would be quite large. On the other hand, a high rate of economic growth or, alternatively, a recession in Jordan or the WBGS would have little impact on Israel, as the volume of trade between those regions and

Israel would constitute only a small share of Israel's total trade. At least in the case of the WBGS, this claim has been demonstrated to be valid (Sagea *et al.*, 1992). Another problem is that Jordan has special trade agreements with other Arab countries that are still in conflict with Israel. Since a customs union would entail Israel's *de facto* inclusion in those agreements, the Arab countries that are unwilling to trade with Israel might oppose allowing Israelis to purchase their products at the special rates that were originally granted only to Jordan.

A customs union also has disadvantages from Israel's perspective, due to high import taxes on labor-intensive products. Within the framework of a customs union Palestinian and Jordanian labor-intensive products will be able to compete freely with expensive Israeli labor-intensive products, which are currently protected by high customs. But even products that are less expensive to produce in Israel might be cheaper to purchase from Jordan or the PA. This is because of a high value-added tax (VAT) in Israel, which raises the price of every product sold in Israel by 17 percent.

For these reasons, prior to the Oslo process, Israel did not allow competitive Palestinian products to enter the Israeli market or even to be exported via Israeli ports. In addition, like Jordan, Israel also maintains special trade agreements with the European Community, the United States and a score of other states. The moment Israel creates a trade union with the WBGS and Jordan, these two regions must be included within the agreements.

If a uniform import regime were to be established for the three economies, another major issue would be how to determine the tariffs on products originating from abroad. Any trade agreement with a fourth party would require the consent of all three parties to the union. Thus, an international institution comprising all members of the union would have to be set up in order to determine the union's trade policy. On the positive side this could increase cooperation and integration within the union. But such an intergovernmental institution could also serve as an arena of conflict and disagreement. Because of the differences in the orientations of the three economies, reaching a consensus would be very difficult. While Israel is oriented toward trade with advanced industrial states, Jordanian and Palestinian trade is conducted with less developed economies (David Boas *et al.*, 1996). The gap between the Arab and Israeli economies would probably bring pressure on Israel to reduce its customs duties, standards, and purchase taxes, contrary to Israeli policy.

A possible compromise is to create a *free trade area* (FTA). This type of trade agreement, which is less liberal than a customs union, involves the elimination of customs barriers between the members only on products manufactured by each. Thus such an arrangement allows each economy to conduct an independent trade policy in regard to products originating outside the area. This solution would eliminate the contradiction between Israeli–Jordanian–Palestinian trade relations and agreements with other countries.

An FTA would be especially beneficial for the PA, which could continue expanding its exports to Israel while at the same time allowing it to purchase imported goods from markets cheaper than Israel. However, the Palestinians are wary about such an arrangement, as Jordanian labor is cheaper than Palestinian. Thus, an FTA between the three regions might result in a loss of the Palestinian share within the Israeli market. The Jordanians too have expressed their concern about such a regime; their major anxiety is that Israeli and Palestinian businesses will successfully compete with Jordan's local industry (Fletcher, 1994).

Negative sectoral effects caused by free trade have been frequently observed in the case of agricultural production. Israeli mass producers have sometimes succeeded in reducing prices in the WBGS to very low levels (Litani, 1996), though Palestinian agricultural production has sometimes forced prices down to unprofitable levels for Israeli farmers. However, in the case of industrial production, the local industry of the WBGS has been quite successful in resisting Israeli competition. This is because it is very difficult for non-local manufacturers to penetrate local markets that are based on high levels of consumer loyalty. Thus, while there might be some justification for the Jordanian fear of Israeli domination, the PA's concerns might be mitigated because of its potential as a more serious source of competition for Israel. In the same manner, Jordanian production is also expected to compete with Palestinian production.

Allowing each government to determine its own independent trade policy could allay the centralist fears of Jordan and the PA with regard to Israeli "economic imperialism" and mutual competition. However, Jordan and the WBGS would lose their special access to the Israeli market because they would be bound by the high Israeli protective customs.

In order to gain access to the Israeli market, while also protecting local interests, Jordan and the PA could opt for a limited FTA, which would encompass a limited number of goods, though the list could be expanded over time. In addition, more Middle Eastern countries could join the agreement in the future. It should be noted that in western Europe, too, the initial trade agreements prior to the creation of the European Market and the European FTA were limited to specific products. Over time, more and more items were included in new FTA agreements. In fact, many of the bilateral FTAs between Israel and foreign countries are also limited. For example, in the FTA between Canada and Israel, which came into effect on January 1, 1997, under Annex 2.1.2A Canada and Annex 2.1.2B Israel, a number of agricultural products were exempt from being entirely duty free, or were subject to a duty free status under a limited quota.

In the long run, mutual access between the markets of the three regions can be expected. In 1996, Israel, Jordan and the PA, along with another twenty-seven countries from Europe, the Middle East, and North Africa agreed to the creation of an FTA between the southern Mediterranean and the EU by the year 2010 (FICC, 1997). In addition, since Israel became a full member of GATT, there are indications that it intends to reduce its protective tariffs. Indeed, since 1989 Israel has been gradually reducing tariffs on many products and in 1991 quotas and license requirements on foreign products were canceled. The objective is to reach a maximum 12 percent customs rate on finished products imported from countries that do not have trade agreements with Israel and a maximum of 8 percent on intermediate products (Lawrence, 1995).

In the future, the removal of protective measures on imports into Israel might have a negative effect on Israeli–Palestinian or Israeli–Jordanian trade, as the Jordanians and Palestinians will then have to compete with products from foreign countries. Yet, they will retain the advantage of geographical proximity to Israel, which will reduce transportation costs as well as facilitate trade in perishable agricultural produce.

Besides economic interests, realist political considerations also motivate the members of the Israeli–Jordanian–Palestinian triangle. From the point of view of Palestinian national aspirations, a common market with Israel is hardly desirable. Enhancing economic autonomy and restricting the movement of commodities and persons across a recognized "border" can be viewed as part of the process of political independence. Thus, for the Palestinians, from a purely political standpoint, a common market would probably not be an optimal solution.

In the case of Israel's realist political interests, the exact opposite is the case. If a common market between Israel and the PA is established, there will be no need to demarcate a border, which might be considered the foundation of a future territorial settlement between Israel and the Palestinians. Moreover, free movement of goods and workers between the PA and Israel would have negative security implications for Israel, diminishing its ability to monitor the passage of arms and terrorists or smuggling across the 1967 Green Line.

The Israeli–Palestinian Negotiations over the Paris Protocol

Nearly every clause in Annexes III and IV of the Israeli–Palestinian Declaration of Principles (DoP) begins with the word "cooperation." Both sides agreed to cooperate in a large variety of developmental resource-allocation projects, and encourage free access to prospective markets (clause 6 in Annex III). As mentioned in the previous chapter, before the signing of the agreement Israel did not impose any customs barriers on products transferred from the WBGS across the pre-1967 cease-fire lines. However, while the Israelis had free access to the Palestinian market, Palestinian access to the Israeli market or to markets abroad was limited to products that did not affect Israeli economic interests.

Following the signing of the DoP in 1993, a team of Israeli and Palestinian economists met in Paris in order to work out an agreement over a new economic regime between Israel and the future PA. According to one of the Israeli representatives, the parties began with two assumptions regarding the agreement. First, since they were negotiating an interim settlement, the economic arrangements to be concluded would need to be revised in the light of the eventual permanent settlement between them. Second, because the current status quo was highly disadvantageous to the Palestinians, Israel would have to make some concessions in order to improve the Palestinians' economic situation in the form of eliminating certain regulations and policies. The problem was how far Israel was prepared to go toward meeting Palestinian demands (Klienman, June 24, 1998). It soon became apparent that contrary to the spirit of a liberal regime enshrined in the DoP, the parties were entangled in a zero-sum bargaining match, with each side striving to maximize economic and political interests.

Unlike a normal economic agreement between two states, in this case the agreement was between a state and an occupied territory. While both sides viewed the status quo as untenable in the new circumstances, each sought a different solution. The problem, according to the Israelis, was that the population under its jurisdiction had suffered from discriminatory policies for many years. Israel thus offered to eliminate the discriminatory economic policies against the WBGS and bring about a common market. However, because the Palestinians would remain under Israeli occupation, all economic policies would continue to be determined by Israel (Arnon and Spivak, 1998).

In contrast to the Israelis, who were attempting to create "friendlier terms of occupation," the Palestinians had a different political agenda. Their solution to Israeli discriminatory practices was to obtain the greatest possible level of administrative functions and gain recognition as a separate political entity, thus limiting the terms of occupation. However, total economic independence from Israel was viewed as very harmful: because Israel imposed protectionist customs against competing industries most Palestinian exports, which until then were directed at the Israeli market, would be subject to these customs duties and would also have to compete with foreign imports. The Palestinian delegation therefore proposed an FTA between Israel and the WBGS. In this manner the Palestinians would be allowed to develop an independent trade policy with foreign countries while maintaining their free access to the Israeli market.

The Israeli representatives opposed the FTA. First, this proposal had obvious political implications. It would entail recognition of Palestinian territorial jurisdiction, as the areas to be exempt from Israeli tariffs would have to be clearly defined. But there was also a purely economic consideration. Allowing the Palestinians to import merchandise from abroad at lower customs rates and low standards would effectively turn the WBGS into a "duty free zone." Israeli consumers would then be able to purchase imports from the WBGS at lower prices, and possibly also at lower standards, thus bypassing the protective barriers imposed on imports to Israel (Maltz, 1994; Barr, April 29, 1999).

In the meantime, Hamas attempts to frustrate the Israeli–Palestinian negotiations through terrorist attacks against Israeli civilians led the Israeli security forces to impose limitations on the entry of Palestinians and Palestinian goods to Israel. Thus, due to realist concerns over security, the Israelis no longer viewed a common market as an attractive option. Instead, Israel suddenly expressed greater willingness to accede to the Palestinian demands to limit economic ties between the WBGS and Israel, mainly by restricting labor mobility.

This turn of events placed the Palestinians in a highly uncomfortable situation. They were now faced with a dilemma between the opportunity to create a border between Israel and the WBGS and the economic costs this would entail. The Palestinians eventually decided on a compromise of their political aspirations in favor of economic welfare, agreeing to retract their FTA proposal and accept the initial Israeli proposal for a common market with a few reservations, which allowed for a limited degree of autonomy.

Under the final agreement, the Palestinians were given full access to the Israeli market with the exception of six agricultural products (poultry, eggs, potatoes, cucumbers, tomatoes, and melons). The Israelis agreed to remove all restrictions over the import or export of these products within a specified period. The Palestinians were also granted free access to trade with foreign countries, but agreed that Israel would continue to bear sole responsibility for determining the customs rates. In spite of this limitation, Israel accepted the Palestinians' request to determine tariffs for motor vehicles and a limited number of products required for Palestinian development. An additional number of products, imported from Jordan and Egypt and some other Arab countries, were also exempted from Israeli customs and standards, thus allowing the Palestinians to expand their economic relations with the Arab world. The Israelis, however, insisted that the lower tariffs for the Palestinians be limited in quantity. The quota imposed on those specific items that could be imported at a lower tariff was intended to satisfy only Palestinian demand, but not sufficiently satisfy both Israeli and Palestinian demands. In this manner the Israelis hoped to prevent competition of Jordanian or Egyptian products with Israeli products.

Another protective measure introduced at Israel's insistence was that the Palestinians would impose a value-added tax on all merchandise sold within the WBGS; otherwise, the price of products sold within the WBGS, even if manufactured in Israel or imported from abroad, would be cheaper than in Israel. It was, however, agreed that the Palestinian VAT would be a few percent lower than the Israeli rate of 17 percent. Still, this "compromise" did not give the Palestinians a significant advantage: taking into consideration the time and transportation costs, the incentive for Israelis to travel to the WBGS in order to make a purchase with a slightly lower VAT was minimal.

The most critical limitation imposed on the WBGS was the Israeli demand to limit the mobility of Palestinian labor. The first sentence of Article VII in the Paris Protocol states clearly:

> Both sides will attempt to maintain the normality of movement of labor between them, subject to each side's right to determine from time to time the extent and conditions of labor movement into the area.

In other words, the agreement allowed the Israelis to continue to limit the size of the Palestinian workforce entering Israel from the WBGS.

Implementing the Paris Protocol

Obstacles and constraints

It should be emphasized that the Paris Protocol is not merely a trade agreement but a comprehensive economic accord. However, while in other areas the negotiators seemed to find common ground, the issues of trade and labor mobility were not satisfactorily resolved. The Palestinians soon discovered that in the case of labor mobility particularly, they were in a disadvantageous position.

Most economists agree that the short clause allowing Israel to impose restrictions on labor mobility had calamitous consequences for the Palestinian economy. In 1994 and 1995, as terrorist attacks intensified, Israel responded by expanding the closure periods, causing a steep decline in remittances from Palestinian laborers in Israel. In addition, Palestinian exports to Israel and abroad were prohibited. In the case of perishable agricultural products, a major exporting sector in the WBGS, these developments were critical.

Since 1996, with the decline of terrorist attacks against Israeli citizens, many of the restrictions imposed on the movement of Palestinians have been relaxed. However, the Israeli government developed complex bureaucratic and security mechanisms to monitor the transport of products from the WBGS into Israel. All Palestinians from the WBGS who seek entry into Israel require a security clearance and a permit. But even obtaining a permit may be insufficient, as there are different types of permits. There are permits for entering Israel and permits to work in Israel. Many permits are granted for a limited time. Obtaining a permit to enter with a vehicle is especially difficult.

The policy of limiting the movement of Palestinians from the WBGS within Israel can be traced back to the pre-1967 era. Between 1949 and 1966, the Palestinian citizens of Israel ("Israeli Arabs") were placed under the rule of a Military Government, which imposed severe restrictions on their movement. Following the war of 1967, a new Military Government was established in the WBGS. The movement of Palestinians and Israelis within these territories was restricted; Palestinians in the WBGS required a permit from the military governor to visit Israel, while Israelis required a permit to travel in the WBGS.

However, the Israeli restrictions on Palestinian movement were more of a formality. The Israeli security forces made no serious efforts to control the entry of Palestinians into Israel, despite frequent acts of Palestinian terrorism. This policy was motivated by political considerations. First, the elimination of barriers between the WBGS and Israel encouraged economic and social relations and thus was thought to heighten the prospects for a future peace settlement. Second, many Israelis hoped to annex parts (or even all) of the occupied territories, and thus did not want a border demarcated. The result was that the "Green Line," which had been made on official maps to show the borders between the WBGS and Israel, vanished from post-1967 Israeli maps. On most roads that crossed the Green Line there were no permanent checkpoints or signs indicating the line's existence, and the old physical barriers, such as fences, walls, and gates were dismantled. Thus, Palestinian workers and merchants could travel freely between Israel and the WBGS, even though they were formally required to obtain permits. In 1971, after the PLO was expelled from Jordan and Palestinian violence against Israel diminished, the Israeli authorities rescinded the order requiring Palestinians from the WBGS to obtain a permit to enter Israel (Gazit, 1985: 220).

The change in Israeli attitudes during the 1990s regarding Palestinian traffic across the Green Line was probably a consequence of the *Intifada*. Although Palestinian violence was not a new phenomenon, between 1974 and 1985 Palestinian factions affiliated with the PLO based outside Israel's borders were responsible for the majority of Arab attacks with Israeli fatalities. In 1986, as the military activity of Palestinian organizations from outside fell off, violence initiated by Palestinian residents of the WBGS for the first time became the dominant source of Palestinian and Arab aggression against Israeli civilians and soldiers. In addition, in the late 1980s a shift occurred in the attitude of the Palestinian population toward armed Palestinian groups operating from the WBGS. While in the 1970s the local population was reluctant to support such military activity, the new wave of Palestinian violence in the 1980s gained popular support (Schiff and Ya'ari, 1990: 138).

The Israeli security forces initially discounted the changes in the pattern of Palestinian violence, since 1986 was unusually calm and the number of Israeli casualties was exceptionally low. During that year Palestinians operating from the WBGS killed seven Israelis, while another three soldiers in Lebanon and a diplomat in Cairo were killed by non-Palestinian or unidentified groups. This was the lowest number of Israeli deaths from acts of political violence (whether by regular military units or non-conventional forces) since the war of 1967. In 1987 and 1988 the number of Israeli casualties caused by Palestinian violence gradually increased, with Palestinian cells from the WBGS responsible for the majority of the lethal attacks, although the overall casualty figure remained comparatively low. It was not until 1989, the second year of the *Intifada*, that the Israeli security forces began to grasp the change that had occurred. Israeli casualties at the hands of Palestinians from the WBGS reached a record high. Groups operating from the WBGS killed more than forty Israeli soldiers and civilians, accounting for more than 80 percent of the total number of Israelis killed by Arab violence that year.

As the Palestinian attacks became increasingly lethal, it became apparent that violence originating in the WBGS posed a greater threat to Israeli civilians than the actions by Palestinian organizations abroad. Eventually, in 1991, in the wake of the Gulf War, in which Israel was subjected to missile attacks and the Palestinians gave massive support to Iraq, a closure was imposed on the WBGS. Any Palestinian resident of the WBGS wishing to enter Israel required a permit from the military authorities. Permission to spend the night in Israel, which had been widely granted in the past, was suspended. Permanent checkpoints were erected on all major highways that crossed the Green Line. Scrupulous searches were carried out and people and goods lacking the appropriate documentation were sent back. Anyone who looked suspicious was detained and interrogated. Crossing the Green Line into Israel became a complicated and time-consuming endeavor.

The closure of 1991 had positive consequences from a security perspective, drastically reducing the number of Israeli victims of Palestinian violence during that period. However, soon after the war ended the closure was lifted and the permit requirement was not enforced, though it was re-introduced more systematically in 1993.

Notwithstanding the permits system and the positive security impact of the closure policy, the IDF was reluctant to seal off the WBGS completely. The Israeli authorities discovered that strict closures had grim economic consequences for the Palestinians. With no alternative source of income, the frustrated Palestinians demonstrated and engaged Israeli soldiers in the streets of their hometowns and villages. Thus the closures had the effect of intensifying the clashes between the IDF and the Palestinians within the WBGS. Israeli policy-makers found themselves caught in a difficult dilemma between the public's demand to prevent terrorism and the need to maintain law and order within the WBGS. In order to alleviate the strain on the IDF and mitigate Palestinian hostility toward the Israeli occupying forces, the Israelis eventually lifted the closures. However, this exacted a heavy security price: along with the laborers and merchants, Palestinians with other intentions were able to enter Israel and perpetrate acts of murderous terrorism.

By 1994 Palestinian violence against Israel reached an unbearable level. In a series of suicide bombings in Israeli cities, Palestinian Islamic groups operating from the WBGS killed over 60 Israeli soldiers and citizens.[1] As in the past, Israel responded by toughening the restrictions on the traffic of commodities and especially on the movement of labor across the Green Line. But by now, under the Oslo process, the Israeli army had retreated from the major city centers, so that the IDF and the Border Police no longer had to confront incensed Palestinians who were cut off from their source of income. As a result, the Israelis were willing to extend the closures for longer periods and introduce more rigorous criteria for issuing permits to enter Israel. Consequently, the Palestinian unemployment surged and the economy of the WBGS deteriorated further.

The Palestinian terrorist attacks also had a significant impact on the Israeli political arena. The Israeli opposition to the peace process became more strident, eventually culminating in the assassination of Prime Minister Yitzak Rabin in November 1995 and the election of a more hawkish government the following May.

The results of the 1996 elections widened the gulf between Israel and the PA. Many joint bodies, including the Israeli–Palestinian Joint Economic Committee, which was supposed to monitor the implementation of the economic agreement, rarely met during the three years that the Likud government was in power. Thus none of the problems that had developed between the two parties were re-negotiated and resolved.

The major victim of the Israeli security policies has been the agricultural sector, which is the major export sector of the WBGS. As noted, the time it takes to cross the border can be critical for agricultural products as they are perishable. For this reason, most WBGS traders turned to imports, only to find that imports can be costly too. One trader interviewed by us said he had found a defect in the item he imported and wanted to return it to the Israeli manufacturer. It took him months to obtain the proper permit in order to return the product.

After a series of terrorist attacks in Jerusalem during the summer of 1997 an "economic war" broke out between Israel and the PA. In addition to the regular closure, Israel refused to transfer funds collected from taxes levied on the Palestinians. The PA reacted by imposing a trade embargo on Israeli products (*ArabicNews.Com*, November 19, 1997). But maintaining the boycott proved difficult. There are two main advantages associated with the import of Israeli products: Israeli suppliers grant Palestinian importers credit, and Palestinian importers are also allowed to sell by commission. Whatever is not sold can be returned. Such flexibility cannot be obtained when importing products from abroad.

Although the trade embargo failed, the PA found other methods of "economic warfare." In 1997 the PA published a decree requiring that a Palestinian agent must represent all Israeli imports. Complaints regarding this policy had already been received by the Federation of Israeli Chambers of Commerce (1996) a year earlier. However, it was not until May 1998 that the president of the Federation complained about this matter, in response to the removal of Israeli products from the shelves of stores in the WBGS and East Jerusalem *(Globes*, May 25, 1998). Despite the restrictions imposed by the PA on trade with Israel, Israelis of Palestinian origin with family ties in the WBGS were able to continue commercial transactions with the WBGS and now constitute a significant percentage of Israelis engaged in such trade.

Another non-cooperative measure initiated by the PA has been the policy of reimbursing the mandatory VAT on all products sold in the PA (although it can sometimes take up to six months to receive the reimbursement). In this manner, while the tax is officially collected, in reality Palestinian merchants can sell their products at a reduced price. The Israeli Ministry of Industry and Trade and the Manufacturers Association requested the Ministry of Finance to consider reimbursing Israelis who sell products to residents of the PA (*Globes*, December 23, 1997). However, the Ministry of Finance has been reluctant to change its policy. Providing a tax exemption for Palestinians could lead to a legalized system of tax evasion. Palestinian middlemen would be able to purchase products from Israelis without paying the VAT and resell them to Israeli customers.

The Israelis also found ways to retaliate against the Palestinians, mainly by not imposing limitations on imports that compete with Palestinian products. All Palestinian requests to have an observer present during trade negotiations between Israel and other countries have been turned down.

The reality described above reveals that in practice a common market between Israel and the PA does not exist. The source of the problem lies in Israel's insistence on monitoring transportation across the Green Line. The Israelis view this as a legitimate defensive measure. But because of the Palestinians' dependence on Israel as a source of labor and trade, the associated costs of closures, delays, and obtaining security clearances, are perceived by the PA as an act of aggression, spurring it to take non-cooperative measures.

As part of the economic tit-for-tat, the PA has imposed its own strict regulations on trade transactions. Israeli exporters to the WBGS who were interviewed by us explained that obtaining a license entails bribing PA officials. In addition, the PA tends to encourage the creation of monopolistic markets by licensing sole suppliers for each product.

An example of the PA's corrupt and anti-liberal practices is the contract between Dor Energy and Palestinian Petroleum. In addition to paying the Palestinian partner, Dor Energy paid a "third" partner half of their profits from their business transactions with the PA, estimated at 42 million Shekels in 1997 and 14 million Shekel during the first quarter of 1998 (*Ha'aretz*, June 21, 1998). Newspaper reports revealed that this third partner was Sheffer & Levy (a petroleum transport company) whose chairman was closely connected to top PA officials. In addition to paying Sheffer & Levy such a high commission, Dor Energy and Sheffer & Levy were required to pay high-ranking PA officials a tribute of half a million Shekels each month. Although this deal may seem a bit expensive, Dor Energy was granted exclusive rights to supply petroleum to a large portion of the WBGS. According to newspaper reports, 40 percent of Dor Energy's profits during the first three-quarters of 1998 were from their business deals with the PA (*Globes*, December 25, 1998; *Ha'aretz*, November 19, 1998). In another instance mentioned by Roy (1996), the PA initiated a self-imposed closure for two weeks until the monopolist importer of gravel to the Gaza Strip was able to rout his competitors.

While the repression of liberal economic practices and the centralization of the economy have deterred many potential investors, this type of regime has certain political benefits, which are advantageous even to Israel. In this manner the PA has been able to control the economic activities of its political adversaries, including the Hamas and other Islamic opposition groups. Like all other organizations in the PA, institutions identified with the Islamic opposition must also pay their token tribute to the appropriate PA officials in order to obtain an operating license. Hence, if the PA chooses, it can easily retaliate and exert pressure on Hamas by imposing demands and limitations on it and on other organizations. Thus, for example, in response to the suicide bomb attack in Jerusalem in the summer of 1997, the PA closed down sixteen social, religious, and charity organizations affiliated with Hamas. A similar reaction of the PA was also observed after suicide bomb attacks against Israel in 1996 (*ArabicNews.Com*, September 30, 1997). Liberalization will thus reduce the PA's ability to monitor Hamas activities, and might even be interpreted by Hamas as a signal to resume its violent activity against Israel.

Fragile range of opportunities

Despite the competitive and conflictive economic relations, according to CBS statistics Israeli–Palestinian trade expanded to more than $1.5 billion in 1996 (*Globes*, May 21, 1997) and more than $2 billion in 1997. This was due mainly to a relaxation in Israeli security measures, thus allowing more Palestinians to work in Israel. In 1997 the borders were closed for sixty-three days, as compared with ninety-two in 1996. In 1998, the situation improved even further. According to PCBS statistics, during 1998 there were only 14.4 days of closures (5.2 percent of the effective working days) in comparison to 56.8 days in 1997.

Israel also increased the number of work permits from 29,000 in 1996 to 47,000 at the beginning of 1997; by May 1997, 55,000 work permits had been issued to Palestinians. According to the Israel Foreign Ministry

Newsline (February 1998), permits were provided based on Israeli demand. In addition, the minimal age requirement for receiving a permit to work in Israel was reduced to 23 and the number of permits for overnight stays in Israel was increased to 4,000. In addition, Israel began to issue closure-exempt permits, which allowed their bearers to enter Israel even during a closure. More than half the work permits provided to the residents of the WBGS fall into this category. In 1998 Israel also eliminated the quota on the number of Palestinian trucks allowed to enter the country. By May 1998, 16,500 Palestinian trucks had obtained permits, in comparison to only 6,374 trucks permitted to enter Israel in 1997 and 3,420 in 1996. This may also explain why Palestinian exports and imports began to rise; as noted above, relying on Palestinian transportation reduces costs.

Israeli restrictions *vis-à-vis* the West Bank are less severe than against the Gaza Strip, probably because it is more difficult to seal the West Bank hermetically. Unlike the Gaza Strip, which is on a plateau and has only a few routes, the West Bank is not fenced in and it is quite easy to bypass the army roadblocks, which are located only on the major highways (Schiff and Ya'ari, 1990: 138).

The more lenient Israeli policies had a considerable impact on the Palestinian economy. Average unemployment levels fell to 20 percent in 1997 and 16 percent in 1998.[2] According to the PCBS, the GDP of the Palestinian Authority increased to $3,950 million in 1997 and $4,050 million in 1998 (PalTrade). Concurrent with the improvement of the Palestinian economy, the violent trend that started in 1987 at last changed its course in 1997. The years of 1998 and 1999 were the most peaceful since 1986. Yet, the security checks and permit system have raised the costs of transportation. In many cases Palestinian merchants have attempted to by-pass the checkpoints system by hiring Israeli drivers. This, however, increases the costs of transportation, since an Israeli driver is more expensive than his Palestinian counterpart.

The situation described above has led many economists to conclude that the Palestinians should build their own port (which was in fact agreed upon during the Arab–Israeli negotiations). While such an enterprise is very expensive – far more so than using the Israeli ports – an independent port will reduce Palestinian vulnerability to Israeli restrictions. A Palestinian port will also affect the Israeli economy: improved access of Palestinians to foreign markets will probably reduce Israeli–Palestinian trade by enabling PA manufacturers to import directly. The port might also compete with the Israeli ports, as it will probably be cheaper to use the Palestinian facility; one cannot exclude the possibility that Israelis or Jordanians might utilize such a port. Overall, though, a greater range of opportunities and reduced dependence will reduce the conflictive nature of relations and replace them with a more competitive pattern.

Israeli–Jordanian Trade Negotiations

On September 14, 1993, in a joint meeting the day after the signing of the Israeli–Palestinian DoP, President Clinton, Prince Hassan of Jordan, and Israeli Foreign Minister Shimon Peres decided to establish a committee for economic cooperation between Israel, Jordan, and the United States. Following this meeting and following the signing of the Israeli–Jordanian peace treaty in 1994, a number of economic agreements were concluded between Israel and Jordan.

At the outset of the Israeli–Jordanian trade negotiations, in line with liberal ideology, the Israelis opted for the creation of an FTA with Jordan. A customs union was not feasible because it would negate Israeli trade agreements with the United States and with the European Union. But the Jordanians were wary of forming an FTA with Israel, fearing that Israeli entrepreneurs would dominate the small Jordanian economy. Thus, the Jordanian representatives demanded that their markets gradually open up to Israeli products, over a period of 10 to 15 years. The Jordanians were also concerned with the effect of Israeli–Jordanian relations on the Palestinian economy and avoided arrangements that might be perceived as having a negative impact on the Palestinians.

The Israelis, for their part, sought to protect certain sectors that would be exposed to competition as a result of free trade. However, Israel was more attentive to Jordanian than to Palestinian needs. This was because Jordanian economic production was small and because the Israelis were more sympathetic toward the Jordanians. In addition, the Israelis believed that trade with Jordan would increase their access to other Arab markets. Thus, in contrast to its approach to the PA, Israel agreed to allow Jordan greater access to its market while limiting Israeli access to Jordan.

The agreement for trade and economic cooperation was signed in October 1995. Although the Israeli desire for an FTA was retracted (paragraph 15 clearly grants each side the freedom to determine its own customs rates), both sides agreed to accord each other preferential trade status. Still, the Israelis insisted that certain quotas and restrictions be imposed on Jordanian imports. The agreement also included a clause (para. 10) allowing each country to prohibit the import of certain goods for security, public safety, or health reasons. Short-term emergency trade policies were also agreed upon in case of a severe decline in the balance of payments (para. 14). Attached to the agreement was a protocol with two tables. The first table included a list of Jordanian products to which Israel would apply a reduced customs rate of 100, 50 or 20 percent; the second consisted of a list of Israeli products on which Jordan would reduce customs by 10 or 5 percent. In December 1996, the number of Jordanian products on the list was increased (Barr, April 29, 1999).

Still, Israeli–Jordanian trade was hindered after the accord came into effect because the sides failed to reach a transportation agreement (*Globes*, December 5, 1996). The transportation agreement took 15 months of negotiations. According to Jordanian sources, this was mainly due to attempts to appease Jordanian sectorial interests. Due to security demands, the initial agreement did not allow for door-to-door transportation, so the system of "back-to-back" transportation, which had existed between Jordan and the West Bank, was adopted. Under this arrangement, merchandise was transferred from trucks parked on one side of the border to trucks on the other side, under the inspection of Israeli security guards. However, at the end of 1996, this cumbersome, time-consuming method was replaced by a door-to-door system. This has proven especially advantageous for the Jordanians for two reasons. First, Jordanian drivers are cheaper than Israelis; and second, because the Jordanian customs offices close relatively early, the Israeli drivers cannot return home the same day and must spend the night in Jordan, raising the costs of employing an Israeli driver (Barr, April 29, 1999).

The Israeli–Jordanian trade agreement marked the first time that Israel was willing to make economic concessions to the other party. In the past, such as with the European and US FTAs, Israel demanded concessions, claiming it was at an economic disadvantage. Still, perhaps because this reversal of roles was new, it was difficult for the Israeli negotiators to be less protective. Thus, although asymmetrical, the Israeli–Jordanian trade agreement to a great extent protects Israeli industries too.

Some members of the Israeli team criticized the negotiators from the Ministry of Industry and Trade for adopting a centralist posture. These critics argued that Israel could have been more forthcoming (Catrivas, 1999). This view does not necessarily express liberal aspirations, as the critics support the asymmetric features of the agreement that favor Jordan. Rather, the argument is that because Israel has a strategic interest in securing an ally along its eastern border, it should have done more to prove to the Jordanians the benefits of allying with Israel, even if this meant compromising Israeli sectoral interests.

While Israelis claimed that Israel was not generous enough to the Jordanians, many Jordanians contended that Amman conceded too much to the Israelis. Indeed, many Jordanians harbor a strong resentment against conducting business with Israel. All the Jordanian professional associations refuse to cooperate with Israel. In January 1997, the first Israeli trade fair in Jordan was met with massive demonstrations (*Globes*, January 27, 1997). But far from the limelight, contacts between Israeli and Jordanian businesses continued. Data published by the Israeli Central Bureau of Statistics shows that Israeli–Jordanian trade increased during 1997, though it remained far lower than Israeli–Palestinian or even Egyptian-Israeli trade. From 1996 to 1997, Israeli exports to Jordan grew by 116 percent, while Jordanian exports to Israel rose by 147 percent (*Globes*, January 21, 1998). This tapered off considerably from 1997 to 1998, when Israeli exports to Jordan increased by about 25 percent, while Jordanian exports to Israel increased by 37 percent (Barr, 1999).

Another result of opening the borders is that Jordanian merchants gained access to the port of Haifa. Besides the fact that Haifa port is larger than the port of Aqaba, it is cheaper and faster when trading with Europe, North Africa, or America. Taxes at Haifa are lower than at Aqaba, and Haifa-bound ships save the time and expense of going through the Suez Canal. Yet these advantages have also generated resentment in Jordan, because of their negative effect on Aqaba (*The Star*, June 18, 1998).

The Jordanian–Palestinian Economic Agreement and its Aftermath

Despite Israel's post-1967 open-bridges policy, which allowed free trade between the West Bank and Jordan to continue, the Jordanians applied protective measures against Palestinian competition. Following the onset of the Israeli–Palestinian peace process, the Palestinians hoped they would be able to reach an agreement to reverse the Jordanian policy. This in fact transpired in January 1994, soon after the signing of the Israeli–Palestinian DoP. The Jordanian-Palestinian economic agreement resembles Annexes III and IV of the DoP. Meanwhile, in May 1994 the Paris Protocol was ratified. This had the effect of subjecting all trade between Jordan and the WBGS to Israeli customs and regulations, with the exception of the items contained in the appendix to the Paris Protocol.

The Paris Protocol eliminated any possibility of creating a bilateral customs union between Jordan and the WBGS. Instead, in January 1995 Jordan and the PA agreed to create a limited FTA, eliminating all customs on goods that were exempt from Israeli customs under the Paris Protocol and manufactured within each other's borders (Lawrence, 1995).

The Jordanians have pressured Israel to increase the number and quantity of goods produced by Jordan and Egypt that are exempt from customs (lists A1 and A2), thus enabling the Jordanian-Palestinian FTA to be expanded. The Israelis have expressed their willingness to negotiate the matter, but have no desire to create a situation in which the PA and Jordan could form an unlimited FTA (Israel Foreign Ministry, March 10, 1998).

As in the case of its trade with the PA, Israel also has control over Jordanian-Palestinian trade in the form of tariffs and security checks at the border. Moreover, the Israelis refused to cancel the back-to-back transportation policy in the case of Jordanian-Palestinian trade. As a result, the cost of transferring products is relatively high. Awartani (1997), for example, estimated that the cost of transferring agricultural produce from the WBGS to Jordan adds $70 to the price of each ton of produce. As a result, most Palestinians have preferred to continue trading with Israel. The upshot is that despite the peace process of the 1990s, Jordanian–Palestinian trade remains at a lower level than in the early 1980s (*Akhbar.Com,* August 31, 1998).

At the end of 1996, in an attempt to allay Jordanian and Palestinian criticism, the Israelis agreed to a Jordanian request to allow door-to-door transportation of cement and fuel from Jordan to the PA. This followed the signing of an Israeli–Jordanian–Palestinian monopolistic marketing arrangement for these items.

Attempts to blame Israeli security inspections for the low level of Jordanian–Palestinian trade are off the mark. Although the inspections raise the cost of trade, the major reason for the minimal economic activity is Jordan's lopsided negative trade balance with the WBGS. According to Dr. Ismail Zagloul, director of research at the Jordanian Central Bank, between 1968 and 1990 the total Jordanian exports to the West Bank amounted to $150 million, while the West Bank exports to Jordan stood at $1.46 billion (Fletcher, 1994). In addition, the Jordanians resent Palestinians' demand to free themselves from linkage to the Jordanian dinar and to create a Palestinian central bank. As a result, despite the FTA agreement between Jordan and the PA, the Jordanians continued to maintain quotas on the import of Palestinian products. Palestinian manufacturers could not export above the amount of the raw material they imported (Sela, 1995). Even after the disagreements between the Palestinians and the Jordanians were settled, in May 1995, trade remained below the quotas set by the Paris Protocol.

Paradoxically, then, the Paris Protocol may have helped to protect Palestinian industry from Jordanian competition. Because Palestinian labor is more expensive than Jordanian, an unlimited FTA between Jordan and the PA might have harmed many Palestinian businesses in the WBGS. However, in 1998, probably as a result of the cement and petrol monopolies, the trade balance between Jordan and the PA was reversed: for the first time Jordan exported more to the West Bank than it imported. But the Jordanians remain fearful of Palestinian competition. Thus, when Israel proposed at the end of 1998 to allow Jordanians and Palestinians door-to-door transportation for two additional items (thus reducing transportation costs for those items), the Jordanians rejected the offer. Still, in the future, if the Jordanians identify a certain industry that will provide them with an advantage, and they can secure the cooperation of a Palestinian monopolist, they will probably seek another door-to-door transportation agreement with Israel.

While Jordanians are wary of Palestinian imports, Palestinian businessmen claim that they too are in a disadvantageous situation. First, they find it difficult to compete with imports from East Asian countries. Second, because of the unstable situation in the WBGS, foreign investment is hard to come by (Sela, 1995).

Despite the mutual fears between the PA and Jordan, the Palestinians have publicly supported Jordanian demands to increase the number of customs-free products. Nevertheless, in 1997, when Israel suggested increasing the number of customs-free products from Jordan and canceling the requirement to obtain an import license from Jordan, the PA rejected the idea. The official explanation was that this would negate the status quo stipulated in the Paris Protocol. The PA was unwilling to provide special exemptions only for Jordan and not for Egypt (Barr, April 29, 1999).

Trade and Conflict within the Israeli–Jordanian–Palestinian Triangle: Future Trends

The Israeli military occupation of the WBGS in 1967 generated increasing trade between those territories and Israel, while their trade with the Arab world gradually declined. Under the new reality of occupation the pursuit of prosaic economic utility prevailed over the poetry of political ideology. This trend was temporarily reversed during the first half of the 1990s, as a result of a change in the Israeli attitude toward the political future of the WBGS and its relation to Israel. The Palestinian attempt to sever the WBGS and Israel, expressed in the *Intifada*, was costly for both sides, although the major victims were ultimately the Palestinians.

While Arab–Israeli trade is partially motivated by political interests, realist political interests seem to be a minor factor in the case of Jordanian-Palestinian trade. Even though the political relations between these two parties are closer than the relations of either of them with Israel, as both share similar concerns regarding Israel's domineering position, their economies are so similar that they have very little to offer each other. For trade between Jordan and the PA to be boosted each region will have to specialize in particular types of industries.

Unlike the Israeli–Palestinian and the Jordanian–Palestinian cases, Israeli–Jordanian trade relations were for many years affected by the realist view of subordinating economic considerations to political interests. Until the peace agreement between Israel and Jordan was signed, trade between the two countries was minimal. However, the signing of the treaty set in motion a steady, if hesitant, growth in their bilateral trade. In fact the expansion of Israeli–Jordanian trade was a step toward filling the vacuum caused by the Arab boycott.

Still, although the prognosis is for Israeli–Jordanian trade to expand, arguably, unless Jordan undergoes significant economic development, such trade will remain limited even if political harmony between all parties prevails. As noted, Israeli exports are oriented mainly toward the industrialized states of western Europe and the United States, and far less toward developing countries. Israeli products are simply too expensive for most Jordanian consumers and industries.

Other Arab countries also have very little to offer Israel. Most goods produced in Arab states are also manufactured in Jordan and the WBGS. Furthermore, foreign products must meet Israeli standards, which are higher than in most Arab states. Jordanian products are often rejected by the Israeli authorities because they fail to meet the requirements of Israeli lab tests (*The Star*, 1997). Thus, the major "export" that the Arabs can offer Israel is cheap labor (*Issues*, March 1996). There are already indications that Jordan has started "exporting" labor to Israel and this trend is expected to grow (*Globes*, August 21, 1996). However, if trade is not limited, exporting labor will not be necessary; instead, Israeli producers can send unfinished products to Jordan or the WBGS for processing, and then send the products back to Israel for their completion.

The possibility that trade will develop in the form of sending unfinished products between Israel and its neighbors for processing various stages of production requires the establishment of a trade regime that will be compatible with the new system that is emerging. In this respect, all three members of the Israeli–Jordanian-Palestinian triangle have not produced a very "user-friendly" arrangement. The trade regime between Israel, Jordan, and the Palestinians is based on three bilateral economic agreements that were signed separately between each of the three parties during 1994. The resulting economic regime has been the target of criticism and dissatisfaction from all three parties. The shortcomings associated with the current trade regime were not necessarily the result of misguided intentions, but rather of the inability of the parties to envision many of the political developments that occurred. Thus, the creation of a new economic regime between Israel, Jordan, and the Palestinian Authority seems to be pertinent.

The trade relations that were established between the three parties show that the negotiators were guided by assumptions derived from a realist mindset and thus perceived themselves to be involved in a series of bilateral relations between monolithic political units with clear and uniform national interests. As a result, realist bargaining tactics colored the negotiations over the trade regimes. Even Israel's willingness to concede to Jordanian demands for asymmetrical trade relations reflects the realist motive of aiding a political ally, rather than a liberal attitude toward international trade.

Still, it is possible to identify certain liberal trends. A complex new political and economic reality has sprung up between the parties. Rather than bilateral relations between monolithic units, dynamic relationships have given rise to a multilateral social network. Thus, all the individuals and groups belonging to each of the three parties are loosely associated and interact among themselves and with the other parties on a variety of planes. Because of the interactive nature of the relations between Israel, Jordan, and the Palestinians, when bilateral agreements are concluded the excluded third party tends to feel threatened and may even attempt to hamper the implementation of the two-party accord. Maintaining the Israeli–Jordanian–Palestinian network will thus require policy-makers to become more aware of the ramifications of bilateral interactions for the third party. Future agreements will therefore probably need to be based on trilateral understandings rather than on separate bilateral-collaborations.

Notes

1   The data regarding Israeli victims of Palestinian violence was collected from the Quantitative History of Arab–Israeli Conflict and Cooperation (QHAICC) project at the Jaffee Center for Strategic Studies, Tel Aviv University. Although this data set is incomplete, official Israeli statistics are inaccurate. For example, according to the Prime Minister's Report, Vol. 2. No. 35 (September 11, 1998), in 1978 twelve Israelis were killed by Palestinian terrorists. According to the QHAICC data, there were over 60 Israeli fatal casualties that year, due to Palestinian violence (in March alone, 35 Israelis

were killed after a group from Lebanon landed on the beach south of Haifa and hijacked a bus).

2   These estimates are based on persons seeking employment. If jobless individuals who do not actively seek employment are included, the unutilized labor force reached 25.6 percent in 1998. While this is quite high, it is lower than in Jordan and many other Arab countries.

5

Transnational Economic Cooperation

While trade between Israel, Jordan and the WBGS is expected to be limited, the WBGS and Jordan do have one attribute that is in great demand – cheap labor. However, instead of Jordanians and Palestinians coming to work in Israel, a more economically efficient solution would be to bring the means of production to those regions, thus reducing rent and employment costs.

Distributing the production process among a number of political entities is the essence of the multinational business enterprise. However, establishing multinational business ventures requires a far higher degree of cooperation than exists in normal trade, since all members of the corporation are mutually dependent. Hence, both the level of commitment and the economic risks are considerably higher. For this reason, the interests of the parties involved in maintaining a peaceful and stable environment are greater than when relations are based merely on trade.

Joint Ventures: An Analytic Perspective

Risks and opportunities

Because the risks and complications involved in the operation of a joint venture between companies located in different countries are much higher than in simple trade relations, it is not surprising that trade is a more common form of transnational economic cooperation. However, although trade still reflects the paramount type of international economic transaction, the number of joint ventures between companies in different countries is growing rapidly. This might indicate that the benefits associated with the creation of multinational enterprises outweigh the higher risks and complications that are involved. It might also reflect the general decline of realism as a leading theory of international order, especially since the end of the Cold War.

As in the case of international trade, there are divergent opinions as to who benefits and who loses in multinational partnerships. While the beneficiaries have an interest in maintaining stability, groups that feel deprived by the activities of transnational organizations may harbor conflictive attitudes toward such enterprises. The problem, though, lies in identifying the groups that gain or lose from the multinational approach.

When a company decides to extend its operations across the state's border, a certain investment is directed to the foreign country chosen to host the production process that is being transferred abroad. That country will earn new capital and tax revenues and gain employment opportunities. For this reason, many countries, including Israel, Jordan and the PA, encourage foreign investments by offering tax breaks as well as government grants to the investors (Mulenex, 1999). While the country hosting the venture gains from this arrangement, the question is whether, as is sometimes argued, the investor's country loses. Because certain functions of the organization are transferred abroad, the country of the investor forfeits employment opportunities and capital growth and thus collects fewer taxes.

However, the advocates of investing abroad refute that argument. Although certain functions of the organization are transferred abroad, they say, if the company did not relocate these elements of production to a more suitable environment (where operating costs are cheaper), it would have to shut down or drastically reduce its output. This would produce an even greater loss of jobs, capital, and tax revenues. In practice, this argument holds, transforming the company into a multinational corporation (MNC) will not necessarily result in a loss of employment opportunities or tax revenues. This is because the establishment of the MNC will require a substantial restructuring of the organization, since new units and functions will be needed in order to communicate and to coordinate activities with the foreign subsidiary. Hence, although persons from certain professions may lose their jobs, other persons with different professions are hired instead.

Even if transferring certain elements of production abroad is economically beneficial for the investor's state, from a realist point of view there is a strategic price to be paid. When certain aspects of production are relocated abroad, the host state acquires the strategic advantage of being able to harm the investor's state by halting production. However, this strategic vulnerability can be overcome if a minimal portion of the production process that was transferred abroad remains active in the home country, or if the production process is dispersed among a number of host countries. Thus, if production in one host country is cut off, it can continue in the other countries or even in the investor's country.

Indeed, contrary to the assumption that the host country benefits from the creation of the joint venture, advocates of the centralist dependency theory, or what Dos Santos (1970) calls the "New Dependency," maintain that the host country actually loses from such an arrangement. This is because the new jobs and capital created by the investment in the host country are usually the least profitable components of production, while the more profitable jobs and advanced forms of production remain in the investor's country (Hymer, 1972). Thus, although the host country profits to a certain extent from this arrangement, the investor reaps far greater profits. As the sole client of the subsidiary company in the host country, the investor controls the level of production and types of technologies that are transferred to the host country. By adopting the realist strategy described above, the investor can maintain considerable leverage over the subsidiaries, since there is always the option of reducing production in one of the host countries in favor of another. In this manner the subsidiaries become totally dependent on the investor.

If the products of the MNC are not export oriented but instead are intended for distribution in the local markets of the host country, the creation of a joint venture might not produce any significant growth in the host country's economy. This depends on whether the product of the joint venture competes with products manufactured locally or with imported products. If the product competes with imports, the host country benefits because it receives a portion of the costs of production. However, if the product of the joint venture competes with local manufacture, the host country might lose. This is because, unlike a regular local firm, which is based on local investments, part of the profits from the joint venture will be transferred abroad to the investor's country, rather than being reinvested in the host country.

The problems associated with distribution of profits can be avoided if the MNC is structured to give all partners an equal share and equal control over all parts of the organization. However, such an ideal arrangement is rare and the distribution of profits is usually uneven. This state of affairs is simply a consequence of the evolution of the MNC. All MNCs originate from independent local companies, which at some stage start cooperating. Since the partners to the joint venture are not equal, usually the terms of the association are not such as to ensure equal distribution of the profits either. The question is whether or not all the partners feel that they are receiving a fair distribution of profits.

Thus a second issue to be considered in connection with joint ventures relates to the social relations between the members of the MNC. Certain structural characteristics of the joint venture encourage a greater or lesser degree of cooperation between the relevant parties. Studies have shown that when power is not distributed equally between members of the MNC, there is a tendency to coerce the weaker members when a disagreement emerges within the firm (Lin and Germain, 1998).

The ability to coerce weaker partners depends on the monopolistic status of the investing company. If there are a number of competing industries seeking deals in a foreign country, this will reduce the investor's bargaining power. However, if the foreign investor is a large, dominant firm or a bank, it can impose its will on its subsidiary partners. Such firms can place the weaker partners in a precarious position of having to choose between signing an unfair deal or suffering the retaliation of the foreign firm.

Attempting to protect local industries from takeover by foreign corporate giants can be hazardous. Unless the host country is very attractive, imposing legal restrictions on the creation of joint ventures can be counterproductive. Countries that impose such restrictions will suffer from a lack of foreign investment, since they will be less attractive than others like them that do not impede foreign investors and allow profits to be transferred abroad. Jordan, for example, in an attempt to boost foreign investment, amended its laws in 1995 to allow total ownership by a foreign concern in some sectors (US & Foreign Commercial Service and US Department of State, 1998). Until then, all joint ventures required at least 51 percent Jordanian ownership and the approval of the Jordanian government.

Although there is no substantive empirical evidence demonstrating that firms dominated by coercive decision-making techniques perform less efficiently than those that are more democratic, this type of relationship can have negative political implications, fueling hostile attitudes toward the more powerful country. This may discourage other firms in the host country from entering into new business deals with the investor's country, as well as causing a break-up of existing joint ventures. Thus, it is sometimes advisable for a powerful partner to forgo part of its clout in order to create a more cooperative atmosphere. This is especially desirable in the case of former enemies where activists of the conflict are striving to rekindle any potential source of tension.

Formal associations and the range of cooperation

Hashai (1993) identifies ten possible formal arrangements between the members of the MNC, reflecting various degrees of cooperation:

1 A merger between companies in order to share production resources.
2 A joint-equity venture between a number of companies.
3 Joint research and development programs.
4 An international partnership or consortium.
5 Joint marketing by companies.
6 Acquisition of a local industry by a foreigner.
7 Foreign investment in a company that is developing a particular product.
8 Limited foreign investment (buying a share in a foreign company).
9 Vertical supply alliances, where a local company receives a license to produce a product carrying the trademark of the foreign company.
10 Subcontracting with a foreign company.

The first five types of formal associations require a very high level of cooperation on a personal basis between the partners, especially if the ownership is split equally. As noted above, if members of the corporation fail to cooperate the venture might falter. The cost of failure is highest in the case of a merger and least in the case of a consortium or joint marketing program, as the costs of breaking up such partnerships are usually lower.

If ownership is not divided equally, there is a risk that major shareholders will dominate the company's management in a manner liable to create animosity among the minor partners. The potential for this is especially high in the case of foreign acquisition of local industries, where the foreign owner wields considerable power over the company.

Limited foreign investment for developing certain products is another example of unequal control. In this case, however, ownership remains in the hands of the local producer. The last two types of joint ventures listed above also preserve local ownership. However, in this case, the foreign investor has the power to revoke and break the contract. This is demonstrated in the case of Israeli–Palestinian joint ventures, which have mainly been in the form of subcontracting. When the *Intifada* broke out in 1987, Israeli businesses severed their connections with the WBGS, preferring to subcontract with Israeli Arabs.

Bargaining and Problem-Solving Strategies

Based on the experience of subcontracting arrangements between Israeli and Palestinian firms in the WBGS, joint ventures of a more cooperative type should be preferred between Israel, Jordan and the PA. However, an examination of such arrangements reveals that when the size of the companies and the management culture are vastly different, difficulties can be expected. Hence, Arab–Israeli cooperation will be likely to encounter serious difficulties in comparison to Jordanian–Palestinian joint ventures (Beamish, 1988).

There are, however, also certain advantages associated with cultural diversity between members of the MNC. It enables the corporation to display greater flexibility as a challenge to competing environments. In negotiations with a third party (a potential customer or supplier), a partner with a close cultural affinity with the third party can contribute to their successful completion (Morosini *et al.*, 1998). Thus, for example, an Israeli–Palestinian MNC has an advantage when confronting either Middle Eastern or western suppliers or customers in comparison to a Jordanian–Palestinian firm (which is at a relative disadvantage when dealing with westerners) or an Israeli–European company (which is at a relative disadvantage *vis-à-vis* Arabs).

Taking into account economic risks and political uncertainties, as well as the alternative world order perspectives associated with the creation of joint ventures, David Boas *et al.* (1996), in a study prepared for the Israeli Foreign Ministry, proposed a set of guidelines for establishing Israeli, Jordanian, and Palestinian joint ventures. The study identified eleven strategies aimed at increasing the benefits of economic cooperation, while circumventing effects that are liable to counterbalance joint ventures between the three parties in question.

1 *Investment in export projects.* The advantage of this type of initiative lies in its ability to offset the deficit in goods and services and the high foreign debt which limit the economic independence of all three economies. Export projects can significantly strengthen the economies of Jordan and the PA. Activity that helps reduce the balance of payments deficit is preferable to economic activity that is geared solely to the local market and competes with already existing local production.

2 *Investment in industrial ventures.* Economic development in Jordan and the PA depends largely on the development, scale, and quality of their respective industries. Industrial development, particularly in exports or

goods that can successfully compete with imports, is critical to tackle major economic challenges: the balance of payments deficit, resulting foreign debt, and relatively high unemployment rates.

3 *Investment in labor-intensive projects.* Because of the job scarcity in the manufacturing sector in Jordan and the PA, priority should be given to labor-intensive projects as a means to reduce unemployment.

4 *Investment in needs shared by the economies.* Economic cooperation will be more likely to succeed if greater focus is placed on shared goals, challenges, and needs, even if the expected rewards are not equally distributed. Joint ventures evolving around shared needs are likely to reduce the fears and suspicions of countries in the region concerning Israeli economic patronage. This pattern contrasts with other forms of cooperation in which Israel sells "know-how" and the Jordanians and Palestinians supply the "work," or situations where the entrepreneurs are Israeli and the sources of production are from the PA or Jordan.

5 *Investment in ventures in which the economic gap is relatively small.* The economic gap greatly reduces the range of possibilities for cooperation between the three economies. In this respect the prospects for successful joint ventures in the field of advanced industries – such as hi-tech, chemistry, and plastics – are very poor in the short term. Joint ventures in areas in which Israel has technological superiority will reinforce its image as a colonial economic power and deter neighboring countries from cooperation in such fields. Consequently, the focus should be on economic sectors in which Israel has a narrow advantage, such as tourism, light industry, construction, transport, and agriculture. As stated previously, the disparity in the development of the three economies leaves only a narrow common base of shared economic needs. However, this base is sufficiently wide to provide a ground for a range of joint projects.

6 *Evenly distributed ownership of ventures.* Israel's position as a dominant player, in terms of scale of investment, current management, and distribution of anticipated profits is liable to deter the Jordanians and Palestinians from entering into cooperative ventures. Therefore, it is important to ensure that Jordan and the PA get an "honorable share" of the ownership in such ventures at the expense of Israel's share, even if this affects Israeli financial profits.

7 *Reduced Israeli presence in Jordan and the PA.* An Israeli presence in the form of management teams, or Israeli goods and advertisements, will deter neighboring countries from participating. Taking this into consideration, it is advisable for the Israeli presence to be low-key, or alternatively for the various ventures to be given a low profile.

8 *Minimal publicity.* As demonstrated in the case of the Israeli trade fair in Amman at the beginning of 1997, publicity is one of the key obstacles to Arab–Israeli economic cooperation. This is particularly true of the private sector. Despite political arrangements and the change in attitude toward Israel in recent years, there are still dominant political groups in the Arab world that reject peaceful relations and economic cooperation. Various parties inside and outside Jordan and the PA do not recognize the legitimacy of the peace agreements and have a vested interest in undermining the process. Public exposure strengthens the opposition and often discourages the advocates of cooperation from engaging in activities that public opinion considers controversial.

9 *Short-time implementation.* Political stability and public security are a necessary and sufficient condition for economic cooperation. Because of the gradual character of the process, priority should be given to ventures with short time frames for preparing the infrastructure and for implementation.

10 *Engagement of foreign, non-Arab parties.* The inclusion of a non-Arab country as a third or fourth party in joint ventures may add to the success of economic initiatives between Israel, Jordan and the PA. True, the inclusion of foreign firms may reduce the share of each country or entrepreneur. Still, the inclusion of a non-Arab party is likely to contribute to strengthening patterns of economic cooperation and joint ventures, and hence political stability, for at least two major reasons. First, it will diminish the perception of Israeli patronage, thus reducing opposition within the Arab world to economic cooperation. At the same time, it will increase the inflow of capital from the West and the concomitant interest in regional stability.

11 *Projects that do not require participation of another Arab state.* The number of potential Arab partners available to participate in cooperative regional ventures is in inverse proportion to the prospects for their implementation; that is, the more partners, the less the chance for success. Thus, the inclusion of another Arab party would delay implementation.

The Proliferation of Israeli–Jordanian Joint Ventures
The textile industry

One of the first joint ventures to be established between Israel and Jordan was the Century Wear hosiery factory located in the Al-Hassan free-trade zone in Irbid (Lautman, May 9, 1998). This project was the product of a meeting between Omar Salah, from the Jordanian Century Investment Corporation, and the executive director of Delta–Galil, Dov Lautman, which took place shortly before the Israeli–Jordanian peace treaty was signed in 1994. Although the Jordanian partner initiated the deal, Delta had already started transferring elements of its production abroad a few years earlier. Hence, Lautman was receptive to the idea of establishing another plant abroad.

The Century Wear factory exemplifies the notion of breaking up production into segments and processing each part in different countries. Israel supplies the Jordanian plant with "kits" that are assembled in Jordan and then sent back to Israel, where the product is finished. The components of the kit, too, are not produced entirely in Israel, but imported by Delta's subsidiaries in Turkey and Egypt.

Unlike Delta, most Israeli textile companies were at the time based solely in Israel. Because textile production is a very popular export industry in less-developed countries where labor is cheap, the Israeli government subsidized the local companies in order to keep them competitive. However, as Israeli wages continued to rise, the subsidies bloated until finally the government could no longer sustain them. The result was that Israeli textile manufacturers had no choice but to start transferring certain elements of the production process abroad. Another alternative was to transfer production to the WBGS, but memories of the *Intifada* made investment in the WBGS seem too risky.

While Lautman was highly receptive to the idea of a joint venture with Salah, he was unwilling to start negotiating until the peace treaty was signed. Immediately afterward a joint-equity venture was created and the Jordanian textile plant was opened in March 1996. As suggested above, the ownership is equally divided between Delta and Century, although it is under Jordanian management.

One of the reasons that Salah sought Delta as a partner was that Delta is a multinational concern associated with Sarah Lee in the United States. Salah was unwilling to form a joint venture with a purely Israeli company. Thus, the factory in Irbid was not financed directly by Delta, but by a Dutch subsidiary of Delta in the Netherlands Antilles. Salah has adhered to this principle in all other business contracts with Israeli firms. Although it is possible to find examples of joint Israeli–Jordanian ventures that do not include a third partner from abroad, most Israeli firms acquiesce in this Jordanian demand, since in many cases the foreign subsidiaries also serve as tax shelters (Peri, 1998; Catrivas, 1999).

The location that was chosen for the plant, as noted, was the Al-Hassan free-trade zone of Irbid. During the period of the military clashes between

Israel, Jordan, and the PLO after the 1967 war, the city of Irbid found itself on the front line. Because of its close proximity to the Israeli border and its large Palestinian population, the city suffered from Israeli attacks. But in the era of peaceful relations, Irbid's location proved highly beneficial. Because part of the production is also carried out in the city of Carmiel in Galilee, material had to be transported back and forth between Israel and Jordan. Thus Irbid was the ideal location, as it is less than a two-hour drive from Carmiel. Lautman has claimed that economically the Irbid plant was a very good deal, although he was partially motivated by his personal passion to promote the peace process. Besides the special tax breaks offered to industrial ventures located within the free-trade zone of Irbid, the high rate of unemployment in Jordan increased the prospects of finding better-educated laborers at lower wages than normally paid in the WBGS. In addition, because there are many empty buildings in Irbid, finding a low-rent location was very easy. In short, the option of transferring the textile industry to Irbid was very tempting.

Egypt also has free-trade zones that offer alluring tax breaks. However, Lautman, who also opened a number of factories in Egypt, has found the Jordanian bureaucracy to be less labyrinthine and more cooperative than its Egyptian counterpart. Besides being more efficient, Jordan's bureaucracy is also less antagonistic toward Israel than Egypt's. Jordan's cooperation may be motivated by the fact that its economy is much smaller than that of Egypt, making it more difficult to attract foreign investors. Thus the Jordanians facilitate deals, even if the foreigner in question happens to be Israeli.

There was, however, one drawback with the location of the Century Wear factory. Irbid has a large community that is associated with the Muslim Brotherhood, which opposes the Israeli–Jordanian peace treaty. To make matters worse, unlike most Israeli–Jordanian joint ventures, this particular venture received extensive public coverage. It didn't take long before the Jordanian opposition started attacking this initiative. Jordanian tabloids published rumors about the disgraceful treatment allegedly suffered by Jordanian employees, claiming that workers were beaten on the job and sent to work as prostitutes at night. According to the *New York Times* correspondent in Jordan, employees of the plant typically denied the Israeli partnership, claiming that the foreign partner was a US-based company (*Globes*, December 30, 1996).

Opposition to the Century Wear factory reached its climax when the Muslim leader in Irbid discovered that his own niece was working in the factory. In response to his demands that she quit her job, the plant's manager invited her family to visit the factory and inspect the working conditions. After the visit the niece received permission to return to her job. Altogether, despite the opposition, Lautman says that the establishment of the Delta–Century joint venture has led Jordanians to take a more conciliatory attitude toward Israel. The plant's workers took a growing interest in Israel and many of them eventually visited Israel.

Following the success of the Irbid enterprise, Delta and Century established three additional factories. Other Israeli companies have also made the move to Jordan. Irbid remains the most popular location, although the industrial free zone in Zarka also has a large number of Israeli–Jordanian enterprises.

It is mostly light industries that have transferred to Jordan from Israel. The leading joint-venture industry is textile production, which was also the fastest growing industry in Jordan during the 1990s. By 1998, seventeen Israeli textile firms had established Jordanian-based plants. According to Gidi Laks, deputy general manager of the Kitan textile company, all major Israeli textile companies will eventually transfer their sewing to Jordan (*Globes*, September 17, 1997).

Unlike the Delta–Century plant, most Israeli–Jordanian joint ventures are kept secret. The Jordanian partners are afraid of public exposure; even Delta's partner was initially unwilling to reveal his identity (Peri, January 16, 1998). Furthermore, as noted above, the reason he chose Delta was that it was not a purely Israeli company, but a multinational. Most of the other Israeli–Jordanian ventures have also abided by the rule of having a third country as a partner.

The fact that most Israeli–Jordanian companies are interested in exploiting the cheap Jordanian labor has caused resentment in Jordan. A frequently voiced complaint is that the Jordanians have replaced Palestinian labor. Furthermore, the Israeli partners have been accused in the Jordanian press of not including Jordan on their product labels (*The Star,* December 4, 1997).

Lautman claims that despite Jordanian feelings of indignation, the high rate of unemployment in Jordan serves as a major motivating force. Regardless of what they may think about their Israeli employers, he insists that the Jordanians, like the Palestinians in the WBGS who negotiated business transactions with Israel and sought employment in Israel, will come to work in Israeli industries too.

While finding Jordanian employees may be relatively easy, marketing to the Jordanian public is a different matter. The Mossad's botched attempt in 1997 to assassinate the Hamas leader Khalid Mash'al in Amman had an extremely negative effect, resulting in the boycott of Israeli products (*Globes*, October 17, 1997). As a result of rumors that Israel had invested

105

in Assyra Dairy, its sales plummeted, and ultimately the company had to publish large ads denying any business contacts with Israel. In another case, the Jordanian Professional Association boycotted the *Al Raj* daily newspaper nearly a month after it published an advertisement which was perceived to imply advocacy of "normalization' with Israel (*The Star,* August 6, 1998). Still, despite the negative public attitudes expressed toward Israel, about half of the Israeli–Jordanian joint ventures market their products in Jordan and at least two companies export to Arab states.

Lautman attributes his successful deals with Jordan and Egypt to his ability to comply with the culture and norms of his Arab counterparts. He argues that in this respect Israelis and Palestinians have a better chance than Europeans, who are less adaptive to the Arab business culture. Delta's success may also be a consequence of the relatively high salaries paid the workers. In comparison to the average wages in Jordan, this is one of the more attractive places of work. It is also possible that the Israeli–Jordanian business connections are based on only a small number of Jordanian businessmen who are willing to cooperate with Israelis. Between 1994 and 1998 fewer than 30 Israeli-Jordanian joint ventures were created. Over a third of them involved the Salah family, the joint owner of Century Wear (*Globes,* May 25, 1997). As a result of these deals, Century has become the largest corporation and largest employer in Jordan (*Globes,* January 1, 1998).

Besides resentment from the Jordanian opposition, the Delta–Century factory in Jordan also drew criticism within Israel. The major argument was that Jordanians were taking jobs away from Israelis. Lautman defiantly denies this. He insists that because Israeli labor-intensive production cannot compete with the cheaper labor-intensive industries in less developed countries, the establishment of factories abroad has actually saved the Israeli textile industry. He points out that only those elements of production that require intensive labor were moved and that many other aspects of the production process remain in Israel. Lautman attributes Delta's competitive advantage to its ability to divide the different phases of production among a number of different countries. Furthermore, contrary to the prediction of the Stolper–Samuelson theorem, Lautman maintains that transferring the labor-intensive components of production to Jordan did not come at the expense of Israeli laborers. No one was laid off, he said: the Israeli laborers were reassigned to different and even better positions. This has not, however, been the fate of laborers in other Israeli textile firms, who simply lost their jobs. Lautman claims that unemployment in the Israeli textile sector was due to mismanagement and lack of foresight. Other textile firms had to lay off many of their employees because they started transferring their labor-intensive production process abroad only after they suffered heavy losses when the government cut subsidies. Lautman insists that if the other firms had restructured themselves earlier, before the subsidies were withdrawn, the massive layoffs characterizing the textile industry could have been avoided.

Assuming that the creation of Israeli–Jordanian joint ventures will prove profitable, Israeli textile firms will start rehiring. However, most of the new recruits will be required for administrative or more professional duties. Thus, the laborers living in Israel's peripheries, where the labor-intensive plants were located, are unlikely to be among the new workforce hired by the textile industries.

Not all Israeli–Jordanian joint ventures succeeded like the Delta–Century enterprise. In fact, the Jordanians showed a high degree of suspicion toward Israel even before the Likud party came to power in May 1996. First, until the Israeli–Jordanian trade and transport agreements were signed, the Jordanian bureaucracy was reluctant to cooperate with Israel. Cooperation was further delayed in the wake of Israel's 1996 "Operation Grapes of Wrath" in south Lebanon. Finally, the majority of Jordanian businessmen are Palestinians, who are ultra-sensitive toward Israel's actions in the WBGS (*Globes*, May 15, 1996).

The bromine production plan

An example of a less successful story, which cannot be attributed to the attitudes of Jordanian businessmen but rather to the smugness of the Israeli negotiators, is the attempt to establish an Israeli–Jordanian bromine plant on the eastern shore of the Dead Sea. The idea for the plant was conceived during negotiations between Dead Sea Bromine (DSB) and the Arab Potash Corporation (APC). Like Delta–Century, this was one of the first Israeli–Jordanian attempts to form a joint venture, and here too the proposed Jordanian plant was to be export oriented. The economic motivation behind this initiative was the growing demand for bromide in world markets and the fact that both countries border on the Dead Sea, which is a major reservoir for bromine products. As in the Delta–Century arrangement, the bromine plant was to have equal Israeli–Jordanian ownership and sole Jordanian management (*Globes*, October 10, 1996). And, like other Israeli industries that have invested in Jordan, DSB hoped to take advantage of the cheaper Jordanian labor and the facility's close proximity to Israel. At the same time, this was to be a far larger deal than Delta–Century or indeed any other Israeli–Jordanian joint venture. Another difference was that the DSB–APC project involved an industry characterized by a large technological gap between Israel and Jordan, thus requiring the Jordanians to undergo intensive training and supervision.

While the advantages of establishing a bromine plant in Jordan were obvious, negotiating the terms of the contract encountered considerable difficulties. The three major sources of contention were:

1   Unwillingness by the Jordanians to pay a high price for Israeli know-how.
2   Difficulties in insuring foreign trade risks because of the plant's location on the Jordanian side of the Dead Sea.
3   The refusal of the Government Investment Center to accord DSB approved enterprise status (*Globes*, March 12, 1997).

From the start, this joint venture took the form of a bargaining match between two unequal partners. The Israelis assumed that as the world's leading producer of bromine products, with a wealth of experience in extracting the minerals from the Dead Sea, the Jordanians should be grateful that Israel was willing to invest in their plant. In this respect the Israeli negotiators completely misperceived the situation. Focused on the risks and costs of creating a plant in Jordan, they failed to appreciate the price of not establishing a plant in Jordan. A bromine plant in Jordan that was independent of DSB could serve as serious competitor, since Jordan shared a unique asset with Israel – access to the Dead Sea. Thus an independent Jordanian enterprise would break DSB's virtual monopoly over this resource.

Overconfidence in the attractiveness of DSB in comparison to other potential competitors proved costly. As the negotiations dragged on, the Israelis began to receive negative signals from the board of directors of APC. Finally, in March 1998, after two and a half years of talks, the Jordanians asked to postpone the signing of the final agreement, which was scheduled for April 1998 (*Globes*, March 12, 1998). The Israelis soon discovered that parallel to the Israeli–Jordanian channel, the Jordanians had been secretly negotiating with Albemarle Holdings, a major US competitor of DSB (*Globes*, March 12, 1998).

DSB blamed the failure of the negotiations on the political tensions that emerged after the election of the Netanyahu government. At least one other Israeli entrepreneur has also complained that an attempt to establish a joint venture in Jordan failed for the same reason (Miller and Shlomot, 1997). Unlike other Jordanian companies that cooperated with Israeli firms, APC is government owned. Furthermore, although the members of the board of directors are Jordanians, more than 40 percent of the shareholders are from other Arab countries.

Still, the US–Jordanian deal seemed to be motivated by more than political considerations. First, DSB's American competitor was very keen to break its Dead Sea monopoly. It was therefore more receptive to the Jordanian demands and offered better terms. An important improvement from the Jordanian standpoint was the willingness of Albemarle Holdings to allow the Jordanians to raise the volume of production above the level that had been agreed upon in the Israeli–Jordanian memorandum. The Israelis were unwilling to allow production by the Jordanian plant to exceed Israeli production (*Globes*, May 24, 1998). Thus, instead of establishing a plant at an $80 million investment, which was the most DSB was willing to offer (*Globes*, October 10, 1996), the Jordanians obtained a $120 million investment together with Albemarle. In addition, the Jordanians might have been subject to pressure from the US administration, which was concerned by dwindling supplies of bromine products in America (*Globes*, May 24, 1998).

The representatives of DSB should have been aware that the establishment of an industry characterized by an Israeli technological advantage might heighten Jordanian animosity toward them. The more critical issue was probably that unlike Lautman, who treated his partners with respect and demonstrated a cooperative approach, the DSB people displayed a patronizing attitude toward their Jordanian interlocutors. Their arrogant behavior might well have induced the Jordanians to cut a deal with a perhaps less attractive company, but one that at least treated them more respectfully (Barr, 1999).

The computer software industry

An unexpected source of economic cooperation has been in the field of computer programming (by 1998 there were three Israeli–Jordanian software companies). Suffering from a shortage of Israeli programmers, Israeli software development companies turned to Jordan. As in other professions in Jordan, the average wages of programmers are lower than in Israel. The major problem in this sphere is that much Israeli software is security oriented. Thus, Israelis have been reluctant to cooperate with Arab companies. Another problem associated with the employment of Jordanian professionals in general and programmers in particular, is that they are often unemployed for lengthy periods. As a result, employers must invest in retraining or updating professionals, even if they are graduates of highly qualified institutions (Barr, 1999). Furthermore, Israeli software companies are disinclined to engage in equity joint ventures. Instead, they seek to maintain as much control and knowledge as possible and subcontract certain parts of production to foreign companies. This was the approach adopted by Malam, which was the first Israeli software company to engage in a joint venture with Jordan, in 1997 (TechWeb News, December 26, 1997).

The tendency of companies to reassure industrial secrets and control over knowledge is not limited to Israel or to the computer software industry. However, foreign countries are especially wary about revealing patents to Jordanian companies. The problem is that in comparison to most countries, Jordanian law does not adequately protect intellectual rights. In April 1998, the US Trade Representative placed Jordan on its "301 Watch List" for failure to provide effective protection of intellectual property rights (US & Foreign Commercial Service and US Department of State, 1998). Although the Jordanians have declared their intentions to rectify the situation, there is strong local opposition because major pharmaceutical firms in Jordan produce unlicensed patented drugs. As long as Jordan does not resolve the issue of intellectual property rights, hi-tech cooperation between Jordan and other countries will remain limited, since companies providing knowledge to Jordan lack any legal means to prevent its free distribution.[1]

The Establishment of the Qualifying Industrial Zone (QIZ)

While the low rent and cheap labor in Jordan provides Israeli–Jordanian companies with a competitive advantage, this arrangement also has certain drawbacks. Israel is a member of many FTAs. Jordan, however, is not a member of most of the FTAs that include Israel, so that any product that is partially manufactured in Jordan might not be eligible for customs exemption (depending on the terms of the FTA). Consequently, both Israel and Jordan sought to have their jointly manufactured products qualify for customs exemption within FTAs to which Israel belongs. However, the other members of the FTAs have usually opposed this, as the Israeli–Jordanian MNCs have a competitive advantage (cheap Jordanian labor, petrol, and rent) unavailable to the other members of the FTAs. Furthermore, such an arrangement would enable the Jordanians to export to members of an FTA without paying duties, while items manufactured by the other members of the FTA would be subject to Jordanian customs. In fact, the Israelis too had their own qualms about this arrangement: it would allow Jordanian entrepreneurs to establish an address in Israel in order to qualify as a joint Israeli–Jordanian company and then take advantage of the FTA by exporting as an Israeli-based company, though most of the income would not reach Israel.

Citing the above reservations, in June 1997 the European Union turned down a joint request by Israel and Jordan to recognize the rules of origin aggregation between the two countries. However, the EU left open the option of granting such recognition in the future. According to EU officials (quoted in *Jerusalem Post,* May 15, 1998), the EU would be willing to reconsider the request after Israel and the Palestinians reached a settlement.

The United States, however, was more accommodating, and in November 1996 the US Congress agreed to recognize the rules of origin aggregation for products manufactured within a restricted area along the Israeli–Jordanian border within the Jordan Valley, to be known as the "Qualifying Industrial Zone" (QIZ). However, because no joint Israeli–Jordanian industrialization of the designated area existed, a number of Israelis and Jordanians who had already established joint ventures in the Al-Hassan industrial zone proposed that the Congress make an exception and also declare that area a QIZ. Following initial hesitation – because the area was exclusively within Jordan and was not a free-trade zone – the Congress agreed in July 1997 to recognize the rules of origin aggregation for products manufactured in the Al-Hassan industrial zone. In November 1997, Israel, Jordan, and the United States jointly signed the agreement at Doha, Qatar, during the Fourth Economic Conference for the Middle East and North African States (*ArabicNews.Com,* October 2, 1998).

Another eight months were needed to finalize the terms of the QIZ. The original Israeli proposal was that Israel and Jordan must bear at least 35 percent of the production costs and that each party must separately contribute at least 11.7 percent of the direct production costs (not including services), or at least 20 percent of the total costs (including all auxiliary expenses). At the request of Jordan and the United States, the Palestinian Authority was also included in the QIZ (Barr, 1999). A committee co-chaired by Israel and Jordan with a US observer was established to grant authorization for products qualifying under the QIZ arrangement (Jordan Industrial Estates Co., 1998).

According to Jordan's Prince Hassan, the special advantage that would accrue to the Jordanians under the agreement outweighed their fear of Israeli economic domination (*Globes*, January 22, 1996). This unique route into the US market has attracted other foreign companies in addition to Israeli and Jordanian firms, as countries outside the QIZ are also granted tariff-free access to the US market as long as they do not contribute more than 65 percent of the costs of production.

Since the establishment of the QIZ some changes have been negotiated.

Already before the QIZ was established, the Israeli and Jordanian Industry and Trade ministers had asked the United States to extend the size of the QIZ beyond the original size of the Irbid free-trade zone (*Jerusalem Post,* June 30, 1997). In March 1998, the United States acceded to this request, as the free-trade zone in Irbid had reached full capacity (*Jordan Times,* May 31, 1998). However, a Jordanian request to include other regions in the QIZ was rejected (Barr, 1999), so that only the Irbid free-trade zone was expanded.

In June 1998, the Jordanians proposed a reduction in the minimal amount of production required in Israel. The Israeli Manufacturers Association strongly rejected this, citing the cheap labor available to Jordanian firms, which would enable them to increase their exports to the United States at the expense of the Israeli producers (*Globes,* July 30, 1998). However, the Israeli government, which was under considerable pressure from the Jordanians since the failed attempt to assassinate the Khalid Mash'al in Jordan, agreed to make concessions. Under the new terms, which were granted for one year only, the minimum required costs of direct Israeli production were lowered to 7 percent for Israeli hi-tech products and 8 percent for all other types of products (Barr, 1999).

The Jordanian opposition has criticized the QIZ, claiming the United States backed it in order to promote Israeli capital investments in Jordan. Another source of resentment is that because the QIZ encourages Jordanians to export to the United States rather than to Asia, Africa, and the Pacific, the port of Haifa has gained at the expense of Aqaba. It is in fact cheaper to ship goods to the United States via Haifa, while Aqaba is preferable for eastbound and southbound routes (*The Star,* June 18, 1998).

Although the QIZ offers a strong incentive to initiate Israeli–Jordanian joint ventures, it has generated only minimal cooperation between the two countries, since there is no requirement to form joint-equity ventures (*The Star,* May 9, 1998). For example, the owner of a Jordanian company that manufactures suitcases asked the Israeli Ministry of Industry and Trade for help in finding Israeli subcontractors to produce the minimal 8 percent of Israeli production costs. The ministry found two manufacturers that provided the minimal production amount, one making the handles for the suitcases and the other producing the cartons for packaging the finished product. Thus, while the Jordanian entrepreneur was required to purchase 8 percent of the components of the suitcases in Israel, whereas the same items could be had more cheaply in Jordan, he increased his sales by gaining duty-free access to the US market (Barr, 1999).

As the example above demonstrates, the QIZ creates an incentive for

Jordanian entrepreneurs to subcontract from Israel. However, the commitment is low. If in the future the Jordanians establish an FTA with the United States, or find alternative markets, many of these joint enterprises will break up and Jordanian manufacturers will likely seek cheaper suppliers. Such joint ventures are also vulnerable to political pressure. Although terminating the contract with the Israeli firms may have the effect of raising the prices of Jordanian products in the United States, few Jordanian companies are exclusively US-oriented, so this arrangement is ultimately expendable. As a result, Israeli subcontractors might be used only for those products earmarked for the US market.

Israeli–Palestinian Joint Ventures

There are supposedly three advantages associated with the creation of a joint venture between Israel and the Palestinian Authority (PA). The first is the close geographical proximity. Most potential sites for Palestinian factories are less than an hour's drive from Israeli main cities and seaports. Thus, transportation costs are much cheaper than with Jordan. Second, under the Paris Agreement there are no tariffs on trade between the PA and Israel. The third advantage is that the PA has secured preferred trade arrangements (duty-free) with the United States and with the EU, so there is no need to establish a QIZ if the Israeli contribution to direct costs of production is less than 35 percent. Despite these advantages, Israeli entrepreneurs have been very reluctant to invest in the WBGS. Even Lautman (1998), who has successfully conducted business ventures with Jordan and Egypt, has publicly announced his unwillingness to embark on a similar project in the WBGS.

The Israeli hesitance to establish joint ventures with the Palestinians is due to a number of political and economic factors. First and foremost is the unstable political situation in the WBGS. A minimal requirement would be the ability to export merchandise, even if there is a border closure. Currently no such guarantees exist. Although Israel has established an insurance fund for joint ventures with the PA, there is no coverage for an Israeli-imposed closure, only for a closure initiated by the PA.

Another Israeli concern is the rampant corruption within the PA and its poor economic and financial reputation. Since Israeli law is no longer applicable in the PA, Israelis fear that their investments will be unprotected by the PA. This is a problem from which many developing countries suffer, and the PA's public record in this respect has not been positive (*The Jerusalem Post*, December 21, 1998). The instability of the situation in the

WBGS is such that even Palestinian foreign entrepreneurs are disinclined to invest there.

Israeli reluctance to engage in joint ventures within the PA is also motivated by the feeling of personal insecurity of Jews who visit the PA. Thus, for example, Hanan Achsaf, president of Motorola Israel, has explained that this is why his company has preferred working with the Jordanians rather than the Palestinians (*Globes*, May 25, 1997).

In addition to the political risks, there are also purely economic concerns. First, Palestinian labor is more expensive than Egyptian or Jordanian labor. Second, unlike Egypt or Jordan, the PA requires that all joint ventures have a 51 percent Palestinian ownership (FICC, 1999). The Palestinians have also opposed Israeli attempts to persuade the EU to recognize the rules of origin aggregation allowing duty-free exports for joint ventures between Israeli and Palestinian companies. This is very problematic, since the minimal European requirements for obtaining tax-free access to their markets are much stricter than US requirements. Under the current system, at least 45 percent of the costs of production must originate from either Israel or the PA, rather than a combined minimum of 45 percent costs of production, as in the case of the Israeli–Jordanian QIZ (Barr, 1999). Thus, even without the problem of closures, there are clear economic incentives to prefer Jordan over the PA.

Although Palestinian restrictions on cooperation with Israel have deterred many Israeli investors, the Palestinians have been unwilling to change their policies. Possibly this is because these policies support the interests of Palestinian monopolists. Conceivably, though, this is also related to the PA's economic war against Israel, since Israeli entrepreneurs also lose from these policies.

Due to the difficulties described above the trend that began during the *Intifada*, when Israeli firms stopped subcontracting in the WBGS, has continued in the post-*Intifada* years. According to Mansour (1997), by 1997 only one major Israeli textile firm was still subcontracting with factories based in the WBGS. According to Nasr (1997), most of the Israeli–Palestinian joint ventures that have survived are small and are owned by Israeli Palestinians. Because these businesses are oriented toward the Israeli market and are not integrated within a multinational production line, it is easier for them to cope with possible closures.

Palestinian companies have made attempts to establish joint ventures with foreign companies rather than with their Israeli counterparts. This has resulted in a loss of markets in the WBGS for Israeli companies. For example, Israel Coca-Cola lost its access to the Palestinian market when the Palestinian company that manufactures and markets soft drinks in the territories, entered into a partnership with the Coca-Cola soft-drink company in the United States (*Globes*, August 13, 1996). The Palestinians are thus able to eliminate imports from Israel by manufacturing products locally themselves. However, most foreign investors, including Palestinians, have shown very little interest in investing in the PA. Thus Palestinians have usually no choice but to settle for Israeli investors or partners. Including an Israeli partner with a good reputation can greatly enhance the attractiveness of the investment.

One attempt to form a joint venture with a foreign company produced an Israeli–Palestinian R&D partnership between Hi-Tek Engineering in Ramallah and Siemens Data Communications (SDC) in the Galilee city of Carmiel. The initiator of the joint venture was Dr. Heinrich V. Pierer, the president and CEO of Siemens in Germany. In response to the peace process launched by the Oslo initiative, Siemens opened an office in Israel in 1993, anticipating that Israel would serve as a headquarters for the Middle Eastern region. By 1999, Siemens had invested in six Israeli companies and twenty start-ups, and had bought the Ornet Software Company (renamed SDC) in Carmiel. In addition, Siemens contracted a number of projects in the WBGS and in Jordan.

Soon after Siemens entered the Israeli and Palestinian markets, Tariq Maayah, the owner of Hi-Tech Engineering, approached the company in hope of becoming its representative in the PA. Maayah was one of the Palestinians who returned to the West Bank in the aftermath of the 1993 DoP. He served as an adviser to the Palestinian negotiating team, in addition to conducting private business in the field of computer communications. Maayah's offer to represent Siemens was rejected as the company preferred to use its Amman office to handle business with the PA. But based on the experience of a previous joint venture between SDC and a group of Jordanian computer programmers, Siemens proposed a joint venture between SDC and Maayah.

According to the manager of SDC, Eden Bental, the joint venture became feasible when Siemens' president in Germany decided that it was in the company's interest to promote the peace between Israel and the Palestinians. The project was also facilitated by the fact that the product is export oriented and unrelated to the Israeli defense industry. Thus the Israelis did not face the conflict of interest that frequently characterizes its software industry.

Despite the good intentions, the ultimate success of the joint venture between SDC and Hi-Tek Engineering remains in doubt. Although there is a strong incentive to seek foreign programmers, due to the scarcity of software engineers in Israel, Bental reveals that recruiting and training

115

Palestinian programmers has proven to be difficult. The first problem confronting an Israeli employer is that, while the qualifications of Israeli programmers who graduate from Israeli universities are well known, Palestinians study in foreign institutions with which Israeli employers are less familiar. Second, because of the closures, it took eighteen months to complete the training of the Palestinian programmers. In addition, Bental found some difficulties with the social norms of the Palestinians. Unlike the Israelis who express themselves freely, the Palestinian programmers were very reserved, carefully weighing every remark or criticism. It took about half a year until they gained enough confidence to speak freely without worrying about the reaction of their superiors. Bental also notes another important trait that is required in order to promote a project in Israel: an aggressive character, which is more common among Israelis. Because the project depends on other suppliers, it cannot progress without continually nagging and pressuring them.

Taking into account the problems described by Bental, the management of Siemens in Israel is still unwilling to grant Hi-Tek Ramallah the opportunity to run its own projects independently. Instead, the Israeli managers prefer to have the Palestinian programmers travel to Israel and work under Israeli supervision. Thus, to a certain extent this joint venture suffers from the same problems that emerged during the attempts to create the Israeli–Jordanian bromine plant. Rather than each side investing equally and sharing profits equally, as in the case of the textile industry, in the software industry, where there is an obvious Israeli advantage, it is impossible for the Palestinians to serve as equal partners. Under these circumstances, bargaining rather than problem-solving becomes the main mode of interaction.

While acknowledging the problems confronting the Ramallah project, Hermann J. Koelle, the managing director of Siemens–Israel, emphasizes that this arrangement was not motivated by philanthropic intentions. Assuming that the peace process will gradually progress, establishing Arab–Israeli joint ventures will serve Siemens' long-term interests in the Middle East (*The Jerusalem Post*, June 13, 1999). In this manner Siemens receives publicity and legitimization in the Arab world.

Israeli–Palestinian joint ventures in the software industry that have been more successful (at least in the short term) have been based on unpublicized and surreptitious associations. According to Barr (1999), there is at least one case in which an Israeli software company is developing a communications project together with a Palestinian software company. Many Israeli firms in fact have experience in forming clandestine arrangements with foreign companies. During the period of the Arab boycott, many countries that shunned diplomatic relations with Israel signed deals via "front companies" located in the United States and Europe.

Jordanian–Palestinian Joint Ventures?

Publicly, Jordanian and PA government officials speak about their common interest in encouraging economic cooperation between them. However, Jordanian–Palestinian economic cooperation is quite limited. Because investment in the WBGS is considered so risky, it is difficult to find Jordanian businesspersons willing to form joint ventures with Palestinian businesses. Thus, most Jordanian–Palestinian joint ventures are based on familial connections, where Palestinians living in Jordan provide financial assistance to their family's businesses in the WBGS. Although these types of joint ventures are rare, the Jordanian authorities have expressed their concern that these business partnerships have resulted in the flow of capital investments from Jordan to the PA (Khalidi, 1994).

Political Conflict and Joint Ventures

Unlike trade, the establishment of joint ventures is inversely related to the level of conflict between Arabs and Israelis. Thus, corresponding to the faltering formal relations between Israel and the PA, Israeli–Palestinian joint ventures have been limited mainly to small subcontractors. On the other hand, in the case of Israeli–Jordanian relations, which are at least officially more cooperative, joint-equity ventures with equal ownership rights began to be formed even before the creation of the QIZ. Despite the political friction and the animosity of the Jordanian public, the sense of stability in the Israeli–Jordanian relationship has encouraged many Israeli and Jordanian businesses to cooperate.

While the level of political conflict and cooperation serves as a good predictor of Arab–Israeli joint ventures, this is not the case with Jordanian–Palestinian joint ventures. There is very little cross-national cooperation between the PA and Jordan, even though Palestinians own most Jordanian businesses. The blame for the lack of economic cooperation between Jordan and the PA is commonly attributed to Israel, which increased transportation costs by its stringent security measures, and to the Paris Protocol, which imposed high Israeli tariffs on Jordanian imports.

However, while increased costs are a factor, the major reason for the minimal Jordanian–Palestinian cooperation appears to be, again, the high risk associated with investing in the PA.

An analysis of the probability of a joint venture being formed in terms of political risks resolves the seemingly contradictory observations within the Israeli–Jordanian–Palestinian triangle. Because the risks of trade are relatively low, there is a willingness to trade with anyone who is interested. Conflict might influence trade trends, but it is not a major variable in the decision to conduct business. In the case of joint ventures, where risks are much higher, conflict becomes a more critical factor. Yet, risks are not simply a function of conflict between the nations to which the entrepreneurs belong. Conflict in general raises risks, whether international or domestic. Thus, the inability of Israel and the Palestinians to resolve their differences has also harmed Israel. The PA, however, is less attractive than Israel because the Palestinians are more vulnerable to Israeli closures and because the PA is viewed as less stable politically.

A second factor that appears to impede the formation of joint ventures between Israel, Jordan and the PA, is the tendency toward bargaining. To a great extent problem-solving modes of interaction have emerged when Israeli and Arab entrepreneurs have attempted to create low-technology joint ventures, where none of the partners had an advantage over the others. However, when the Israeli partner had an obvious advantage in comparison to the Arab partner, problem-solving modes of negotiation were usually abandoned.

Note

1   Israel also has a bad reputation in the area of protecting intellectual property rights, especially in the case of the software and music industries. As a result Israel has also been placed on the 301 Watch List. However, unlike Jordan, the Israeli government and legal system does not sanction this behavior and is willing to prosecute without hesitation any illegal replication of patented or copyrighted products.

6

Regional Infrastructure Development

As observed in the previous chapters, government policies have a considerable impact on the volume of trade and the creation of joint ventures. Governments can easily create obstacles, such as demanding various permits or imposing taxes, and thus reduce the profitability of economic cooperation. On the other hand, when governments want to encourage cooperation, taxes can be reduced and bureaucratic measures can be simplified. Still, these policies may not be sufficient. In order to increase the profitability of economic cooperation, a suitable infrastructure is required. Its absence can raise the costs of production, transportation, and marketing (Biehl, 1991).

When relations between neighboring states are peaceful, an infrastructure supporting the movement of commodities and persons usually allows routine and unimpeded cross-border transportation. Often the citizens of the neighboring country can enter the other simply by showing any type of identification card, such as a driver's license. However, an undeveloped infrastructure system that fails to support adequate transportation and communication is to be expected between two states that are in a state of war. As the conflict drags on, transportation links and communication lines that existed before the war are not maintained. Instead, each party, to reduce the possibility of an attack or of intelligence gathering, attempts to seal its borders and prevent transportation and communication between the two states. Thus, for example, following the 1994 Israeli–Jordanian peace agreement, one of the first infrastructure projects between the two countries was rebuilding the King Hussein Bridge located in the Jordan Valley south of the Sea of Galilee. The Israelis destroyed the bridge on the eve of the 1948 war in order to block the advance of the Arab Legion into Israel. Nowadays, as in the pre-1948 period, this bridge serves as the main transportation link between Israel and Jordan. Another way to reduce costs is to share services for regions near the border, such as monitoring pollution, sharing ports and harbors, using common electricity and water systems, etc. By the same token, sharing sources of finance, such as grants, loans, guarantees, and insurance will reduce the costs and risks of joint economic ventures.

While the suggestions above are economically sensible, sharing infra- structures is anti-realist in its nature. According to the realist approach, the idea of two or more states joining forces and sharing with one another a portion of their sovereign responsibilities, rather than each state indepen- dently striving to increase its own national capacities, has an adverse effect on national security. Thus, a critical and essential prerequisite for any such joint venture is a firm willingness of the states involved to abandon the realist mode of thinking.

Once the realist security fears are overcome, the countries that want to cooperate must bridge social discrepancies and economic differences. Since different political rules and bureaucratic norms exist in Israel, Jordan and the PA, the success of a joint venture requires a higher degree of mutual adaptation than a simple trade transaction. In the case of establishing a large-scale inter-state project, the ability to cooperate at the bureaucratic level is a *sine qua non*.

Success in creating joint infrastructures also depends heavily on the size of investment involved and its imprint on the physical environment. "Soft infrastructures," such as joint legal systems, or joint institutions, require small investments and hence are easier to establish. However, frequently such systems lack real authority, fulfilling a more symbolic role. "Hard infrastructures," such as pipelines or railway networks, which require large investments and entail physical changes in the environment rather than merely founding social institutions, are more difficult to agree upon, since the stakes in case of failure are very high. These types of infrastructures are more rare, and usually the parties involved will agree upon them only after they are fully assured of their success and the stability of the relations between the states.

Despite the obstacles and difficulties associated with sharing infrastruc- tures, the study by David Boas *et al.* (1996) proposed that the members of the Israeli–Jordanian–Palestinian triangle should make an effort to support such initiatives. Taking into account the inherent economic and social dif- ferences between Israel and its neighbors, the study made the following six recommendations in order to secure cooperation between the parties:

1 *Catering to different qualitative needs of each economy.* Each of the economies is in need of infrastructure development. The development

needs, however, vary from one economy to another due to differences in existing level of infrastructure, economic structure, etc. Furthermore, the infrastructure needs of each economy tend to change over time. It is therefore necessary to examine both short-term and long-term needs and to take anticipated changes into account. A preliminary examination of an infrastructure project should examine the solution it provides for the needs of each of the economies. The better suited it is to those various needs, the greater its viability.

2 *Relating maturity of the infrastructure with the level of economic development.* As noted, large differences exist in the infrastructure level of the various economies, thus producing significant differences in their development needs. An examination of the projects must address the existing infrastructure level. On the one hand, there is no need to close reasonable gaps at any price; for example, there is no point in building a multi-lane freeway when the number of vehicles is small in relation to the population and the basic infrastructure is adequate. On the other hand, an effort should be made to ensure that the projects constitute a significant step forward in development, particularly in the case of Jordan and the PA.

3 *Aligning project scale with size of the economy.* Infrastructure projects are characterized by large-scale investments. The size and strength of each economy affect its capacity to handle various scales of investment. In examining a project's feasibility, care must be taken to align its scale with the share of each of the economies involved.

4 *Expanding spheres of influence.* One of the distinctive characteristics of an infrastructure is that it is simultaneously an end product and a production factor. A water supply infrastructure, for example, is an end product for the individual but also a key production factor in agriculture and industry. As production factors, infrastructure projects such as roads, communications, and energy have an indirect impact on various sectors of the economy. Roads provide direct savings in time costs. However, they also play a crucial role in creating a basis for other types of infrastructure, thereby expanding their spheres of influence. In reviewing an infrastructure project, a detailed examination must be made of all the potential spheres of influence. The more sectors the project is anticipated to contribute to, and the greater the impact, the greater the project's viability.

5 *Private and governmental participation.* Because of the scale of investment and the manner of implementation, infrastructure often constitutes a "public product." However, it is possible to establish an arrangement where the users can be made to pay, thereby enabling private sector intervention in financing and implementation. An example of this is the supply of electricity or gas. In these cases, private-sector intervention is an

accepted practice. The greater the number of "normal product" components in the project, and the smaller the number of "public product" components, the higher the interest of the private sector, and the greater the prospects for its implementation.

6 *Securing potential funding sources.* The large-scale investments necessary for infrastructure projects require close attention to be given to the sources of financial backing. The successful implementation of a project is dependent on the ability to mobilize the required funds to set it up. To the degree that funding for a project, by private or public sources, is known and guaranteed, the greater the prospects for its implementation.

Israeli–Jordanian Shared Infrastructure Initiatives

Both Israel and Jordan clearly understood the importance of creating joint infrastructures. Even before the signing of the 1994 peace treaty, the Israeli negotiators proposed joint projects with the Jordanians. However, the process of agreeing on the terms of these projects has been laborious. In the first five years after the peace treaty, only two joint projects requiring physical investments actually started, though neither has been completed. In both cases, Israeli political–bureaucratic procedures, rather than lack of cooperation, are stalling the projects.

The Eilat–Aqaba Airport

The first regional development project was a 1996 agreement to develop the cities of Aqaba and Eilat at the southern tip of Jordan and Israel (State of Israel, 1997: chapter 2). The intention of joint management of this region was stipulated in Article 15 of the Israeli–Jordanian peace agreement. The logic of joint regional development along the southern Israeli–Jordanian border was noted in 1996 by Nachmias *et al.* in a document prepared for the Foreign Ministry:

> The border in this area has increased the costs of mobilization of commodities and people because each state, Israel and Jordan, had to build a separate transportation system. Consequently two parallel roads, two airports, and two commercial harbors were built. The duplication of transportation systems results in a sub-optimal utilization of resources.

A major advantage regarding this area in terms of joint cooperation is that it is relatively undeveloped, with hardly any industry. While there are many opportunities for investment, there is no need to restructure old foundations. Thus, the area can be effectively treated as a single unit.

An important issue associated with the development of the Aqaba-Eilat region is the possible deterioration of the environment. This is crucial because the major industry of the region is tourism. In this case, cooperation is essential. Borders cannot stop the spread of pollutants. To meet the threat of environmental deterioration, Israel and Jordan established joint committees for pest and sewage control (*Jordan Times*, May 12, 1998).

Based on forecasts regarding tourist volume to the Gulf of Aqaba, it was anticipated that expanded transportation facilities to the area would be needed. The airport in Eilat had already reached its maximum capacity and international flights were landing at an airforce base north of the city. Extending the airport in Eilat was impossible because of its close proximity to the city, so plans were drawn up for a new airfield five kilometers north of the city, with the site of the current airport to be used for new hotels.

In the meantime, the Israeli–Jordanian negotiations got underway and a cheaper option emerged: the underutilized Aqaba airfield. On the Israeli side, however, two problems arose. The first was that Eilat-bound tourists would have to pass through Jordanian border control and pay taxes to Jordan, thus raising the cost of the visit (*LINK*, September 1995). The second problem was that in the long run the Jordanian facility would not be large enough and a new airport would in any case have to be built.

It should be noted that a number of bi-national airports operate in Europe. The most famous is the EuroAirport (1999) located on the intersection of the borders of France, Germany, and Switzerland, which has been functioning since 1949. Like the Eilat–Aqaba project, this initiative also grew out of the need to expand an international airport at Basel. However, due to geographic limitations, the most suitable site was on the French side of the border. The Swiss proposed a bi-national joint venture: France would provide the land and Switzerland would build the airfield. The EuroAirport authority is a totally independent organization and its board of directors consists of an equal number of Swiss and French nationals. In 1987 the airport was transformed into a tri-national enterprise and two German representatives were added to the board of directors.

While the agreement to build the Swiss–French airfield required only two months of negotiations and another three years to complete the entire project, the process has been much more complicated in the case of the Eilat–Aqaba airport. The Israelis and Jordanians decided to progress through three stages. The first would be a pilot project. During this stage some Israel-bound flights would land in Jordan and the passengers would be bused to Eilat. In the second stage a new terminal would be financed, built, and managed by Israel (on the Israeli side of the border), adjacent to the Aqaba runway. All Eilat and Aqaba bound flights would land in Jordan. The Jordanians would service the airplanes and the Israel-bound passengers would enter Israel through the new terminal, while Jordan-bound passengers would enter that country through the old terminal. In the final stage, as in the case of the EuroAirport, an additional runway would be built in Jordan and a joint Israeli–Jordanian airport authority would be established to manage the airport facilities.

Because Eilat is far more developed than Aqaba, this joint development project could be viewed as an experiment which encapsulated all the hopes and fears of the Jordanians *vis-à-vis* Israel. On the one hand, the creation of good transportation links between Aqaba and Eilat would increase tourism to Aqaba, which lags well behind Eilat in this sphere. Another paramount consideration was that the joint airport would enhance Jordanian revenues by significantly increasing the volume of air traffic to the traditionally sleepy airport at Aqaba. On the other hand, the Jordanians feared that the Israelis would pocket most of the profits from the area's development. And even though Israel has agreed to transfer to Jordan the responsibility of servicing all Eilat bound planes at the airport, the Jordanian opposition parties, espousing realist arguments, vehemently objected to the project. The initiative, they argued, was an infringement of Jordan's sovereignty (*ArabicNews.Com*, April 7, 1997). Thus, despite the Jordanians' interest in joint regional development, Amman insisted on advancing by small, carefully measured steps in order to appease the Jordanian opposition.

Israel, in contrast, seemed to be highly receptive to the idea of sharing infrastructures with Jordan. The Likud government, which came to power in 1996, approved the continuation of the joint projects that were agreed upon by the previous Labor government (*Globes*, July 29, 1996). However, certain sectors in Israel expressed their own concerns. First, due to the cheap labor and fuel in Jordan, the creation of good transportation links might cause investors to prefer Aqaba to Eilat. The plan to have Jordan service the planes in the second stage of the agreement generated consider-able resentment, as all the firms that serviced Eilat bound flights would lose their source of income.

Another concern of the tourist industry in Eilat was that designating the flight destination as Jordan might deter some tourists who had reservations about Arab countries, thus causing a loss in tourism (*Globes*, March 26, 1998). A possible terrorist attack, facilitated by Jordan's comparatively lax security procedures, would have a devastating impact on tourism. Yet another concern was that the Aqaba seaport, which is larger and more advanced than Eilat's port, would take away business from the latter. The joint airport project, then, would seriously jeopardize Eilat's two major industries, tourism and the port.

Nevertheless, the two governments overrode their respective oppositions, and in 1997 launched the first stage of the plan, the trial period, which lasted four months. During this period, the Israelis were supposed to eventually land 10 percent of the incoming flights of El-Al and Arkia airlines from Europe, estimated at about fifteen to twenty a week, at Aqaba and then bus the passengers to Israel. The Israelis also agreed that the Israeli carrier El Al would pay Royal Wings, a subsidiary of Royal Jordanian, a landing fee equal to that charged by Israeli airports, which was four times that charged by Jordanian airports. The Jordanians agreed to allow Israeli security personnel to enter Jordan in order to escort the passengers from the moment the plane landed until they entered Israel. In addition, it was agreed that joint Israeli–Jordanian security teams would guard the planes and passengers in Aqaba.

To the chagrin of the Jordanians, nearly two months passed before the first Israeli flight landed in Aqaba. Moreover, the Israelis redirected no more than three flights a week to Aqaba, claiming that the volume of tourists to Eilat was lower than expected. As a result, the Jordanians demanded an extension of the trial period. They claimed that with such a small number of incoming flights they could not collect sufficient data to assess the technical and administrative aspects of the program (*Jordan Times,* February 7, 1998; March 2, 1998). The Israelis, however, seemed quite satisfied with the results of the pilot program and to demonstrate their commitment to the project, announced their intention to start building the new terminal, thus launching the second phase of the project.

Despite the declared intentions of the Israeli government, the construction of the terminal was postponed. The Israeli Ministry of Environment intervened, demanding that an environmental survey be conducted before building began. Gabi Golan (1999), adviser for planning and construction in the Prime Minister's Office, explains that the Environment Ministry stepped in because certain bureaucratic procedures were circumvented in an attempt to expedite the construction of the new facility. Indignant Israeli bureaucrats retaliated by supporting environmental organizations, which threatened to petition the High Court of Justice.

Thus, over a period of five years, despite the bombastic declarations regarding Israeli–Jordanian joint administration of the Eilat–Aqaba region and a specific clause in the peace treaty to that effect, cooperation in the southern region has remained minimal. With the exception of tourists from Eilat spending a day in Jordan's ancient city of Petra, there is very little cross-national traffic. Even though Aqaba is cheaper than Eilat, the services there are undeveloped and modest bathing suits are required. Under these circumstances, the Israelis continue to reap most of the profits from tourism, since most tourists prefer Israeli accommodation and tourist guides. Only Arab tourists, who constitute a small portion of the vacationers flocking to the area, are attracted to hotels and services offered in Aqaba.

Since the Jordanians demand a very high port tax, Israeli fears of competition from the port of Aqaba have so far also not materialized. It is still cheaper to use Eilat's harbor. If future peace treaties are signed between Israel and Syria or Iraq, the Jordanians may be forced to reduce these tariffs, since those two countries will then have the alternative of using Eilat's facilities.

Eventually, when authorization is obtained to build the new terminal, the second phase of the airport project will get under way. According to Golan (1999), the third phase will probably not be implemented in the near future: the costs of building a new runway are very high, and the old runway, together with the new terminal, should be sufficient to accommodate current air traffic. Although Israel will relinquish the servicing of the planes to Jordan, this will be cheaper than servicing them in Israel. The new terminal, however, will be exclusively handled by Israel and is expected to be profitable.

From a realist point of view, the second phase of the Israeli–Jordanian airport project will place Israel in a disadvantageous position because the Jordanians will hold the runway hostage. After Israel completes the construction of the terminal and closes the old airport, the realist approach argues, the Jordanians could raise the price of using the runway and even forbid landings if they choose. The only choice Israel would then have would be to divert incoming flights to the Ovdah military airport north of the city, far from the new terminal. It should be noted that a similar situation exists in the case of the EuroAirport, which is on French soil. So, if relations between Israel and Jordan are as stable as those between France and Switzerland, there is no reason why the Jordanians should suddenly attempt to change the terms of the agreement. Also they would lose economically, since most of the flights are expected to be for Eilat bound passengers.

While the realist interpretation of the project identifies the Jordanian advantage, from a centralist perspective the Jordanians will be at a disadvantage. The Israelis, who own the new terminal, will earn more profits than the Jordanians, who will only service the runway and airplanes.

Although this predicament cannot be denied, the fact is that if the Jordanians had refused to allow the Israelis to use their runway, the Israelis would have built their own runway. In this case both sides would have lost. The Jordanians would be left with an underutilized, unprofitable airport, while the Israelis would have to spend an enormous amount of money to construct a new runway. In this respect, the Eilat–Aqaba airport serves as a typical example of a situation where both parties gain more by cooperation than if each side were to develop a separate infrastructure independently.

The Jordan Gateway Project

A second plan for joint regional development is in the Jordan Rift Valley region. As in the case of Eilat–Aqaba, there was an agreement to cooperate in all aspects of resource utilization. The agreement encompassed pollution and pest control, monitoring water salinity, and sharing the waters of the Yarmouk and Jordan Rivers (Jordan Bureau of Information, October 1997). One major outcome of this agreement was the initiative to establish the Jordan Gateway Project (JGP), located eight kilometers south of the Hussein Border Station. Unlike the Al-Hassan industrial zone in Irbid, this area was designated a free-trade zone to be connected by a bridge to an industrial park on the Israeli side of the border. But what makes this project so unique is its joint Israeli–Jordanian administration. Persons entering the parks on both sides of the border will be able to move freely back and forth between them without a passport.

The idea of building industrial parks along the borders that will include Arab and Israeli enterprises is not new. It was put forward already in 1975 by the Egyptian journalist, Said Ahmed (1976: 73–5) who argued that the incentive for Arabs or Israelis to resume the armed conflict would diminish since this would lead to the destruction of joint economic units. Besides the political implications, building industrial parks along the border also has economic advantages, especially in the case of a relationship between a highly industrialized country and a neighbor with low labor costs. The most typical example of such a policy is the case of the US–Mexican border. In 1965, in an effort to attract American businesses, the Mexican government initiated the Border Industrial Program, widely known as the maquiladora program. Under this program, foreign companies (mainly from the United States and Asia) could establish factories in Mexico and import parts and materials to them duty-free. Mexican law allowed 100 percent foreign ownership and management. However, the labor force had to be Mexican and the majority of the products had to be exported out of Mexico, with duty paid only on the "value added" during manufacture or assembly. Thus the Mexicans built industrial parks along the US border with appropriate infrastructures to support the maquiladora companies.

The US–Mexican experience inspired US Senator Hank Brown, the chair of the Senate Foreign Relations Subcommittee on Near Eastern and South Asian Affairs, to propose to Gil Dekel (1999), an Israeli businessman, that a similar project be initiated along the Israeli–Jordanian border. Dekel, who had developed close relations with the Jordanians as the IDF representative during the aviation negotiations between Israel, Jordan and the Palestinians, persuaded the Jordanian government to go ahead with the project. He found a Jordanian businessman of Palestinian origin who was willing to participate as a Jordanian partner, despite the increasing domestic opposition against the peace agreement with Israel.

Amman, which was interested in proving that the peace with Israel could be economically beneficial, considered the proposal positively. At the same time, the Jordanian regime, unlike the Palestinians, was unwilling to allow its nationals to commute to work in Israel, since this would have highly negative political implications, as well as increase costs. At bottom, moreover, the Jordanian administration and business community were reluctant to cooperate with the Israeli side. The US–Mexican model was not viewed as appropriate for the Israeli–Jordanian arena.

As explained in the previous chapter, full Israeli ownership and management was not viewed positively. On the other hand, the support of international investors required Israeli participation. In order to strike a balance in the Israeli–Jordanian relationship, a twin park was created on the Israeli side of the border and the entire area was defined as a QIZ and a free-trade zone.[1] Dekel was able to monopolize the status of the industrial park. He reached an agreement with the Jordanians that no additional industrial parks would be established within ten kilometers of the JGP for the next ten years, and a requirement to obtain his consent for any such project afterward. This combination made the JGP an especially attractive site.

While a maquiladora type of industrial park has certain economic benefits, it can also produce negative side-effects. Besides the argument that transferring production to a neighboring country where labor is cheap creates unemployment, another source of criticism is that the maquiladoras create health and environmental hazards near the border due to poor working conditions and no regulation of waste disposal and safety. Only during the NAFTA negotiations were environmentally concerned groups able to impose clauses for creating joint institutions to monitor health and environmental hazards. Thus, the North American Commission for Environmental Cooperation (NACEC), a tri-national organization headed by the environment ministers of the United States, Mexico and Canada, was established in order to address a variety of environmental and trade issues, including environmental management in the US–Mexico border region. The NAFTA side agreements also resulted in the establishment of the Border Environment Cooperation Commission (BECC) and the North American Development Bank (NADBank). Working in tandem, these two new bi-national institutions are intended to help fund new infrastructure facilities to deal with water supply, wastewater treatment, and municipal solid waste needs in the border area. In addition to the institutions above, which were formed between federal governments, local organizations at the state and municipal levels have also been created. However, the effectiveness of all these organizations is questionable and private groups complain that environmental and health hazards along the border have not been ameliorated.

There is very little that US environmentalists can do about companies operating in Mexico. But in the case of the JGP, which is partially located in Israel, environmentally concerned groups were able to take advantage of the Israeli judicial and administrative system to promote their cause. Thus, the Israeli Ministry of Environment, along with other groups, adopted the same strategy they used to frustrate the Eilat–Aqaba airfield, intervening in the various committees authorizing construction permits on the site and threatening to take the developers to court. What made this case so special for the environmentalists was that the area designated for the park was right on the banks of the Jordan River. Besides the fact that this is one of the very few rivers in Israel that is not heavily contaminated by pollutants, thanks to a combination of running water and high temperatures, an ecological system unique to the Middle East exists there.

Although the area next to the Jordan River is defined as a free non-development zone, it was never declared an official nature reserve. Still, the wildlife within this area is well protected. This is a by-product of the post-1967 attempts of Palestinian terrorists to infiltrate into Israel and the West Bank, which led the IDF to install an electronic fence system parallel to the river. As a result, the entire area between the Jordan River and the fence became an off-limit military zone, enabling the unique fauna within this area to thrive for thirty years without any interference.

Dekel (1999) tried to reach a compromise with the Israeli environmentalists, offering to create a nature reserve next to the JGP and possibly even obtain Israeli–Jordanian cooperation to preserve the environment on the Jordanian side of the river as well. However, the Israeli groups, backed up by international environmental organizations, refused to yield. Thus, while on the Jordanian side the park is being developed, all work on the Israeli side has been suspended, even though the Israeli government officially approved the area of the project as a QIZ on May 20, 1999.

The Ministry of Environment has suggested that the Israeli portion of the industrial park be transferred to one of the two Israeli industrial parks nearby. This, of course, would eliminate territorial continuity between the Israeli and Jordanian sides of the JGP. Dekel claims that this alternative is unacceptable to the Jordanians, as it would defeat the unique purpose and quality of the project.

Nor is it only the environmentalists who must be dealt with. In order to obtain the proper licenses and start developing the Israeli side of the park, Dekel had to form coalitions in each of the committees that authorizes each aspect of the project. Thus he must identify potential allies who are willing to oppose the environmentalists and offer them some *quid pro quo* in return for their support. With this strategy, his prospects were quite good. Since Dekel's company is better connected and has far greater financial means than the environmentalists, and because the JGP is located in Israel's periphery, which is suffering from high levels of unemployment and emigration, there was strong local and governmental support for the initiative.

Eventually, in the fall of 1999, Dekel overcame Israeli and foreign opposition. The JGP received the final approval from the Israeli authorities.

Attempts to Establish Israeli–Palestinian Shared Infrastructure Projects

While Israel and Jordan have succeeded in embarking on a number of joint infrastructure projects, Israel and the PA have been less successful in co-operating with each other, despite the intentions that were declared upon the signing of the DoP.

The major physical infrastructure projects that the Israelis and Palestinians agreed upon involved the establishment of industrial parks, similar to the JGP, which would house Israeli and Palestinian businesses. However, there seems to be no linkage at all between the JGP and the joint Israel–PA ventures. According to Catrivas (1999), who was then an official in Israel's Ministry of Industry and Trade, the idea of creating these industrial parks was raised by the Minister of Industry and Trade, Micha Harish, during the first Economic Conference for the Middle East and North African States in Casablanca. Harish thought this idea might offset the negative effect of the Israeli closure policy in the WBGS. Rather than the Palestinians coming to work in Israel, the work would be brought to them. In addition, such projects would save the Palestinians time and transportation costs. Since the parks would provide high-quality services and reduce production costs, they would need advanced infrastructures, which would spur the development of the Palestinian economy.

Harish's concept was not entirely new. Prior to the DoP, Israel had built one industrial park near the Erez border station on the Israeli side of the Green Line on the border with the Gaza Strip. But in contrast to the JGP, Harish's proposal was not viewed positively by the Israeli public. Unlike Israel and Jordan, the borders between Israel and the PA remained to be negotiated. Thus, Israel's agreement to allocate land for the creation of a Palestinian industrial park might lead to a legitimate Palestinian claim to the area, as Israel has claimed areas in the WBGS settled and developed by Jews. Another problem with Harish's approach was that most Palestinian workers in Israel are employed in jobs that cannot be relocated, such as agriculture, construction, and services. Whenever possible, Israeli entrepreneurs have usually been willing to subcontract work in the WBGS. However, as explained in the previous chapter, due to the *Intifada*, and possibly also the Jordanian alternative, subcontracting to the Palestinians has declined. Finally, a third problem with the idea of Palestinian industrial parks is finding the funds to finance such large projects. This has not been easy, particularly because the legal status of these parks has not been clarified and is open to negotiation as part of the permanent Israeli–Palestinian settlement.

The Gaza Industrial Estate (GIE)

In July 1996, after the Likud party came to power, the question of establishing parks for Israeli and Palestinian industries was raised once again. The first industrial park was conceived at a meeting in Washington, D.C. between Natan Sharansky, the new Israeli Minister of Industry and Trade, and World Bank President James Wolfensohn (*The Jerusalem Post*, July 31, 1996). The site chosen for the park was in Al-Muntar, near the Karni border pass between Israel and the Gaza Strip. Unlike the JGP, which straddles the border, the park proposed by the Israeli government was to be situated exclusively within a Palestinian controlled area. Because there was a relatively high level of public consensus in Israel to withdraw from most of the areas unsettled by Jews in the Gaza Strip, it was relatively easy to obtain the approval of the Israeli government. In addition, the location of the park was designated in the Israeli–Palestinian redeployment agreements as Area A, which anyway granted the PA full administrative and security responsibility.

The park near the Karni pass, known as the Gaza Industrial Estate (GIE), was officially opened in January 1999. A special organization, the Palestine Industrial Estate Development and Management Company (PIEDC), was established in order to manage the project, although the World Bank, which was the major investor, has had a high level of involvement, mainly in demanding commensurate Palestinian legislation. Many of the donor countries for the project expressed serious concern about environmental issues, particularly the disposal of industrial waste (Press, 1998). Israel also contributed to the establishment of the park, investing $15 million for the erection of an advanced and faster passage and clearance facility for the products manufactured in the industrial estate. Israel was also to serve as the supplier of water and electricity to the park.

While many Israeli officials term the GIE as a joint infrastructure project, in reality there has been very little cooperation between Israel and the PA. The bulk of cooperation is limited to security problems. The Israelis were involved in determining the security guidelines for the park. But unlike the JGP, there was no Israeli attempt to extend cooperation into other "civilian" matters, which are managed exclusively by the PIEDC, under the guidance of the World Bank. When the park was officially opened, in the presence of US President Bill Clinton, in December 1998, no Israeli official was invited. This was explained as a consequence of the tension between Israel and the PA, as well as Egyptian pressure on the PA (*Globes*, December 14, 1998).

Since the establishment of the GIE, very few foreign or Israeli companies have been willing to open factories there; similarly, the number of Palestinians willing to lease a site in the park has been minimal. As of August 1999, only 22 companies had signed leases (Barr, 1999).

To a great extent, the park's failure can be attributed to the minimization of Israeli involvement. Unlike the Erez industrial park, which is on the Israeli side of the Green Line, or the Jordan Gateway Project, which is located on both sides of the border, there is no closure exemption and these parks are managed entirely by Israelis. Hence the investment risks are higher than at Erez or the JGP. Because of Israeli involvement in planning the park's security system, it is simpler to transfer products across the border into Israel. In fact, the time that will be saved processing merchandise produced inside the park, in comparison to goods originating elsewhere, is expected to become negligible. This is because there are plans to make the Karni checkpoint so efficient that Israel intends to require all

Israeli commerce with the Gaza Strip to transfer through that crossing station. Under these circumstances, the park has no significant competitive advantage over any other location within the Gaza Strip. Even though the GIE has a highly developed infrastructure and efficient security measures, leasing costs there are high in comparison to alternative locations, and because most Israeli subcontracting involves small-scale enterprises the less developed infrastructure at other locations is sufficient.

Besides the relatively higher expenses of investing in the GIE and the lack of a special closure exemption, there are no special legal guarantees or protection against monopolistic interests. It should be noted in this connection that the Mexican attempt to establish the maquiladora industries also initially failed, even though there was, of course, no threat of a US closure. Like the PA, the corrupt and unstable political regime of Mexico deterred many American businesses. Only after the devaluation of the peso in 1982, when the price of Mexican labor drastically declined, were Americans drawn to start manufacturing in Mexico.

A month after the park was officially opened Israel announced the establishment of an industrial estate on the Israeli side of the GIE. This industrial zone had been planned a year before, and was supposed to serve as a complementary facility to the GIE – mainly servicing the trucks transporting merchandise to and from the Karni pass and possibly building offices for Israeli managers, as in the case of the JGP. Many complementary industries have also been established on the US side of the border with Mexico. But the unilateral Israeli announcement, combined with a general lack of coordination between Israel and the PA, generated considerable suspicion and criticism by the PA. The prevalent attitude was that the lack of collaboration between Israel and the PA indicated the intention of the Israelis to compete with the Palestinian project by taking advantage of Israel's closure and regulation policies across the Karni pass (*The Jerusalem Post*, February 6, 1999).

Industrial Parks in the West Bank

After the GIE was approved, Israel agreed to allow the Palestinians to open three more industrial parks, all in the West Bank: one north of Jenin at Mukeibila, a second near Tulkarm, and a third near Nablus. All three parks were supposed to be under exclusive Palestinian control, rather than jointly managed by Israelis and Palestinians.

The largest of the parks, located north of Jenin, is owned by the chairman of the Commercial Bank of Jordan, Tawfik Fakhoury (who is originally from Jenin), and financially supported by the German government. The park is located in Area C, meaning that it is under full Israeli control, thus obviating the need to negotiate security arrangements. The Israelis also agreed to supply the park with water and electricity. However, after a positive feasibility report was submitted, and despite a positive response from the Matam industrial zone in Haifa, both the Israeli Civil Administration in the West Bank and the Industry and Trade Ministry refused to allow the developer to start building. The reason for the Israeli delay was a declaration by the PA's Minister of Industry and Trade announcing that this was a PA project and not private. This was viewed as a Palestinian violation of the redeployment agreement, since Area C is strictly under Israeli control.

The industrial park near Tulkarm, which is intended to serve as a hi-tech incubator, was also delayed by the Civil Administration (*The Jerusalem Post*, February 7, 1997; *Globes*, July 15, 1997), although eventually it was authorized, since it is located in Area A, which is undisputedly Palestinian. In the case of the third industrial park, near Nablus, the project failed because of a negative feasibility test (Crystal, 1999). All the other industrial parks that were supposed to be established in the WBGS have not even entered the planning stage.

A fourth park, to be connected to the QIZ of the Jordan Gateway Park, was suggested by Israel's Foreign Minister at the time, Shimon Peres. However, Gil Dekel, the manager of the JGP, found this suggestion to be nearly impossible to implement. Finding a Palestinian partner who would be acceptable both to him and his Jordanian associate was extremely difficult, so he preferred to exclude the Palestinians from the project.

The Jewish settlers in the West Bank have raised vociferous objections to the creation of Palestinian industrial parks. They prefer that Palestinian entrepreneurs bring their businesses to the existing industrial areas that are annexed to the Jewish settlements. According to the testimony of Ron Nachman, the mayor of the city-settlement of Ariel, Natan Sharansky, the Minister of Industry and Trade, supported the idea of Palestinians basing their factories in the Jewish industrial areas (*The Jerusalem Post*, October 4, 1998).

It is doubtful that the development of additional industrial parks will be agreed upon as long as no permanent settlement is reached between Israel and the PA. However, once a settlement is achieved, which grants the Palestinians some degree of sovereignty, even if not the status of a state, there will probably be no need to obtain Israeli permission anyway. Under such circumstances, when the Palestinians are regarded as an equal partner (like the Jordanians), there might be an attempt to create a project similar to the JGP, which would involve a true joint project.

Meanwhile, there have been other alternatives. In 1999, a private initiative was launched by the Israeli industrialist Stefan Wertheimer to build three industrial parks at the intersection of the borders of Israel, Egypt, and the Gaza Strip. One park would be located in each of the three territories. Wertheimer's initiative had a smooth beginning and he obtained construction permits from Israel and the PA (but not Egypt). The acceptance of the project by all parties was due to the informal nature of the interaction between the Israeli and Palestinian sites. In the meantime, each park will operate independently, though the hope is that this project will serve as the basis for a bi-national or even tri-national joint infrastructure.

Dekel (1999) is also planning to establish an industrial park in the WBGS with a Palestinian partner. Unlike Wertheimer, Dekel preferred first to obtain a commitment from a Palestinian partner before approaching the PA and Israeli authorities. His plan is to duplicate the concept of a joint administration, as with the JGP. However, he claims that the political atmosphere in the PA is not yet suitable and is waiting for appropriate conditions to develop.

The Dilemmas of Sharing Infrastructures

The sharing of infrastructures among a number of nations exemplifies the highest degree of cooperation. If such projects require physical intervention in the environment, which requires a large investment, the cost of dissociation in comparison to trade or joint ventures, which require smaller capital investments, is significantly high. Because the risks are so great both economically and politically, such projects require a very high level of stability between the partners. In this respect, it is possible that the notion of sharing infrastructures in the Middle East is still premature. Instead, at this stage, projects that service links on both sides of the border should be developed; such projects mostly require coordination, not joint management.

It is undeniable that coordinated, mutual infrastructure development can encounter serious obstacles. The problem is not necessarily a realist approach or mutual suspicion factors, but existing bureaucratic, cultural, and legal structures. Even domestic infrastructure projects in a country like Israel are tedious and frustrating affairs. Obtaining a permit to construct a building is a complicated business. Attempting to coordinate between two or more cumbersome bureaucracies can be self-defeating. This was clearly demonstrated in the case of the Israeli–Jordanian projects. While the obstacles confronting the developers were to be expected, the fact that these are not regular domestic projects has international consequences. Thus, rather than encouraging cooperation, these projects have created new sources of tension.

The Israeli experience in joint infrastructure development may serve as a good example of what Allison termed the bureaucratic politics model of foreign policy. According to Allison (1971), because each bureaucracy has its own agenda and interests, foreign policy is the consequence of bargaining and haggling between government organizations and even private interest groups. A major criticism of Allison's model was that because the authority of the US President overrides that of the bureaucrat, the internal conflicts with his "court" are negligible (Perlmutter, 1974). This argument might be relevant for explaining Jordanian foreign policy, and in certain situations, Israeli or US foreign policy. But in the specific case of infrastructure development, the Israeli Prime Minister, who is bound by the country's legal system, cannot force members of the various committees to abide by his wishes, just as the President cannot force Congress to always adopt his policies. Hence, structural limitation must be taken into account in the case of regional infrastructure development.

While the Israeli–Jordanian ordeals may lead to the conclusion that joint infrastructures in the Middle East should be avoided, not to embark on them can sometimes be quite costly. The lack of Israeli–Palestinian joint infrastructures is especially worrying. Most probably, if the GIE had been under joint Israeli and Palestinian management (like the JGP), the site would have been more attractive. Thus, the possibility of creating joint parks should be seriously considered.

Another main infrastructure project that may have to be considered in the future involves the problem of water. The lack of sufficient water in the region for individual, industrial, and agricultural use obliges cooperation by all parties if a serious conflict is to be avoided. In order to satisfy the demand for water, desalination plants, or a system to transport water from Lebanon or Turkey, such as a pipeline, might be required. However, such projects are prohibitively expensive. While in the short term cheaper solutions will probably be preferred, as demand for water increases due to rising needs, the more expensive alternatives may nevertheless be the only viable solution. Under these circumstances all parties in the region might benefit by sharing expenses and managing such a project together (Libiszewski, 1995).

The example of assuring an adequate water supply, as well as other health and environmental issues, demonstrates that eventually, despite the difficulties involved, the political entities within the Israeli–Palestinian–Jordanian triangle will almost certainly need to establish joint infrastructures that support all parties. And as in Europe, to overcome local political–bureaucratic obstacles, special legal provisions might be required in order allow inter-state institutions to be established that will implement cooperative policy with optimal effectiveness.

Note

1   The Israeli government has only approved the status of a QIZ, but there is considerable hesitation regarding the creation of free-trade zones, for fear that they will be used for money laundering. In the meantime, the status of a free-trade zone applies only on the Jordanian side.

7

Conclusion: The Future of Arab–Israeli Economic Relations – Risks and Opportunities

Conflicting Trends and Shifting Priorities

Much of the analytical dispute regarding the nature of the interaction between political conflict and economic cooperation remains unresolved. The question of whether identities and interests of purposive actors are constructed and primarily determined by shared ideas and political aspirations or by material forces, continues to occupy social science and political studies agendas. In the case under discussion the material perspective underlay the major explanation for the growth of transnational economic relations between Israel and a number of Arab states since the signing of the Israeli–Palestinian Declaration of Principles in 1993. Following the DoP, the economic boycott against Israel was rescinded, and Arab and Israeli entrepreneurs and merchants took advantage of the readily available products, services, and labor that they could obtain from each other instead of being imported from overseas more expensively. However, the expansion of Arab–Israeli economic relations has not necessarily been associated with an improvement of political relations. The majority of Arab states have declined to sign a peace treaty with Israel, and political relations with those few countries that concluded peace treaties with Israel are strained.

If economic profit was the primary force motivating human affairs in the Middle East the Arab boycott would never have endured for so many years. However, the enforcement of the boycott since Israeli independence in 1948 indicates that apparently more pressing and fundamental interests overrode the potential benefits of economic relations. This does not mean that material considerations should be disregarded or that they are always secondary human objectives. Rather, as noted earlier, a mixture of different goals motivates behavior. A key factor in this regard is perceived existential threats at a particular time. Priority may accrue to economic interests or in other conditions to social interests.

Throughout most of the past century, the political scene of the Middle East was viewed through the prism of realist dogma, which considers economics a secondary social interest. Indeed, it was the aspiration of Jews and Arabs to live within sovereign states that induced them to engage in a violent conflict in order to achieve their national goals, even if this meant paying a heavy human and material price. The fierce competition for territorial sovereignty required definite borders to be drawn between the adversaries, together with the institution of rigidly hierarchical and centralist modes of government in order to control the movement of people, goods, and information across borders as well as within the jurisdiction of each state. Under these circumstances, the Arab boycott, despite its economic costs, was considered a rational policy by those who implemented it.

A similar pattern can be identified on the Israeli side. Despite Israel's democratic political system, sections of the Israeli public have been willing to tolerate the imposition of limitations on basic human rights, such as freedom of information or movement. Similarly, in the economic sphere, a deep sense of vulnerability provided the normative basis for the government's tight control and regulation of the economy.

Although the realist perspective does not exclude the possibility that enemies might decide to end a conflict and sign a peace treaty, this is expected to occur as the result of a shift in the balance of power. It is the absence of such a shift that might explain why the stalemate in the Middle East endured for so long. The US backing of Israel and the Soviet Union's support of the Arab states preserved the Arab–Israeli conflict in a state of equilibrium. Although neither opponent was able to defeat the other decisively, the conflict lingered on at a low level of intensity, spotted with occasional crises and flare-ups (Azar *et al.*, 1978). With the demise of the Soviet Union as a major world power at the end of the 1980s, the traditional Arab–Russian alliance dissolved and the Arab world was compelled to come to terms with the existence of the Jewish state in its midst.

Realist calculations that underlay the Middle East peace process have been equally dominant in Arab–Israeli economic agreements. Both sides have attempted to maintain the greatest possible control over economic transactions. The Arab parties were especially wary of the possibility that Israel would enhance its relative economic advantage, thus increasing its political leverage and power. The Israelis, on the other hand, have focused mainly on security risks associated with opening borders and returning Arab and Palestinian territories conquered during the war of 1967.

Some students of political behavior tend to argue that as long as ethnic groups aspire to achieve the ideal of statehood, the security threats posed by competing states will continue to surpass all other interests (Waltz, 1979). So, one should expect a highly inimical future for the Middle East. This situation can be compared with the case of Europe following the First World War. As in the period between the two world wars, this view holds that "peace" will persist as long as one side maintains its strategic superiority. Hence, if for some reason the balance of power shifts back in favor of the Arab states, then arguably, as in Europe at the end of the 1930s, the status quo will break down, followed by possible violence.

If the realist assessments are accurate, then the prospects for economic cooperation are quite grim. The risks of establishing long-term joint ventures or sharing infrastructures will be high. And under conditions where stability is perceived to be a temporary status quo, preference will be to avoid long-term commitments and confine economic exchange to trade agreements or limited forms of joint ventures.

The fact that Israeli–Palestinian and Israeli–Jordanian relations have been restricted mainly to trade and limited forms of joint ventures seems to support the realist argument. Similar realist interpretations of the predicament of western Europe were also quite common during the past fifty years, yet political developments within Europe have shown that the realists' doom-saying was unfounded. Contrary to the expectations of most realists, the post-1945 period saw an erosion in the priority of "national security" with other interests being advocated (Morgenthau, 1950).

Does this mean that statehood and nationalism will be sacrificed and new ideals, such as maintaining the environment or tending to the social welfare of humanity, will prevail? Although some scholars actually believe that this is the trend of the future (Sprout and Sprout, 1971), the quest of ethnic groups for autonomous fulfillment and institutional representation remains a potent factor. Summarizing the argument, one may conclude that states and societies are undergoing two opposite processes. On the one hand, ethnic groups are demanding their right to political independence or autonomy, while on the other hand, there is a willingness to impose limits over centralized forms of authority, and over military build-up (Hanrieder, 1978).

In the case of Israel, the anti-realist notions sweeping across Europe and North America have fallen on fertile ground. For example, according to the realist theory, following the collapse of the Soviet Union and the consequent weakening of the Arabs' strategic position, Israel should have taken advantage of the Arab enfeeblement and heightened its demands at the negotiating table. Indeed, this has been the major argument of the Israeli opponents of the peace process. However, they have failed to comprehend that as the Israeli economy strengthened and developed, and as the Arab threat declined, the sense of living on the brink of extinction has gradually faded. Consequently, large segments of the Israeli public became reluctant to pay the high economic and social costs of occupying Palestinian and Lebanese territories and continuing the state of war.

The change of attitude within the Israeli public is not only limited to the peace process, it has also contributed to the proliferation of liberal values. It became very difficult for the Israeli government to justify violations of human rights and basic liberties by invoking "national security." A similar pattern is discernible in the economic sphere. In the past, the government justified regulation and control of the Israeli economy on the basis of Israel's precarious security situation. As threats to the survival of the state diminished, and demands grew for an improvement in the standard of living, the government gradually reduced its control over the economy.

The new liberal thrust that has begun to gain a foothold in Israel runs counter to many institutional arrangements that were required to maintain the realist system. The liberalist demands for decentralization, the break-down of political and bureaucratic barriers, and freedom of information and transportation, all interfere with the traditional realist agenda. Coinciding with the process of decentralization of the state, new transnational coalitions have been forged between Israelis and foreigners. These include employees of multinational corporations, interest groups, and international governmental organizations. And it is not uncommon for these bodies to join forces against the government in order to promote their interests.

In the Arab world too one can discern a hesitant willingness to reassess and challenge realist values. At least two key reasons underlie this development. First, the Arab perception of Israel as a highly aggressive state is starting to change. With the exception of Lebanon, and the Israeli attack on Tunis in 1985 and on the Iraqi nuclear reactor in 1981, Israel has avoided applying military force against Arab countries since it signed cease-fire agreements in 1974 with Egypt and Syria. As demonstrated in the disengagement agreements of 1974 and 1975 with Syria and Egypt, and later in the peace agreements with Egypt, Jordan and the DoP with the Palestinians, the Israelis were willing to withdraw from territories they had conquered, even when this did not completely stop Arab aggression toward Israel. The second reason for the Arab shift toward abandoning realist principles is the growing economic difficulties facing the Arab world. Most Arab countries, and especially those that were directly engaged in war with Israel, have failed to achieve sustainable economic development and growth. Instead they suffered high levels of unemployment and poverty. Thus, even though Israel is viewed as a stronger power, the social and economic threats encountered by these Arab regimes are perceived to be more intimidating than the possibility of Israeli aggression.

While voices within Arab states calling for a reduction of defense budgets and for greater investment in economic and social programs are growing stronger, in contrast to Israel, this change of priorities has not been accompanied by a large coalition demanding economic liberalization. This is apparently due to the pervasive fear that under a liberal regime the disadvantaged Arab businesses will be unable to compete with more experienced foreign entrepreneurs. Thus, although Arabs engage in commerce and other types of economic activity with Israelis, and even work for Israeli companies, there is a demand to keep these ties under strict regulation. Usually their willingness to establish an economic alliance requires parity between the Arab and Israeli partners. As a result Arab–Israeli joint ventures have been established mainly in light industries, where Israel does not enjoy a relatively advantageous position and thus is not perceived to have the capacity to exploit its partners. In rarer instances, an unequal distribution of management and control can be negotiated if the Arab partners reach the conclusion that they have no other choice. But because unequal relations are discouraged, so far most Arab partners usually prefer to keep their connections with Israel discreet.

Economic Cooperation, Conflict Mitigation, and Future Trends

The events unfolding within the Middle East indicate that a critical transformation of the political and economic systems has occurred. Despite heavy clouds of suspicion and animosity, Arabs and Israelis have found ways to cooperate and have created thriving, albeit limited, social and economic networks. The old realist order, where citizens find themselves in hierarchically structured mutually combative states, is gradually being replaced with a new complex network of transnational alliances, based on narrow interests and multiple loyalties.

Cooperation, however, is far from being ideal. While one can identify a minority within the Arab business community that espouses the liberal approach, demonstrating willingness to cooperate with Israeli partners, centralist and protectionist elements are still abundant within the Arab and even the Israeli business community. Furthermore, there is still a widespread feeling among large segments of the Arab and Israeli publics that the new status quo that evolved over the last decade will not bring peace and prosperity to the majority of the inhabitants within the Middle East. Thus, although the costs associated with the eruption of a large-scale war have significantly increased, the new political order emerging in the Middle East is still not very suitable for the establishment of large-scale regional development or long-term joint ventures. Under these conditions, an intermediate situation has arisen: While far-reaching liberalization of Arab–Israeli relations is unacceptable, total regulation of these relations is also rejected.

The conflictive nature of Arab–Israeli economic relations might lead one to conclude that Israel should avoid conducting business with its Arab neighbors, and that Arab countries should seek investments and economic cooperation elsewhere. Although such a policy would not ameliorate the disadvantageous position of these countries, it would at least prevent Israel from being considered the villain responsible for their lowly status (Avineri, 1994). Moreover, some scholars contend that open borders between Israel and the Palestinians will in the end be more costly than any economic benefits that may be achieved. According to this argument, allowing free movement of people and commodities across the border will pose problems for Israel in several spheres (Schueftan, 1999). First, as Israel has already experienced, Palestinian terrorists can infiltrate into Israeli cities and murder defenseless civilians. Open borders have also tempted Palestinians to rob their more affluent Israeli neighbors. Besides the risk of criminal and terrorist activities, the porous borders between Israel and its neighbors serve as an easy route for illegal immigrants seeking work in Israel. Many people who cannot obtain a visa into Israel can enter a neighboring Arab country and then slip across the border into Israel. A fourth threat to Israeli society is corruption. Many Israeli businesspersons are willing to cooperate with corrupt Palestinian circles and earn easy profits; a large portion of Israeli money entering the PA is not redistributed among the Palestinian public but ends up in the hands of a few powerful monopolists. Finally, because Israel is viewed as the major exploiter of the Palestinians, it will be expected to invest in their economic development and underwrite their social welfare.

While one cannot ignore the high risks associated with the deterioration of the realist approach, advocates of economic separation underestimate the costs of resisting the forces of interdependence. The major problem is that as much as the Palestinians would probably like to detach themselves from Israel, they have no visible alternative to dependence. Because of the close proximity and low transportation costs, it will still be cheaper to import from Israel. Although Palestinians could turn to Jordanian and Egyptian services and markets, they have discovered that it is more reliable to rely on Israeli infrastructures and markets where they have a competitive advantage in certain sectors such as agriculture and the light industries.

It has been suggested that with proper investment, Jordan could replace Israel as an alternative source of employment and trade for the Palestinians (Schueftan, 1999). As attractive as this proposal sounds, this is wishful thinking. Jordan is teetering on the verge of economic collapse. Like the PA, Jordan is not attractive for foreign investment or as a trading partner. Its economy is small and the costs associated with its non-liberal and monopolistic practices are extremely high. Already facing difficulties in attracting foreign investors and trading partners, Jordan's efforts to limit also the access of Israeli businesses explains in part why it has not benefited from the peace process. As its economy continues to falter Jordan might in the end be obliged to start encouraging business relations with Israel even if this means becoming dependent on the Israeli economy.

The situation confronting Arabs and Jews in the Middle East to some degree resembles the dilemmas that faced western Europe at the end of the Second World War. On the one hand, like the Middle East, Europe was suffering from centuries of ethnic strife and nationalism: on the other hand, driven by domestic economic interests, even the most realist leaders, such as de Gaulle, accepted, however reluctantly, the breakdown of economic barriers (George, 1996: 9–10). While the establishment of economic co-operation was not easy, in the long run, over a period of fifty years, realism failed and problem-solving attitudes prevailed over bargaining strategies.

Despite the success of the western European policy, which is based on liberal–idealist perceptions, there are substantive differences that call into question its relevance for the Middle East region. Unlike the situation among the core member-states of the European Community, the contrasts between Israel and its Arab neighbors, whether economic, political or social, are overwhelming. Thus, although Europe suffered from a history of conflict and violence, there was no fear of one state achieving preeminence. Arab awareness that Israel will be in a more advantageous position in a liberal regime prevents the Middle East from following the European path.

A more relevant comparison than the European experience regarding the position of the PA and Jordan *vis-à-vis* Israel is that of Mexico in its relation to the United States. The United States has been the major country harboring political and economic concerns regarding Mexico's welfare. In addition, in the US–Mexico case there was an attempt, for many years, to maintain a well-guarded border and resist economic integration. But in the end this approach was abandoned. The new agenda, established in the creation of NAFTA, might actually prove to be a more efficient method for reducing illegal immigration into the United States from Mexico. Since many US companies are now tempted to establish plants in Mexico, where it is cheaper, many Mexicans can more easily find employment at home, rather than across the border.

The US–Mexican experience may lead to the conclusion that it is useless to resist the forces that are binding Israel and its Arab neighbors together. Rather than attempting to build a massive wall to stave off the economically less well-to-do Jordanian and Palestinian neighbors, who are suffering from political and social ailments, Israel's alternative strategy might be to share responsibility for their economic welfare. Such an approach requires a strategy that is designed to help shore up their regimes.

Because Jordanians and Palestinians are likely to interpret economic integration as part of an Israeli centralist scheme to subordinate them, what is required is a policy that can accommodate the conflicting perceptions regarding economic integration. Within the broad spectrum of alternatives ranging from total economic integration to total economic separation, it should be possible to devise an international economic regime that can mitigate the tensions that are generated by the structural differences between Israel and its neighbors. This could be accomplished by establishing graduated levels of economic integration. Jordan, Syria, Lebanon and the Palestinians and other Arab states could create an economic regime that excludes Israel, such as the recent Arab Free Trade Zone Agreement (AFTZA) of 1997 (*ArabicNews.Com*, August 1,1998). The AFTZA could be used to negotiate limited economic regimes with other countries, including Israel. An agreement between Israel and the AFTZA would not necessarily be based on a liberal economic agenda, which treats each political entity equally. Probably some economic restrictions should be imposed on the parties involved, especially on the most developed side, Israel.

The concept of an asymmetric economic regime that favors one side over another is not new. Israel benefited from such an arrangement when it signed a free trade agreement with the United States in 1985. Israel persuaded the Americans by emphasizing its disadvantageous position *vis-à-vis* the United States. Its negotiators argued that because the Israeli economy was so small, the competitive advantage that would accrue to Israel would have little effect on the US economy. The Israeli–Jordanian trade agreement followed the same pattern: lower customs were leveled on selected Jordanian goods entering Israel, while relatively high tariffs were applied to Israeli products imported into Jordan (Barr, 1999). However, despite the high customs, many Israeli products are still cheaper and more attractive than similar products produced overseas. Consequently, the Israeli–Jordanian trade balance is still in Israel's favor.

The precedents of the Israeli–US and Israeli–Jordanian trade agreements may set an example for the future Arab–Israeli economic regime. Israel is abandoning light industry such as textiles and shifting its local production to hi-tech and other sophisticated industries – a process that would have occurred irrespective of the peace process. Hence, rather than viewing the Jordanians and Palestinians as competitors against Israeli labor, they should be seen as competitors of other countries outside the Middle East. It follows that Israel has a political interest in preferring Jordanian and Palestinian subcontractors and laborers.

A major question is whether Israel can behave magnanimously and agree to the establishment of an economic regime that favors Arab entrepreneurs. According to the centralist perspective this is unlikely because the more developed centers have a vested interest in maintaining the unequal situation in their favor. If the periphery starts to develop, the commodities it produces will become more expensive and compete with the advanced industries in the center. Thus, from a centralist economic point of view, Israel would be interested in preserving its economic advantage and repressing Arab development. Israeli policy toward the West Bank and the Gaza Strip (WBGS) during the first 25 years of the occupation clearly reflected this approach. However, from a political point of view, Israel has an interest in developing the economies of its neighbors, since this presumably will mitigate the tension between them. Although Israeli generosity entails an economic price, it will in the long run reduce Arab mistrust and suspicion toward Israel.

In any event, Israel's trade policy with its Arab neighbors is not the major problem facing the region's economies. The Arab states must first come to terms with their own internal political problems; it is far from clear whether they can even succeed in instituting an intra-Arab economic regime. Previous attempts to establish some form of Arab economic integration have failed, largely because the Arab world is still entrenched within realist dogma (Moustafa, 1996). Taking into account the inequalities of power and economic prosperity between the Arab parties, it would have made more sense to sustain asymmetric arrangements within the AFTZA too, or have the FTA include only those Arab states with similar levels of economic development.

Because realist and centralist ideals still haunt the Middle East, Israel and its Arab neighbors may prefer to sign separate bilateral trade agreements instead of establishing a broader multilateral order. There are certain advantages, though also disadvantages, in this approach. On the one hand, in the case of bilateral agreements, Israel is more likely to come to terms with Jordanian or Palestinian concerns and accept certain provisions that favor one or both of these political entities. However, serious problems could arise if Israel were to grant one of its Arab neighbors special preferences that are denied to others. An example of this type of reaction was the Israeli decision in the beginning of 2000 to allow Jordanian trucks free passage across the border. Prior to the new policy, merchandise transported between Israel and Jordan, or between Jordan and the PA, had to be transferred from trucks on one side of the border to trucks parked on the other side. Although Israel's neighbors had long resented this practice, which Israel insisted was a necessary security precaution, the Palestinians and Egyptians rejected the new Israeli policy since it was granted only to Jordan (Crystal, 1999), providing its truck drivers an advantage over others.

Even if an asymmetric and balanced economic regime between Israel and one or more of its Arab neighbors can allay Arab fears of economic imperialism, this might still not prove sufficient to resolve Arab–Israeli frictions. Mutual distrust is expected to persist as long as the Arab economies fail to develop and industrialize. Before the Arabs can overcome this feeling of inferiority and the concomitant sense of vulnerability, their economic development will need to achieve parity with Israel, or at least reach a level at which such feelings begin to be overcome.

As in most of the other developing countries, the future of the Arab economies will depend primarily on the internal policies of their governments and on their policies toward one other. Many newly industrialized countries have demonstrated that less developed economies can undergo development, though this is a contingent process, as industry requires foreign investment and should be export oriented. In order to increase their attractiveness the Arab countries will have to go through the same process as Israel, namely to liberalize their economies. However, because economic liberalization entails reduced political control, such an initiative will pose a serious dilemma for countries with authoritarian regimes, where control over the economy serves as a means of political leverage. Furthermore, as the eastern Europe experience demonstrates, even if the leadership has good intentions and is willing to embark on the path of liberalization, the abandonment of tight control and the risks of higher unemployment in the name of efficiency can produce political turmoil.

In the long run, Arab leaders will probably have no choice but to yield to the pressures of liberalization. As unemployment and poverty levels rise, it will be impossible to disregard the public's perception that the state is responsible for relieving their economic duress. Although Arab leaders can try and place the blame on Israel or on other foreign countries, the expansion of the Internet and satellite television is making it increasingly difficult for states to maintain the monopoly over information and to manipulate public opinion. The pressures for liberalization will continue to intensify.

In Jordan, liberalization of the economy at the expense of traditional sectorial interests is readily observable since 'Abdallah was crowned. As a result, it has become much easier for Israeli firms, as well as other foreign companies, to access the Jordanian economy. If 'Abdallah's liberalization policy succeeds, there is a good possibility that long-term Israeli–Jordanian enterprises and joint infrastructure projects will eventually become a reality.

While there is a glimmer of hope in the case of Israeli–Jordanian relations, the future of Israeli–Palestinian relations looks less promising. Anti-liberal practices and high levels of corruption in the PA are scaring off not only Israeli and foreign entrepreneurs, but even Palestinians. Probably the high level of bilateral trade and Palestinian subcontracting for Israeli companies will continue. Still, under such unstable circumstances, the possibility of long-term joint ventures or shared Israeli–Palestinian infrastructures is inconceivable.

The difficulties associated with the Palestinian economy are likely to affect Jordanian–Palestinian relations too. While for many years, the trade balance between the WBGS and Jordan favored the Palestinians, in the mid-1990s this trend was reversed. Newly introduced Palestinian policies that stifle production by raising its costs might encourage entrepreneurs to shift production to Jordan, especially if the Jordanians build industrial parks along the Israeli border. The weak position of the Palestinians will be eroded even further if other Arab countries, such as Syria, seek economic cooperation with Israel. Since Syria's economic structure resembles the PA's and Jordan's, the Palestinian disadvantage will become more pronounced.

As occurred in the case of other less developed countries, it is doubtful that any developed country will be interested in the welfare of the Palestinians. Still, because the PA's social instability will most probably be perceived as a threat to both the Israelis and the Jordanians, both states, even if they pursue centralist or realist practices toward the Palestinians, might reach the conclusion that to prevent the Palestinian economy and political system from collapsing and destabilizing the region, they will be obliged to take upon themselves the responsibility of sustaining the Palestinian economy.

Investment in Peace

Although a comprehensive peace settlement and economic development in the Middle East seem to face almost insurmountable obstacles, this does not necessarily mean that the region will regress back into the old realist mold. Since the costs of maintaining highly centralized and regulated states, where people and information are confined within clearly defined boundaries, have become so high, the gradual development of close economic relations between states in the region, as well as with the rest of the world, will continue at a fast pace. As the Israeli opponents of open borders and close economic relations with Israel's Arab neighbors maintain, this type of political and economic order might be conducive to spreading inter-ethnic violence and terrorist activity. Moreover, this type of environment might also provide large and powerful corporations with numerous opportunities to exploit weaker sectors within the region. However, while the risks are high, the costs of the old realist approach are far higher.

Indeed, the brief history of the relations between Israel and the PA encapsulates the structural dilemmas associated with the Arab–Israeli peace process. The old political order inspired by realist dogma was presumably safer. States expended considerable energy toward developing systems for deterrence and defenses against military or terrorist attacks. Even during periods when the level of Arab–Israeli violence was low, large-scale resources continued to be earmarked for defense and war. Nevertheless, the resolve of all parties to inflict damage on one another meant that even the best defenses were circumvented, and the civilian population suffered from mutual acts of aggression. Under the political agenda of the peace process all sides may be more vulnerable to violence, but the costs of war are much higher. This is not only because states are investing fewer resources on defense, but also because the alternative of not fighting has actually produced genuine benefits.

The realization that the dilemma between war and peace is more acute than in the past is still difficult to comprehend for a generation that has been socialized by realist dogma, but gradually more and more people are adjusting themselves to the new political reality. This may explain why attempts by Arab and Israeli political and religious extremists to derail the peace process have failed to shift the Middle East from its course.

In 1999, despite the continued fighting in South Lebanon, and sporadic acts of Palestinian terrorism in Israel, as well as clashes between Israelis and Palestinians in the West Bank and the Gaza Strip, the aggregate level of Arab–Israeli violence was in fact the lowest in more than a decade. Yet, due to the perceptional gap and to the social, political, and economic gulf between Israel and its Arab neighbors, in the following year the short lull in Arab–Israeli violence collapsed and a new wave of violence erupted.

One way of assuaging political tensions and lowering the level of economic disputes and disagreements might be to narrow the perceptional gap between the parties. Along this line, one might argue that all that is needed for all parties is to "see the light of liberalism." This would bring about a common approach by the parties and enhance patterns of economic cooperation. However, it would require the parties to reinvent themselves by totally erasing their ingrained fears and anxieties.

Still, there is another option. In a world of alternative perceptions, conflicting interests and shifting priorities, *perceptional pluralism* may replace the ordinary pluralistic approach. Concretely, this means negotiating asymmetric arrangements rather than each side insisting on mutual accommodation.

In this respect one may argue that since Israel is very anxious about its security, its Arab neighbors could mitigate those fears and suspicions by providing Israel with security assurances, without imposing similar demands on Israel. And, since Israel's Arab neighbors fear Israeli economic imperialism, Israeli access to their markets should be limited, while Israel allows its neighbors free access to its markets. The existence of an asymmetric security regime may entail a military cost for the Arab partners, but will not overwhelm them; and allowing an asymmetric economic policy will involve an economic cost for Israel but will not overwhelm it. In the long run such a strategy may heighten Arab interests in maintaining good relations with Israel and perhaps allow more Israeli access to their markets, while Israel will be in a position to reduce its military expenditure. Thus, rather than being entrenched in symmetric security and economic regimes, the political stability of the Middle East requires the encouragement of institutional mechanisms that can accommodate perceptional contradictions without succumbing to them.

The concept of perceptional plurality might seem a fantastic idea. Why should someone agree to be a member of a regime that puts the others in a more advantageous position? This type of behavior is irrational if we assume that the states that are in conflict with each other adhere to realist or centralist perspectives of reality. According to these perspectives the status quo that emerges between actors reflects the relative strength of one in relation to the other. Stronger actors frequently enforce asymmetric arrangements in their favor, and the weaker parties accept their derogatory status until the balance of power changes. This interpretation of world order is based on the assumption that all members of the international community share the same perceptions regarding the priority of security. But what if security has a different meaning for the parties involved or if security is not necessarily the highest priority of all parties? This is the case of Arab–Israeli relations. Each party has a different perception of the concept of security. While the Israelis are mainly concerned with the strategic–realist aspects, the Arabs are more concerned with the economic and internal political aspects. Thus each party can satisfy its most basic needs for security precisely by adhering to its own interpretation of security.

A perceptional pluralistic settlement is possible when there are alternative interpretations of interests, such as the case described above, where security priorities are not overlapping. This, however, is not always plausible. For example, in the case of the territorial dispute between the Israelis and Palestinians, and especially the status of Jerusalem, the concept of perceptional pluralism is invalid. This is because overlapping spiritual aspirations rather than alternative security concerns inspire this issue. Therefore the negotiations over territory will require compromising the degree of authority granted to each party over this area. Reaching compromise will most likely be accompanied with all the negative aspects of bargaining.

Even when there exists a situation where priorities are not overlapping, negotiations can take the course of a bargaining match rather than problem-solving. This occurs when each issue is discussed separately. Then, like in the case of the territorial dispute, a compromise is sought over the division of a single value among two or more parties. Since each party attempts to maximize its advantages in relation to this single value, the negotiation regresses toward aggressive bargaining tactics.

The tendency of Arab and Israeli negotiators to discuss military and economic issues on separate tables in different locations has in fact impeded the ability of the discussants to reach a mutually functional settlement. Even if the negotiators produce symmetric security and economic agreements, both parties will be dissatisfied. The Israelis might feel that they have compromised their military security, while the Arabs might feel they have compromised their economic security. Therefore, what is required instead is a simultaneous negotiation over all issues rather than a sequential addressing of each topic. If all issues are discussed concurrently on one table, as part of a larger and more total settlement, then both sides could agree on the creation of asymmetric packages as part of a final peace agreement. In this case each party would compromise certain interests in return for advantages granted on another issue. This would allow each party to receive benefits where they really count.

Bibliography

Books, Articles and Manuscripts

King 'Abdallah Ibn Husayn. 1951. *Memoirs.* Amman (Arabic).

Abidi, Aqil. 1965. *Jordan, A Political Study 1948–1957.* New York: Asia Publishing House.

Alger, Chadwick F. 1977. "'Foreign' policies of US publics." *International Studies Quarterly* 21(2): 277–83.

Allison, Graham T. 1971. *Essence of Decision: Explaining the Cuban Missile Crisis.* Boston: Little, Brown and Company.

Amnesty International. 1999. *Annual Report on Palestinian Authority.*

——. December, 1996. *Palestinian Authority: Prolonged political detention, torture, and unfair trials.*

Anderson, Betty. 1997. "Liberalization in Jordan in the 1950s and 1990s: similarities or differences?" *Jordanies* (December 1997), pp. 207–17.

Arad, Ruth W. and Seev Hirsch. 1981. "Peacemaking and vested interests: International economic transactions." *International Studies Quarterly* 24(3): 349–468.

Aref al-'Aref, *Al-Nakba* (The Disaster) (Beirut: undated).

Arian, Asher. 1985. *Politics in Israel.* Chatham, NJ: Chatham House.

——. 1973. *The Choosing People.* Ramat Gan: Masada.

Arnon, A. and A. Spivak. April, 1998. "Economic aspects of the Oslo peace process." Ben-Gurion University, unpublished paper.

Art, Robert J. 1973. "Bureaucratic politics and American foreign policy: A critique." *Policy Sciences* 4: 467–90.

Augé, Jean-Chrisophe. 1997. "Privatization in Jordan: An assessment." *Jordanies* (December 1997), pp. 131–47.

Avineri, Shlomo. 1994. "Sidestepping dependency." *Foreign Affairs* 73: 12–15.

Awartani, Hisham. 1997. "Palestinian-Jordanian agricultural relations: Constraints and prospects." Center for Palestine Research and Studies.

——. 1991. "The future of Palestinian and Israeli economic relations." Israel-Palestinian Peace Research Project 2. Jerusalem: Arab Studies Society.

Axelrod, Robert and Robert O. Koehane. 1983. "Achieving cooperation under

---

152

anarchy: Strategies and institutions." In *Cooperation Under Anarchy*. Edited by K. A. Oye. Princeton, NJ: Princeton University Press, pp. 226–54.

Azar, Edward, Paul Juriedini and Ronald McLaurin. 1978. "Protracted Social Conflict: Theory and Practice in the Middle East." *Journal of Palestine Studies* 8: 41–60.

Barbieri, Katherin. 1996. "Economic interdependence: A path to peace or a source of international conflict?" *Journal of Peace Research* 33(1): 29–49.

Barham, Nassim. 1997. "Industrialization in Jordan." *Jordanies* (December), pp. 195–206.

Beamish, John W. 1988. *Multinational Joint Ventures in Developing Countries*. London and New York, Routledge.

Ben-Gurion, David. *Diary*. Sde Boker: Ben-Gurion Archive.

Ben Porath, Yoram. 1989. "Nuances and disparities in the population and the labor force." In *The Israeli Economy – Maturing through Crises* (Hebrew). Edited by Y. Ben Porath. Tel Aviv: Am Oved.

Ben Shahar, Haim, *et al.* 1989. *Economic Cooperation and Middle East Peace*. London: Weidenfeld and Nicolson.

Ben Zvi, Shmuel. 1993. *Jordan's Economy* (Hebrew). Tel Aviv University: The Armend Hammer Endowment for Economic Cooperation in the Middle East.

Benvenisti, Meron. 1986. *1986 Report: Demographics, Economic, Legal, Social and Political Development in the West Bank*. Jerusalem: West Bank Database Project.

Bergles, Arik. 1989. "The burden of defense and the Israeli economy." In *The Israeli Economy – Maturing through Crises* (Hebrew). Edited by Y. Ben Porath. Tel Aviv: Am Oved.

Biehl, David. 1991. "The role of infrastructure in regional development." In *Infrastructure and Regional Development*. Edited by R. H. Vickerman. London: Prion, pp. 9–35.

Boulding, Kenneth E. 1975. "Twenty-five theses on peace and trade." *Collected Papers*, Vol. V. Boulder, CO: Colorado Associated University Press, pp. 25–7.

Cady, Duncan L. 1989. *From Warism to Pacifism: A Moral Continuum*. Philadelphia: Temple University Press.

Carr, E. H. 1939. *The Twenty Years' Crisis, 1919–1939*. London and Basingstoke: St. Martin's Press and Macmillan.

CIA (Central Intelligence Agency). 1997. *The World Fact Book*.

Clark, Grenville and Louis B. Sohn. 1966. *World Peace Through World Law*. Cambridge, MA: Harvard University Press.

Claude, Inis L., Jr. 1962. *Power and International Relations*. Random House, Inc.

Cohen, Amnon. 1982. *Political Parties in the West Bank under the Jordanian Regime, 1949–1967*. Ithaca: Cornell University Press.

Cohen, Ohad. 1998. *Qualifying Industrial Zone*. Ministry of Industry and Trade, Division of Middle East and North Africa.

Dann, Uriel. 1984. *Studies in the History of Transjordan, 1920–1949*. Boulder, CO: Westview Press.

David Boas Ltd. May 1998. Unpublished memo. Ramat Gan.

Bibliography

——. 1996. *Economic Cooperation Israel – Jordan – Palestinian Authority*. Ramat Gan.

Dos Santos, Theotonio. 1970. "The Structure of Dependence," *American Economic Review* 60: 231–6.

Easton, David. 1965. *A Framework for Political Analysis*. Englewood Cliffs, NJ: Prentice-Hall.

EIU (The Economist Intelligence Unit). 1998. *Jordan Country Profile*.

——. 1997. *Israel and Occupied Territories Country Profile*.

EuroAirport. 1999. *About Us*.
http://www.euroairport.com/web/euroairport.nsf/$$pages/infonews_fr_index.htm

Evron, Yair. 1987. *War and Intervention in Lebanon: The Israeli-Syrian Deterrence Dialogue*. Washington D.C.: Johns Hopkins University Press.

Federation of Israeli Chambers of Commerce (FICC). July 18, 1998. *Obstacles in the Trade Relations between Israel and the Palestinians*. Unpublished report.

Feiler, Gil. 1993. "Palestinian employment prospects." *Middle East Journal* 47: 633–51.

Feiler, Gil, *et al.* 1993. *Labor Force and Employment in Egypt, Syria & Jordan*. Tel Aviv: Histadrut-General Federation of Labor in Israel.

Findlay, Allan M. 1994. *The Arab World*. London and New York: Routledge.

Fischer, Stanley and Leonard J. Hausman (eds.). September, 1994. *Near East Economic Progress Report*. The Institute for Social and Economic Policy in the Middle East. John F. Kennedy School of Government.

Fletcher, Elaine. March 1994. "New realities, old fears." *LINK Magazine*.

Frank, André Gundar. 1966. "The development of underdevelopment." *Monthly Review* 18: 17–31.

Freenstra, Robert C. and Gordon H. Hanson. 1996. "Globalization, outsourcing, and wage inequality." *American Economic Review* 86(2): 240–5.

Gabbay, Yosef. 1979. "The fiscal policy of Israel, 1948–1978." In *Israel – A Developing Society*. Edited by A. Arian. Tel Aviv: Zmora, Bitan, Modan – Publishers, pp. 305–24.

Gazit, Shlomo. 1985. *The Stick and the Carrot*. Tel Aviv: Zmora, Bitan – Publishers (Hebrew).

George, Stephan. 1996. *Politics and Policy in the European Union*, Third Edition. Oxford and New York: Oxford University Press.

Gharaibeh, A. Fawzi. 1985. *The Economies of the West Bank and Gaza Strip*. Boulder and London: Westview Press.

Gilpin, Robert. 1981. *War and Change in World Politics*. Cambridge: Cambridge University Press.

——. 1975. "Three models of the future." *International Organization* 29(1): 37–60.

Government of Israel. November, 1997. *Partnerships in Development 1998*.

Gultung, Johan. 1971. "A structural theory of imperialism." *Journal of Peace Research* 7: 81–117.

Haider, Aziz. 1995. *On the Margins: The Arab Population in the Israeli Economy*. New York: St. Martin's Press.

Bibliography

Hamarneh, Musstafa. 1997. "The opposition and its role in the peace process – a Jordanian view." *Palestine, Jordan, Israel: Building a Base for Common Scholarship and Understanding in the Area of the Middle East.* Jerusalem: PASSIA, pp. 49–55.

Hanrieder, Wolfram F. 1978. "Dissolving International Politics: Reflections on the Nation State." *American Review of Political Science* 72(4): 1278–87.

Hashai, Niron. 1993. *Business Cooperation during Peace between Firms in Israel and Firms in Arab Countries in the Textile and Clothing Sector.* Unpublished MA thesis, Tel Aviv University (Hebrew).

Heckscher, Eli F. and Bentil Ohlin. 1991. *Heckscher–Ohlin Trade Theory.* Cambridge, MA: The MIT Press.

Heiberg, Marianne and Geir Ovensen. 1994. *Palestinian Society in Gaza, West Bank and Arab Jerusalem: A Survey of Living Conditions.* Oslo, FAFO–report 151.

High Court of Justice. September 6, 1999. *Public Committee Against Torture in Israel vs. State of Israel.*

Hirschman, Albert O. 1967. *Development Projects Observed.* Washington, D.C.: Brookings Institution.

Hobbes, Thomas. *Leviathan.*

Huntington, Samuel Phillips. 1968. *Political Order in Changing Societies.* New Haven: Yale University Press.

Huri, Rami J. Aug 30, 1999. "The Privatization Train has Embarked." *Ha'aretz.*

Hymer, Stephan. 1972. "The Multinational Corporation and the Law of Uneven Development." In *Economics and World Order.* Edited by J. H. Bhagwati. London: Collier-Macmillan.

Institute for Social and Economic Policy in the Middle East. 1994. *Securing Peace in the Middle East: Project on Economic Transition.* Cambridge, MA, John F. Kennedy School of Government, Harvard University.

Israel Foreign Ministry. March 10, 1998. Joint Statement of the Crown Prince of the Hashemite Kingdom of Jordan Prince El Hassan Bin Talal and the Prime Minister of Israel, Mr. Benjamin Netanyahu. http://www.israel.org/peace/pmhassan.html

Jaber, Hana'. 1997. "The Impact of Structural Adjustment on Women's Employment and Urban Households." *Jordanies* (December), pp. 149–66.

Jordan Industrial Estates Corporation. 1998. http://www.jiec.com/

Jordan Information Bureau. 2000. *Government and Politics.*

———. October, 1997. *Jordan's Peace-Making Efforts Attempt to Promote Bilateral Gains to Offset Regional Tensions.*

Kanovsky, Eliyahu. 1997. "The Middle East Economies." *MERIA* 1(2).

Kant, Immanuel. 1983. *Perpetual Peace and Other Essays on Politics, History, and Morals.* Indianapolis: Hackett Pub. Co.

Keohane, Robert O. and Joseph S. Nye. 1977. *Power and Interdependence.* Boston: Little, Brown.

Khader, Bichara, and Badran Adnan (eds.). 1987. *The Economic Development of Jordan.* London: Croom Helm.

Khalidi, Suleiman. 1994. "Jordanian-Palestinian capital and investment in the West

Bank," *Peace Media 1994: Economic Dimensions of the Middle East Peace Process.* Economist Intelligence Unit. Chapter 6.

Khatib, Nabil. 1994. "Private-sector investment in the West Bank and Gaza Strip: obstacles and opportunities." *Peace Media 1994: Economic Dimensions of the Middle East Peace Process.* Economist Intelligence Unit. Chapter 5.

Kimche, Jon and David Kimche. 1973. *Both Sides of the Hill,* 2nd edition. Tel Aviv: Ma'arakhot (Hebrew).

Klienman, Ephraim. 1998. "Is there a secret Arab–Israeli trade?" *Palestine Economic Pulse.* http://www.palecon.org/pulsedir/jul98/feature.html

Lawrence, Robert Z. 1995. *Towards Free Trade in the Middle East: The Triad and Beyond.* Cambridge, MA, Report by a Team of Israeli, Jordanian and Palestinian Experts, Kennedy School of Government.

———. 1994. "Trade, multinationals, and labor." National Bureau of Economic Research Working Paper: 4836.

Lee, Eddy. 1996. "Globalization and employment: Is anxiety justified?" *International Labor Review* 135(5): 485–97.

Lerner, Daniel. 1958. *The Passing of Traditional Society.* New York: The Free Press.

Lewis, Bernard. 1992. "Rethinking the Middle East." *Foreign Affairs* 71: 99–119.

Libiszewski, Stephan. August 1995. "Water disputes in the Jordan basin region and their role in the resolution of the Arab–Israeli Conflict." ENCOP Occasional Paper No. 13, Center for Security Policy and Conflict Research/Swiss Peace Foundation. Zurich/ Berne. http://www.fsk.ethz.ch/encop/13/en13.htm

Lin, Xiaohua and Richard Germain. 1998. "Sustaining satisfactory joint venture relationships: The role of conflict resolution." *Journal of International Business Studies* 27(1): 179–96.

LINK Magazine. September 1995. "Airport Problems I."

Litani, Yehuda. January–February, 1996. "Doing business, the Palestinian way." *LINK Magazine.*

Luciani, Giacomo. 1990. "Allocation vs. production state: A theoretical framework." In *The Arab State.* Edited by G. Luciani. London: Routledge.

Malik, Mueti. 1999. "Elites bargains and the onset of political liberalization in Jordan." *Comparative Political Studies* 32(1): 100–29.

Maltz, Judy. 1994. "Ending 27 years of one-sided trade: implications of the Israeli–Palestinian economic protocol." PEACE-MEDIA 1994: *Economic Dimensions of the Middle East Peace Process.* Economist Intelligence Unit.

Mansfield, Edwin. 1994. *Power, Trade and War.* Princeton, NJ: Princeton University Press.

Ma'oz, Moshe. 1984. *Palestinian Leadership on the West Bank.* London: Frank Cass.

Mersheimer, John J. 1990. "Back to the future: Instability in Europe after the Cold War." *International Security* 15: 5–56.

Metzer, Yaacov. 1989. "Slowdown of the economic growth in Israel." In *The Israeli Economy – Maturing through Crises.* Edited by Y. Ben Porath. Tel Aviv: Am Oved (Hebrew), pp. 74–107.

Miller, Stacey and Oded Shlomot. 1997. "The ties that bind." *LINK Magazine*.

Mishal, Shaul. 1978. *West Bank/East Bank, The Palestinians in Jordan, 1949–1967.* New Haven: Yale University Press.

Mishal, Shaul and Reuven Aharoni. 1994. *Speaking Stones: Communiques from the Intifada Underground.* Syracuse, NY: Syracuse University Press.

Morgenthau, Hans J. 1950. "Another 'Great Debate': The National Interest of the US." *American Political Science Review* 46(4): 971–8.

Morosini, Piero, *et al.* 1998. "National cultural distance and cross-border acquisition performance." *Journal of International Business Studies* 29(1): 137–58.

Moustafa, Moustafa Ahmed. 1996. *The Political Economy of the Peace Process in a Changing Middle East.* Helsinki: UNU World Institute for Development Economics Research (UNU/WIDER).

Mulenex, Elana. 1999. *Investment Led Export Opportunities (Israel, Jordan), Industry Sector Analysis*, U.S. Department of Commerce.

Myrdal, Gunner. 1956. *Development and Underdevelopment.* Cairo: National Bank of Egypt Fiftieth Anniversary Commemoration Lectures.

Nachmias, David, *et al.* 1996. *Preliminary Document: Regional Cooperation between Israel and Jordan – The Joint Airport of the South Arava Region.* Tel Aviv University, unpublished document (Hebrew).

Naor, Aryeh. 1986. *Government at War: The Role of the Israeli Government During the War in Lebanon (1982).* Tel Aviv: Lahav (Hebrew).

Nevo, Joseph. 1975. *'Abdallah and the Arabs of Palestine.* Tel Aviv: Tel Aviv University, Shiloah Center.

O'Brien, D. P. 1975. *The Classical Economists.* Oxford: Clarendon Press.

O' Neal, John, *et al.* 1996. "The liberal peace: interdependence, democracy, and international conflict, 1950–85." *Journal of Peace Research* 33(1): 11–28.

Owens, Edgar and Robert Shaw. 1972. *Development Reconsidered.* Toronto and London: Lexington Books.

Palestinian Trade Center. 1999. *Export–Import Procedures.*
http://www.paltrade.org

Pianet. 1998. "Palestinian economy." *Palestine: The Promising Land.*
http://www.palnet.com/archive/inv/iiieco.htm

Peri, Smadar. January 16, 1998. "The underwear of peace." *Yedioth Ahronot 7 Days Magazine*.

Perlmutter, Amos. 1974. "The presidential political center and foreign policy: A critique of the revisionist and bureaucratic-political orientations." *World Politics* 27: 87–106.

Polachek, Solomon William. 1980. "Conflict and Trade." *Journal of Conflict Resolution* 24: 55–74.

Portugali, Yuval. 1996. *Contained Relations.* Tel Aviv: Am Oved (Hebrew).

Razin, Assaf and Efraim Sadka. 1993. *The Economy of Modern Israel: Malaise and Promise.* Chicago, IL: University of Chicago Press.

Reuveny, Rafael and Heejoon Kang. 1996. "International trade, political conflict/cooperation, and Granger causality." *American Journal of Political Science* 40(3): 943–70.

Bibliography

Richards, Alan and John Waterbury. 1990. *Political Economy of the Middle East: State, Class, and Economic Development*. Boulder, CO: Westview Press.

Roy, Sara. 1996. "Economic deterioration in the Gaza Strip." *MERIP* 26. http://www.merip.org/mer/mer200/roy.htm

Safran, Nadav. 1969. *From War to War*. New York: Pegasus.

Sagea, Eli, *et al.* 1992. *The Palestinian Economy and its Dependence on the Israeli Economy*. Tel Aviv: Pinhas Sapir Center for Development.

Said Ahmed, Mojammed. 1976. *When the Canons Silence*. Tel Aviv: Am Oved (Hebrew).

Schiff, Zeev, and Ehud Ya'ari. 1990. *Intifada*, Tel Aviv: Schoken Publishing (Hebrew).

——. 1984. *Israel's Lebanon War*. New York: Simon and Schuster.

Schueftan, Dan. 1999. *Disengagement: Israel and the Palestinian Entity*. Tel Aviv: Zmora-Bitan Publishers & Haifa University Press.

Sela, Michal. February, 1995. "Hanging on in Hebron." *LINK*.

Shihadah, Aziz. 1970. "The Purposes of the Jordanian Legislation in the West Bank." *Ha-Mizrah he-Hadash* 20.

Shikaki, Khalil. 1998. "Palestinian Public Opinion, the Peace Process and Political Violence," *MERIA* 2(1).

Sobelman, Daniel. October 28, 1998. "Four years of disappointment." *Ha'aretz* (Hebrew).

Spechler, Martin. 1979. "Israel's achievements at the end of thirty years: comparative perspectives." In *Israel – A Developing Society*. Edited by A. Arian. Tel Aviv: Zmora, Bitan, Modan – Publishers, pp. 333–54 (Hebrew).

Sprout, Harold and Margaret Sprout. 1971. *Towards Politics of the Planet Earth*. New York: Van Nostrand.

State of Israel. 1997. Partnership in Development. http://www.israel.org/

Tal, Nahman. 1999. *Domestic Conflict: Egyptian and Jordanian Confrontation with Extreme Islamists*. Tel Aviv: Papirus, Tel Aviv University (Hebrew).

al-Tall, 'Abdallah. 1964. *Memoirs*. Tel Aviv: Maarakhot (Hebrew).

The World Bank. 1993a. *Developing the Occupied Territories: An Investment in Peace*. Washington DC.

Truman, David B. 1951. *The Governmental Process*. New York: Alfred A. Knopf.

Tuma, Elias H. 1991. "Industrialization in the occupied territories." Jerusalem: Israeli-Palestinian Research Project.

United Nations. 1951. *Assistance to Palestine Refugees: Interim Report of the Director of the United Nations Relief and Works Agency for Palestine Refugees in the Near East*. New York: General Assembly, Office Records, Fifth Session Supplement No. 19 (A/1451/Rev.1).

——. 1949. *Yearbook of the United Nations*, 1949, New York: United Nations Dept. of Public Information.

United Nations Special Co-ordinator (UNSCO). 1999. *Report on the Palestinian Economy*.

US & Foreign Commercial Service and U.S. Department of State. 1998. *FY 1999 Country Commercial Guide*.

Walker, Francis A. June 1896. "Restriction of immigration." *The Atlantic Monthly* 77(464): 822–9.

Wallerstien, Immanuel. 1974. "The rise and future demise of the world capitalist system." *Comparative Studies in Society and History* 16(4): 387–414.

Waltz, Kenneth N. 1979. *Theory of International Relations.* Reading, MA: Addison-Wesley.

Weisskopf, Thomas E. 1972. "Capitalism, Underdevelopment and the Future of the Poor Countries." In *Economics and World Order.* Edited by J. H. Bhagwati. London: Collier-Macmillan.

World Bank. 1995. *Atlas.* Washington, D.C. and Oxford: Oxford University Press.

——. 1993a. *Developing the Occupied Territories: An Investment in Peace. Volume I: Overview.* Washington, D.C.

——. 1993b. *Developing the Occupied Territories: An Investment in Peace. Volume III: Private sector development.* Washington, D.C.

News Services

Akhbar.Com

Al-Hayat (Beirut)

ArabicNews.Com

Federation of Israeli Chambers of Commerce (FICC) Newsletter

Filastin al-Thawra (Beirut)

Globes (Tel Aviv)

Ha'aretz (Tel Aviv)

Israel Export Institute

Israel Foreign Ministry Economic Survey

Israel Foreign Ministry Newsline

Issues (Jordan)

Jordan Economic Monitor

Jordan Times

TechWeb News. http://Techweb.com/wire

The Jerusalem Post

The Star (Jordan)

Interviews and Lectures

Barr, Gabi. July–August, 1999. Ministry of Industry and Trade, Interviews.

——. April 1999. Lecture at Forum for Arab–Israeli Trade. Tel Aviv.

Catrivas, Danny. August 1999. Ministry of Finance, Interview.

Crystal, Moti. July–August, 1999. Ministry of Defense, Interviews.

Dekel, Gili. August–September, 1999. Director of Jordan Gateway Project, Interviews.

Golan, Gabi. August, 1999. Prime Minister's Office, Interview.

Klienman, Ephraim. 1998. Comment during discussion in a workshop at Ben-Gurion University, Beer Sheva.

Bibliography

Lautman, Dov. May 9, 1998. Lecture at Tel Aviv University, Tammy Steinmetz Center for Peace Research.

Mansour, Antoine. July 3, 1997. "Subcontracting Arrangements between Israeli and Palestinian Firms," lecture at MAS.

Nasr, Mohamed. August 28, 1997. "The impact of the peace process on the textile and garment industry in Palestine," lecture at MAS.

Pines, Offir. February 16, 1998. Chairperson of Knesset Special Committee Relating to Foreign Workers, Interview to Galei Zahal Radio Station.

Press, J. June 25, 1998. "The state of the industrial zones," lecture in a conference on the Palestinian Economy after the Paris Protocol at Ben-Gurion University in Beer Sheva.

Statistical Data

CBS (Central Bureau of Statistics). 1997. *Statistical Abstract of Israel* 48.

Eurostat. 1996. *Basic Statistics.*

IPR (Info-Prod Research). 1998. Unpublished data regarding Jordan's economy. Ramat Gan, Israel.

JCSS (Jaffee Center for Strategic Studies). 1998. Quantitative Analysis of the Israeli-Arab Conflict and the Israeli-Arab Peace Process, 1948–1997. Electronic Data Set.

PCBS (Palestinian Bureau of Statistics). http://www.pcbs.org/inside/selcts.htm

Index

Page numbers in bold type indicate a main or detailed reference. Arabic names beginning with al- are filed under the letter following the hyphen. References beginning with a numeral are filed as if spelt out in words.

'Abdallah I, king of Jordan, 28, 29, 53, 54, 55
'Abdallah II, king of Jordan, 29–30, 148
Abidi, Aqil, 52
Achsaf, Hanan, 114
agriculture, 31, 38, 39
    trade in produce, 43, 49, 75, 76, 78, 80, 83, 90, 144
Aharoni, Reuven, 43
airport development, Eilat–Aqaba, 122–7
Akhbar.Com, 90
al-Bira, 63, 64
Al-Hassan free trade zone, 102, 103, 111, 112
al-Madina, 64
Al Raj, 106
Albemarle Holdings, 108, 109
Alger, Chadwick F., 13
All-Palestine Government, 52
Allison, Graham T., 12, 136
America *see* United States
Amnesty International, 35
'Anabta, 63
Anderson, Betty, 28
Aqaba, 89, 112
airport development, 122–7
Arab Free Trade Zone Agreement (AFTZA), 145, 146
Arab–Israeli conflict, 47–51
    1948 war, 28–9, 36, 53–4, 119
    1967 (Six Day) war, 21, 31, 66
    1973 (October) war, 25, 31, **50**, 51
    1982 invasion of Lebanon, **50–1**, 64
    1996 Operation Grapes of Wrath, 107
Arab League, 52, 69
Arab Legion, 29, 52, 119

Arab Potash Corporation (APC), 107, 108
ArabicNews.Com, 83, 85, 111, 124, 145
Arabs, **141–3**, 144, 146, **147–8**
    boycott of Israel, 26, **48–9**, 69, 138, 139
    Israel and, 22–3, 141, 143, **145–7**
Arad, Ruth W., 69
Arafat, Yasser, 46, 58
Aref al-'Aref, 52, 53
Arian, Asher, 20
arms trade, 25, 49, 50
Arnon, A., 77
Assyra Dairy, 105–6
Augé, Jean-Chrisophe, 31
Avineri, Shlomo, 143
Awartani, Hisham, 42, 43, 90
Axelrod, Robert, 4
Azar, 139

balance of payments, 25, 26, 33, 87–8
balance of power, 6–7, 50, 139
balance of trade, 25, 30, 91
banking, 45, 90
Barbieri, Katherin, 3
bargaining approach 14, 15, 17, 68
    strategies, 100–2
Barham, Nassim, 29
Barr, Gabi, 132
    on joint ventures, 109, 111, 112, 116
    on trade, 78, 88, 89, 91, 146
Basic Law of Freedom of Occupation, 21
Basic Law of Human Dignity and Liberty, 21
Ba'th party, 52
Beamish, John W., 10, 100
Bedouin, 29
Begin, Menachem, 64

161

Index

Beit Jala, 63
Ben-Gurion, David, 21
Ben Porath, Yoram, 25
Ben Shahar, Haim, 15
Ben Zvi, Shmuel, 31, 32, 33
Bental, Eden, 115, 116
Benvenisti, Meron, 41
Bergles, Arik, 25
Biehl, David, 119
Bir Zeit University, 64
Boas, David, 42, 74, 100, 120
Border Environment Cooperation
    Commission (BECC), 129
Border Industrial Program, 127–8
Boulding, Kenneth E., 71
Britain, British, 28, 31
British Mandate, 20, 53
bromine production, 107–9
Brown, Hank, 128
bureaucratic politics model, 136

Cady, Ducan L., 8
Canada, 75–6
capital-intensive industries, 71–2
Carmiel, 104, 115
Carr, E. H., 7
Catrivas, Danny, 88, 103, 130
Central Bureau of Statistics (CBS), 25, 37,
    41, 44, 46n2, 85, 89
centralism, 9–10, 11, 12, 13, 14, 97, 150–1
    Middle East and, 66–7, 68, 88, 126, 143,
    146
    trade and, 15, 16, 70, 73, 88
Century Wear hosiery factory, 102–5, 106
Channel 2 News in Israel, 35
CIA World Fact Book, 35, 37
Clark, Grenville, 8
Clinton, Bill, 87, 132
Coca-Cola company, 114–15
Cohen, Amnon, 52
Cold War, 1, 51, 96
common markets, 69–71
competitive relations, 13–14, 16, 17
computer software industry, 109–10,
    115–16
conflictive relations, 3, 13, 14
construction industry, 39, 44–5
cooperative relations, 3, 4–5, 14, 15–16,
    100–2
corruption, 45, 84–5, 113–14, 143
cost-benefit approach, 3–4
costs of dissociation, 15, 17, 135
Crystal, Moti, 134, 147
customs unions, 71, 73–4, 87

Da'mas, Wadi', 53
Dann, Uriel, 28
Dawud, Bishara, 63
Dayan, Moshe, 63, 64
Dead Sea Bromine (DSB), 107, 108, 109
Declaration of Principles (DoP), 1, 65, 115,
    141
    economic relations and, 18, 44, 77, 87, 89,
    138
defense budgets, 50, 142, 149
Dekel, Gil, 128, 129, 130, 134, 135
Delta-Galil textile company, 103, 105, 106
democracy, 8, 11
dependency, ix, 2, 3, 97
development towns, 21
diamond industry, 25
discrimination, 22–3, 77
Dor Energy, 84–5
Dos Santos, Theotonio, 97

East Bank, 29, 54, 55
Economic Conference for the Middle East
    and North African States,
    First, 130
    Fourth, 111
economic relations, ix–x, 15–17, 138–51
    Israeli–Jordanian, 67, 87–9
    Israeli–Palestinian, 18, 67, 77–87
    Jordanian–Palestinian, 89–91
    peace process and, ix, 65–8
Economist Intelligence Unit (EIU), 34, 44,
    45, 46n1
economy
    Israel, 21, 23–7
    Jordan, 29, 30–4
    Palestinian Authority, 35, 36–46
Egypt, 36, 49, 104, 132, 135
    Israel and, 50, 141, 147
    trade, 43, 79, 90, 91, 147
Eilat–Aqaba airport development, 122–7
El Al airline, 125
electricity consumption, 32, 36
environment, 120, 123, 128–30, 132, 135
Erez industrial park, 131, 132
EuroAirport, 123, 126
European Union (EU), 75, 144
    Middle East and, 34, 45, 74, 87, 111, 113,
    114
Eurostat, 37
Evron, 50
exports, 100
    Israel, 24, 25
    Jordan, 30, 32–3, 34
    Palestinian Authority, 42–3, 44, 80

Index

Faisal, king of Iraq, 28
Fakhoury, Tawfik, 133
Fatah Organization, 56
Federation of Israeli Chambers of
  Commerce (FICC), 83, 114
Feiler, Gil, 33, 37
Filastin al-Thawra, 58
finance, 45, 120
Findlay, Allan M., 38
Fischer, Stanley, 44
Fletcher, Elaine, 75, 90
foreign aid, 31, 32, 45
foreign investment, ix, 45, 49, 96, 98, 99,
  102, 103, 144
foreign labor, 23
foreign policy, 136
foreign workers, 23, 29, 66
France, 123
Frank, André Gundar, 10
free trade areas (FTAs), **74–6**, 87, 110–11,
  113
  AFTZA, 145, 146
  Jordanian–Palestinian, 89–91
  NAFTA, 128–9
free trade debate, 69–73
  Middle East and, 73–6
Freenstra, Robert C., 72
frontier settlements, 21

Gabbay, Yosef, 25
Gaulle, Charles de, xi, 144
Gaza Industrial Estate (GIE), **131–3**,
  136
Gaza Strip *see* West Bank and Gaza Strip
Gazit, Shlomo, 61, 81
General Agreement on Tariffs and Trade
  (GATT), 76
Geneva Conference, 51
George, Stephan, 144
Germain, Richard, 98
Germans, 133
Gharaibeh, A. Fawzi, 41
Gilpin, Robert, 7, 11
Globes, 22, 46
  on infrastructure projects, 124, 132, 134
  on joint ventures, 104, 105, 106, 107, 108,
    109, 111, 112, 114, 115
  on trade, 69, 83, 84, 85, 88, 89, 92
Golan, Gabi, 125, 126
Grapes of Wrath operation, 107
Green Line, 76, 80–1, 82
gross domestic product (GDP), 3
  Israel, 23, 24, 26, 27, 38
  Jordan, 23, 24, 30, 31, 32, 33, 34, 38

Palestinian Authority, 23–4, 35, 37, 38,
  39, 43, 44, 45, 46n1, 86
gross national product (GNP),
  Israel, 25, 26
  Jordan, 30–1, 32, 33
  Palestinian Authority, 36, 39
Gulf War, 1, 33, 44, **51**, 82
Gultung, Johan, 10

Ha'aretz, 84, 85
Haifa, 48, 89, 112
Halhul, 61, 63
Hamarneh, Musstafa, 29
Hamas, 78, 85, 105
Hamdallah, Wahid, 63
Hanrieder, Wolfram F., 140
Hanson, Gordon H., 72
Hanan, Hilmi, 63
hard infrastructures, 120
Harish, Micha, 130
al-Hasan, Hani, 58
Hashai, Niron, 99
Hashemite dynasty, 28, 55
Hashemite Kingdom *see* Jordan
Hassan, Prince, 87, 111
Hausman, Leonard J., 44
health, 32, 35, 36, 37, 46n2
Hebron, 61, 63, 64
Heiberg, Marianne, 22, 46n2
Hekscher-Ohlin theorem, 71
Hi-Tek Engineering, 115, 116
hierarchical social order, 12, 13
High Court of Justice, Israel, 21
Hirsch, Seev, 69
Hirschman, Albert O., 11
Hobbes, Thomas, 12
human rights, 20–1, 35, 139, 141
Huntington, Samuel Phillips, 11
Hussein, king of Hijaz, 28
Hussein, king of Jordan, 29, 33, 64
Hymer, Stephen, 97

idealism, **7–9**, 12–13, 14, 144
  Middle East and, 48, 49, 68
illegal employment, 40–1
immigration, 21–2, 26, 31, 43
imports, 24–5, 30, 42, 44
industrial parks, **130–1**, 148
  Gaza Industrial Estate, **131–3**, 136
  Jordan Gateway Project, **127–30**, 132,
    134, 137n1
  West Bank, 133–5
industry, 100–1
  Israel, 24–5

Index

Jordan, 24, 30, 31, 32, 34
  Palestinian Authority, **37–8**, 43–4
  see also individual industries
infant mortality rate (IMR), 35, 36–7, 46n2
Info-Prod Research (IPR), 34, 38
information systems, 5
infrastructure development, 17, 18, **119–22**, 140
  Israeli–Jordanian, **122–30**, 148
  Israeli–Palestinian, **130–5**, 148
  problems with, 135–7
Institute for Social and Economic Policy in the Middle East, 37
intellectual property rights, 110, 118n1
inter-state relations
  political, 13–15
  economic, 15–17
International Monetary Fund (IMF), 33
Intifada, 23, 26, **43–4**, 51, 64, 81, 91, 99, 103, 114, 131
Iran–Iraq war 32–3
Iraq, 32–3, 34, 44, 51, 82, 141
Irbid, 102, **103–5**, 112
Israel
  Arab boycott of, 26, **48–9**, 69, 138, 139
  economy, 21, **23–7**, 38
  Foreign Ministry, 44, 90
  infrastructure developments, **122–35**, 148
  joint ventures, **102–17**, 140, 148
  peace treaty with Jordan, 18, 87, 92, 122
  political system, **20–1**, 136, 139
  population, 21–3
  trade with Jordan, 34, **87–9**, 92, 93, 145–6
  trade with Palestinian Authority, 41–2, **77–87**
  trade with US, 24, 30, 74, 87, 92, 111, 112, 145
  workforce, 23, **39–41**, 43
  wars *see* Arab–Israeli conflict
Israel Business Arena, 45
Israel Defense Forces (IDF), 22, 23, 44, 82, 128, 129
Israeli–Palestinian Joint Economic Committee, 83
Issues, 92

al-Ja'bari, Shaykh Muhammad 'Ali, 53
Jaber, Hana', 29, 34
Jaffee Center for Strategic Studies (JCSS), 25, 27, 30, 33, 37, 38, 93n1
Jenin, 133
Jericho Conference, 53
Jerusalem Post, 43, 111, 112, 113, 116, 131, 133, 134

Jewish Agency, 21
joint ventures, 16–17, 18, **95–102**, 142
  Israeli–Jordanian, **102–13**, 117, 140, 148
  Israeli–Palestinian, **113–17**, 140, 148
  Jordanian–Palestinian, 117
  political conflict and, 117–18
Jordan
  economy, 23, 24, 29, **30–4**, 38, 74, 111, 112, 144
  infrastructure development, **122–30**, 148
  joint ventures, 98, **102–13**, 117, 140, 148
  Palestinians and, 28–9, 47–8, **52–62**
  peace treaty with Israel, 18, 87, 92, 122
  political system, 27–8
  population, 28–9
  trade with Israel, 34, **87–9**, 92, 93, 145–6
  trade with Palestinian authority, 42, **89–92**
Jordan Bureau of Information, 28
Jordan Economic Monitor, 30
Jordan Gateway Project (JGP), **127–30**, 132, 134, 137n1
Jordan Industrial Estates Corporation, 111
Jordan Times, 112, 123. 125
Jordanian Professional Association, 106

Kang Heejoon, 3
Kanovsky, Eliyahu, 28
Kant, Immanuel, 8
Khalaf, Karim, 60, 63
Khalidi, Suleiman, 117
Kimche, David, 53
Kimche, Jon, 53
King Hussein Bridge, 119–20
Klienman, Ephraim, 69, 77
Knesset, 20, 221
Koehane, Robert O., 4
Koelle, Hermann J., 116
Kuwait, 33, 51

Labor Alignment, 62, 63, 64
labor force *see* workforce
labor-intensive industries, 10, **71–2**, 101
labor mobility, 79, **80–3**
Laks, Gidi, 105
Lautman, Dov, 102, 103, 104, 105, 106, 109, 113
Lawrence, Robert Z., 71, 72, 73, 76, 89
Lebanon, 49, 55, 136, 145
  conflict with Israel, **50–1**, 64, 81, 107, 149
Lee, Eddy, 72
Lerner, Daniel, 55
less developed countries, 9–10
Lewis, Bernard, 1

Index

liberalism, **10–11**, 12–13, 14, 65–6, 144
 Middle East and, 68, 87, 88, 93, 141, 142, 145
 trade and, 15, 16, **69–70**, 71
liberalization, 26, 27, 28, 29, 85, 142, 147–8
Liberation Party, 52
Libiszewski, Stephan, 136
life expectancy, 35, 37, 46n2
Likud party, 62–3, 64, 83, 107, 124, 131
Lin, Xiaohua, 98
LINK Magazine, 123
Litani, Yehuda, 75
Luciani, Giacomo, 31

Maayah, Tariq, 115
Madrid Conference, 51, 65
Malam software company, 110
Malik, Mueti, 28
Maltz, Judy, 78
Mansfield, Edwin, 3
Mansour, Antoine, 114
Ma'oz, Moshe, 63
maquiladora factories, xi, **127–8**, 133
Marxism, 10
Mash'al, Khalid, 105, 112
Metzer, Yaacov, 25
Mexico, xi, **127–8**, 129, 133, 144–5
Milhim, Muhammad, 61, 63
Miller, Stacey, 108
Mishal, Shaul, 43, 47
Morgenthau, Hans J., 140
Morosini, Piero, 100
Mossad, 105
Moustafa, Moustafa Ahmed, 20, 28, 146
Mukeibila industrial park, 133–4
Mulenex, Elana, 96
multinational corporations (MNCs),
 95–102, 110 *see also* joint ventures
Muslim Brethren, Brotherhood, 52, 104
Myrdal, Gunner, 71, 72

Nablus, 45, 60, 63, 64, 133, 134
Nachman, Ron, 134
Nachmias, David, 122
Naor, Aryeh, 50
Nashashibi faction, 53
Nasr, Mohamed, 114
al-Nassir, Amin, 63
National Guidance Committee, 60, 64
National Religious Orthodox Jews, 22
National Socialists, 52
nationalism, **56–8**, 59–60, 62, 140
neo-Marxism, 11
Netanyahu, Benjamin, 46

Nevo, Joseph, 53
New Dependency, 97
New York Times, 104
North American Commission for
 Environmental Cooperation
 (NACEC), 128–9, 145
North American Development Bank
 (NADBank), 129
North American Free Trade Agreement
 (NAFTA), xi, 128–9

O'Brien, D. P., 70
October War, 25, 31, **50**, 51
oil, 25, 31, 32, 43, 49
O'Neal, John, 3
Ornet Software Company, 115
Oslo agreement, 26, 44, 45, 51, 82, 115
Ovensen, Geir, 22, 46n2

Palestine Industrial Estate Development
 and Management Company (PIEDC),
 132
Palestine Liberation Organization (PLO),
 35, 44, 81
 Israel and, 50, **63–4**, 65
 Jordan and, **57–60**, 65, 81
 West Bank leaders and 56, **60–2**, 63–4
Palestinian Authority
 economy, 23–4, **36–46**
 infrastructure development, **130–5**, 148
 joint ventures, **113–17**, 140, 148
 political system, 34–5
 population, 35–6
 trade with Israel, 41–2, **77–87**
 trade with Jordan, 42, **89–92**
Palestinian Bureau of Statistics (PCBS), 45,
 85, 86
Palestinian Congress, 53
Palestinian Monetary Authority, 46n1
Palestinian Petroleum, 84
Palestinian Trade Center (PalTrade), 43, 86
Palestinians
 employment in Israel, **39–41**, 43
 Jordan and, 28–9, 47–8, **52–62**
pan-Arabism, 1, 52, 55, 56
pan-Islamism, 52
Paris Protocol, **77–80**, 89–90, 91, 113, 117
peace process, viii–ix, 65–6, **149–51**
 opposition to, **66–7**, 83, 102
perceptional pluralism, 18–19, **150–1**
Peres, Shimon, 63, 87, 134
Peri, Smadar, 103, 105
Perlmutter, Amos, 136
pharmaceutical industry, 110

Index

Pianet, 45
Pierer, Heinrich V., 115
Pines, Offir, 23
pluralism, 12–13
  perceptional, 18–19, **150–1**
Polachek, Solomon William, 3, 71
political relations, 13–15
political systems
  Israel, 20–1
  Jordan, 27–8
  Palestinian Authority, 34–5
ports, 86, 89, 112, 124–5, 126
Portugali, Yuval, 41
Press, J., 132
privatization, 26, 27, 29
problem-solving approach, 14, 68, 118
  strategies, 100–2
public opinion, 141, 147–8
public sector, 27, 31
publicity, 102, 104, **105–6**

Qalqilya, 63
Qawasima, Fahd, 61, 63
Qualifying Industrial Zone (QIZ), **110–13**,
  128, 130, 134, 137n1
Quantitative History of Arab–Israeli
  Conflict and Cooperation (QHAICC),
  93n1

Rabin, Yitzak, 83
Ramadan (October) War, 25, 31, **50**, 51
Ramallah, 60, 63, 64, 115
Razin, Assaf, 26, 43
realism, **6–7**, 12, 13, 14, 15, 143, 144, 150–1
  Arab–Israeli conflict and, ix–x, **48–51**, 66,
    68, 76
  joint ventures and, 96, 97
  peace process and, 66, **139–42**, 149
  shared infrastructures and, 17, 120, 126
  trade and, 91–2, 93, 146
refugees, 33, 36, 48, 49
religion, 22
rentier model economies, 31
Reuveny, Rafael, 3
Ricardo's theorem, 70
Richards, Alan, 24, 27, 73
Roy, Sara, 45, 46n2, 85
Royal Wings airline, 125
Russia, 26, 49, 50, 51, 139, 140

Sadka, Efraim, 26, 43
Safran, Nadav, 54
Sagea, Eli, 36, 74
Said Ahmed, Mojammed, 127

Salah family, 106
Salah, Omar, 103
Saudi Arabia, 64
Schiff, Zeev, 50, 81, 86
Schueftan, Dan, 143, 144
security, 21, 68, 76, 125
  attitudes to, 120, 140, 141, 150, 151
  mobility restrictions and, 78, **80–3**, 85–6
  transportation and, 88, 147
Sela, Michal, 90, 91
al-Shak'a, Bassam, 60, 63
Sharansky, Natan, 46, 131, 134
Sharon, Ariel, 46, 64
Sheffer & Levy petroleum transport
  company, 84–5
Shihadah, Aziz, 53
Shikaki, Khalil, 45
Shlomot, Oded, 108
Siemens Data Communications (SDC), 115,
  116
Six Day War, 21, 31, 66
Sobelman, Daniel, 28, 34
social structures, 5, **12–13**
soft infrastructures, 120
Sohn, Louis B., 8
Soviet Union, 26, 49, 50, 51, 139, 140
Spechler, Martin, 27
Spivak, A., 77
Sprout, Harold, 140
Sprout, Margaret, 140
standard of living, 32, 36, 37, 41
Star, The, 89, 92, 105, 106, 112
Stolper-Samuelson theorem, **71–2**, 106
Switzerland, 123
Syria, 26, 49, 50, 55, 141, 145, 148

al-Tall, 'Abdallah, 53
Tawil, Ibrahim, 63
taxation, 26, 31, 46, 74, 79, 83, 84, 89
TechWeb News, 110
terrorism, 21, 85, 93–4n1, 129, 143, 149
  mobility restrictions and, 41, 44, 78,
    80–3
textile industry, **102–7**, 114
  301 Watch List, 110, 118n1
tourism, **38**, 123, 124, 125–6
trade, **15–16**, 66, 48–9,
  free trade debate, 69–76
  future trends, 91–3
  Israel, 24–5, 30, 74, 87, 92, 111, 112,
    145–7
  Israeli–Jordanian, 34, **87–9**, 92, 93, 145–6
  Israeli–Palestinian, 41–2, **77–87**
  Jordan, **30**, 32–3, 34, 111, 112

Index

Jordanian–Palestinian 42, **89–92**
Palestinian Authority, **41–3**, 44
Transjordan, 28, 52, 54, 55
transportation, 76, 86, 88, 90, 91, 113,
    119–20, 147
Tulkarm, 63, 133, 134
Tunis, 141
Turkey, Turks, 28, 136

Ultra-Orthodox Jews, 22
unemployment, vii, 71, 72
    Israel, 21, 25, **26–7**, 106–7, 130
    Jordan, 33, 34
    Palestinian Authority, 45, 86, 94n2
United Nations (UN), 52
    Arab–Israeli conflict and, **48**, 49, 50
    Charter, 8
    Iraq and, 33, 34, 51
United Nations Relief Works Agency
    (UNRWA), 48
United Nations Special Co-ordinator
    (UNSCO), 41, 45
United Nations Truce Supervision
    Observers (UNTSO), 48
United Nations Yearbook, 48
United States (US), 12, 31, 71, 113, 136
    Mexican border, xi, 127–8, 128–9, 133,
    144–5
    Middle East role, 1, 49, 50, 51, 139
    trade with Israel, 24, 30, 74, 87, 92, 111,
    112, 145
    trade with Jordan, 34, 111, 112
US & Foreign Commercial Service and US
    Department of State, 98, 110
USSR, 26, 49, 50, 51, 139, 140

value-added tax (VAT), 74, 79, 84

Walker, Francis A., 71
Wallerstien, Immanuel, 10
Waltz, Kenneth N., 6, 140
water consumption, 32
water supply, 121, 136
Waterbury, John, 24, 27, 73
Weisskopf, Thomas E., 70
Weizman, Ezer, 63, 64
Wertheimer, Stefan, 135
West Bank and Gaza Strip (WBGS), 23, 32
    economy, 24, 35, **36–46**, 49, 67, 79,
    89–91, 92
    industrial parks, 131–5
    Israeli policy on, 57, 58, **62–5**, 79, 91, 146
    Jordan and, 29, 52, **54–60**
    local leadership, 53, 54, 55–6, **60–2**, 63–4,
    65
Wolfensohn, James, 131
workforce,
    foreign, 23, 29, 66
    Israeli, 22, 38
    Jordanian, 29, 38, 66, 67, 92
    Palestinian, 38, **39–41**, 44, 66, 67
World Bank, 23, 36, 38, 39, 45, 46n2, 132
world order, **5–11**, 12–13, 150–1
World War I, ix, 28, 140
World War II, x, 9, 48, 144
World Zionist Congress, 20

Ya'ari, Ehud, 50, 81, 86
Yom Kippur (October) War, 25, 31, **50**, 51

Zagloul, Ismail, 90
Zarka, 105
Zionist movement, 20, 47